HISTORY
OF THE
BUCCANEERS
OF
AMERICA

HISTORY
OF THE
BUCCANEERS
OF
AMERICA

James Burney

DOVER PUBLICATIONS, INC.
Mineola, New York

Published in the United Kingdom by David & Charles, Brunel House, Forde Close, Newton Abbot, Devon TQ12 4PU.

Bibliographical Note

This Dover edition, first published in 2002, is an unabridged republication of the book originally published in 1950 by W. W. Norton & Company Inc., New York. The Burney text is from the 1816 edition of his work.

Library of Congress Cataloging-in-Publication Data

Burney, James, 1750–1821.
    History of the Buccaneers of America / James Burney.
      p. cm.
    Originally published: London : L. Hansard & Sons, for Payne and Foss, 1816. With introd. from the 1950 ed., originally published: New York : W.W. Norton.
    ISBN 0-486-42328-X (pbk.)
    1. Buccaneers. 2. Pirates—Caribbean Area—History. 3. Caribbean Area—History—To 1810. 4. French—Caribbean Area—History. 5. British—Caribbean Area—History. I. Title.

F2161 .B91 2002
910.4'5—dc21

2002071630

Manufactured in the United States of America
Dover Publications, Inc., 31 East 2nd Street, Mineola, N.Y. 11501

INTRODUCTION

JAMES BURNEY was born on the 13th June, 1750, the second child and elder son of Dr. Charles Burney, musician and author, the talented father of a family so talented and esteemed that its name is inseparable from the cultural and social history of England in the 18th and early 19th centuries. The fame of the father and of his third child, Fanny (later Madame d'Arblay), has somewhat obscured the very real accomplishments of other members of the family ; but so highly regarded were all of them in their own day that William Hazlitt has put it on record that " There is no end of the Burney family or its pretensions. It produces wits, scholars, novelists, musicians, artists in numbers numberless. The name is alone a passport to the Temple of Fame."

In point of fact the children were seven, including the only child of Dr. Burney's second marriage, and it is worth recording here that these included, apart from James, the subject of this note, and Fanny, the diarist and novelist, Charles (one of the greatest classical scholars of the period) and Sarah (a novelist of considerable repute in the early 19th century). They were a deeply devoted family all their lives, as Fanny's diary records, and in a letter to Mrs. Thrale on the occasion of James Burney's appointment to the *Latona* in 1781, Dr. Johnston wrote, " I love all that breed whom I can be said to know, and one or two whom I hardly know, I love on credit, and love them because they love each other".

James—" Jem " to Fanny—had little formal schooling. He attended the Grammar School at King's Lynn, where

Eugene Aram the murderer, immortalised by Hood, was a teacher at the time, and in later years Burney is said to have recalled to his friends how, in 1758, he saw Aram arrested, handcuffed and removed to prison. He had scarcely reached his tenth birthday, however, before he started his naval career, enlisting as " captain's servant " on the *Princess Amelia*, a ship of Hawkes' squadron then blockading the French in the Bay of Biscay. In this ship, and subsequently in the *Magnanime*, to which his captain transferred, he served in the closing stages of the Seven Years' War, and obtained his discharge in September 1762, at the mature age of twelve years.

He did not remain long ashore. From June 1763 until June 1765 he served in the *Niger*, again as captain's servant; and from February 1766 until June 1769 in the frigate *Aquilon*, enlisting as a midshipman and serving finally as an able seaman. By this time he was a young man of nineteen and Fanny describes him in her diary as " the same as ever—honest, generous, sensible, unpolished; always unwilling to take offence, yet always eager to resent it; very careless and possessed of an uncommon share of good nature; full of humour, mirth, and jollity . . . his heart is full of love and affection for us . . . a most worthy, deserving creature, and we are extremely happy in his company".

In February 1770 he was off to sea again, this time in an East Indiaman, the *Greenwich*, bound for Bombay. It was the normal thing to use such a voyage for private gain, by indulging in a little trading on one's own account, but Burney—to judge from an entry in his sister's diary—does not seem to have followed the practice and he came back in May 1771 neither the richer (except in experience) or the poorer for the journey.

But it was in this same year, two months after the *Greenwich*, that Lieutenant James Cook, returning from his first voyage of discovery, anchored the *Endeavour* in the Downs and filled London with enthusiasm for the results of his expedition. The Admiralty having immediately decided to fit out a second expedition, James used his father's influence to make known his wish to participate, and having been introduced to Cook and Banks at the home of Lord Sandwich, First Lord of the Admiralty, his request was agreed to and he was shortly afterwards entered on the books of the *Resolution* as an able seaman. It was not until he was at the Cape, in November 1782, that he received his promotion and was appointed second lieutenant of the sloop *Adventure*, the second ship of the expedition, under Captain Furneaux.

This is no place to recapitulate the details of the two voyages which Burney made with Cook : the first (Cook's second voyage) lasting from April 1772 until July 1775 and involving a complete circumnavigation of the southern hemisphere as well as an exploration among the islands of the South Pacific, and the second (Cook's last) from August 1776 until October 1780, having as its object to discover a northern passage from the Pacific to the Atlantic and involving on the way the further exploration of the South Seas. In the interval between these voyages Burney served as lieutenant in the frigate *Cerberus* in the war against the American Colonies, but his service was brief, for having made known his wish to sail with Cook's new expedition he was allowed to return home after only a few months. He was commissioned as first lieutenant in the *Discovery* under Captain Clerke, and after the deaths of both Cook and Clerke in the Northern Pacific, Burney became first lieutenant of the *Resolution* and, on the final stage of the journey home, commander of the *Discovery*. It might be added here that Phillips, who commanded the marines on the last voyage, married Burney's sister, Susan ; and that amongst his other comrades was Bligh, later of *Bounty* fame, with whom he remained in touch in after years.

These two voyages were unquestionably the high point of Burney's life. Whatever his achievements as an officer aboard ships of war, these voyages of discovery were better suited to his temperament, if we are to judge by his later career as a scholar and geographer, and in them he undoubtedly achieved his greatest ambition. He kept journals, as did others, of both expeditions, and these documents supplement with interesting details, and often in graphic style, the facts contained in the official histories. His experience provided him with an unrivalled background for the literary work which occupied his later years, the *Chronological History of the Voyages and Discoveries in the South Sea or Pacific Ocean*, and served eventually to establish him as a geographer with few rivals in his generation.

A year after his return from the last voyage of discovery, Captain Burney was appointed to command the frigate *Latona*. Fanny records his joy at the news : " He sang, laughed, drank to his own success and danced about the room " ; while Dr. Johnson avowed, in the letter to Mrs. Thrale which has already been quoted, " I question if any ship upon the ocean goes out attended with more good wishes than that which carries the fate of Burney ". It was a brief command, however, lasting only three months, Johnson referring to it as Burney's " vicarious captainship " ; but shortly thereafter he was appointed captain of the *Bristol* and ordered to the East Indies, where his ship served in Hughes's squadron in the war against the French, until ill-health forced his return.

This was his last command. Why he did not receive any further appointment is quite obscure, but there are reasons to believe that his relations with the Admiralty were not of the best, for his troubles in later years about his rank reveal scant courtesy on the part of the department. It is at least clear that, in 1790, when he considered the probability of war with Spain, he vainly sought employment ; so much Fanny's diary records concerning an interview he had with Lord Chatham, First Lord of the Admiralty. And in a memorial to the King in 1806 he referred to the fact that he had not been employed in the war with the French, but claimed that this was not his fault, having offered his services at various times. In 1804 he was overlooked in the promotions and placed in retirement ; his plea to be reconsidered was rather coldly rejected and it was not until 1821 that he received his promotion to Rear-Admiral (retired). He died four months later.

Before we leave the summary of his sea career, it is interesting to read, in the obituary notice which can be found in the *Gentleman's Magazine*, the following observations on Burney's character as an officer : " Admiral Burney was particularly remarkable for his great and enlightened humanity to those under his command ; at a period, too, when severity in discipline was generally considered as a proof of zeal, of spirit, and of ability, and when the wiser and more generous opinions and practice of the present day were considered as heterodox and pernicious". Is it possible that a man so far in advance of his time was not to the liking of the Admiralty and he was overlooked for his very humanity ?

The last twenty years of his life were devoted to literary pursuits. His *Chronological History* was begun in 1800, the first volume was published in 1803 and the fifth and last in 1817. *The History of the Buccaneers of America*, here reprinted, forms the first half of the fourth volume of this *magnum opus*. These volumes involved much laborious work, with wide research in several languages and the careful collection and sorting of every known voyage in the South Seas, but Burney carried out his very ambitious project with such conscientiousness and skill that it has remained the standard work on its subject for generations. The plan of the work was submitted first of all to Sir Joseph Banks, President of the Royal Society, and on publication was dedicated to him.

Among Burney's other works were several pamphlets, including a "Plan of Defence against Invasion" and "A Commentary on the Systems which have been advanced for Explaining the Planetary Motions ". In 1809 he submitted two papers to the Royal Society, which few members seemed to have understood, at which Burney took such offence that, although elected a Fellow, he did not actually take up his Fellowship until 1815. In 1819 he published *A Chronological*

History of North-Eastern Voyages of Discovery and of the Early Eastern Navigations of the Russians, and in 1823 a little work entitled *An Essay by Way of Lecture on the Game of Whist* —a game at which both he and his wife were expert, for James had married Sarah, daughter of Thomas Payne the bookseller, in 1785, on his return from his last command.

To literary folk James Burney is best remembered for his long association with Charles and Mary Lamb. He is Lamb's " Admiral ", and his wife Sarah is the " Mrs. Battle " of Elia's essay. Burney was a constant figure at the Lamb's Wednesday evenings, even as Lamb himself was at the parties held by James and Sarah at their James Street home, and he was beloved by all the literary figures which formed the Lamb circle. Lamb's well-known essay, *The Wedding*, actually describes the marriage of Burney's daughter, Sarah, to her cousin, John Payne, and the essay provides a vivid picture of the " Admiral " and his home in Burney's closing years :

" I do not know a visiting place where every guest is so perfectly at ease ; no where, where harmony is so strangely the result of confusion. Everybody is at cross purposes, yet the effect is so much better than uniformity. Contradictory orders ; servants pulling one way ; master and mistress driving some other, yet both diverse ; visitors huddled up in corners ; chairs unsymmetrised ; candles disposed by chance ; meals at odd hours, tea and supper at once, or the latter preceding the former ; the host and the guest conferring, yet each upon a different topic, each understanding himself, neither trying to understand or hear the other ; draughts and politics, chess and political economy, cards and conversation on nautical matters, going on at once, without the hope, or indeed the wish of distinguishing them, make it altogether the most perfect *concordia discors* you shall meet with. . . . He has learnt, as Marvel expresses it, to ' make his destiny his choice '. He bears bravely up, but he does not come out with his flashes of wild wit so thick as formerly. His sea-songs seldomer escape him."

Amongst his many friends in these years may be numbered Southey, Rickman (Secretary to the Speaker), Hazlitt (until they quarrelled over Hazlitt's attack on Miss Burney's novel *The Wanderer*), Crabb Robinson, and even Leigh Hunt, who confesses that although he had met the Admiral " fifty " times he had never dared to speak to him because he " appeared to be so wrapped up in his tranquility and whist ".

When the Admiral died, Lamb wrote to Wordsworth ; " There's Captain Burney gone ! What fun has whist now ? What matters it what you lead, if you can no longer fancy him looking over you ? " Martin Burney, his son, ugly, eccentric, capricious Martin, remained the constant companion of the Lambs for the rest of their days.

More might have been said of the relations between this " frank-hearted voyager " and other members of the Burney family, or with the wits and *literati* of this brilliant period, for in diaries and letters references are many and affectionate ; but this would not have been relevant to the present note, whose purpose is to light the background to a work whose reputation has survived the memory of that lovable seaman, its author. *The History of the Buccaneers* has survived, not because of any special pretensions, but because it is the work of a man who was both a great scholar and a great sailor, who knew from experience what he was writing about. It is a thoroughly " seamanlike " job, to quote a term used by a contemporary reviewer.

Burney was primarily interested in the Buccaneers insofar as they contributed to the exploration of the South Pacific, and the bulk of his *History* is devoted to those exploits ; but in order to get a true perspective to them he found it necessary also to relate their earlier activities in lesser detail. Not least among the sources on which he drew was the narrative of Esquemeling, a Dutchman who was himself a Buccaneer and whose account of his own adventures was first published in Amsterdam in 1678, with the title *De Americæ neche Zee Roovers*. This book was quickly translated into other languages, including English, but the translators dealt very freely with the original, each one adding much and manipulating the story to the glory of his compatriots. Esquemeling, however, makes no mention of the Buccaneers in the South Seas, since those events developed subsequently, for it was not until 1680 that Coxon and others crossed the Isthmus and first erupted upon the Pacific. For information of these later activities there are several sources, principally the journals of participants, including Sharp and Cowley, Dampier and Wafer, and most notably Mr. Ringrose, a pilot on Sharp's voyage who was killed by the Spaniards in 1688, some ten years before the Buccaneers were finally dispersed. But James Burney's *History*, deriving from these and other records, still today remains the most comprehensive and accurate account of Buccaneering in all its aspects.

MALCOLM BARNES.

CONTENTS

HISTORY

OF

THE BUCCANEERS OF AMERICA.

CHAPTER I.

Considerations on the rights acquired by the discovery of unknown lands, and on the claims advanced by the Spaniards.

THE accounts given by the buccaneers who extended their enterprises to the Pacific Ocean are the best authenticated of any which have been published by that class of adventurers. They are interspersed with nautical and geographical descriptions corroborative of the events related, and more worth being preserved than the memory of what was performed. The materials for this portion of buccaneer history, which it was necessary should be included in a history of South Sea navigations, could not be collected without bringing other parts into view; whence it appeared that, with a moderate increase of labour, and without much enlarging the bulk of narrative, a regular history might be formed of their career, from their first rise to their suppression; and that such a work would not be without its use.

No practice is more common in literature than for an author to endeavour to clear the ground before him by mowing down the labours of his predecessors on the same subject. To do this where the labour they have bestowed is of good tendency, or even to treat with harshness the commission of error where no bad intention is manifest, is in no small degree illiberal. But all the buccaneer histories that hitherto have appeared, and the number is not small, are boastful compositions, which have delighted in exaggeration ; and, what is most mischievous, they have lavished commendation on acts which demanded reprobation, and have endeavoured to raise miscreants notorious for their want of humanity to the rank of heroes, lessening thereby the stain upon robbery, and the abhorrence naturally conceived against cruelty.

There is some excuse for the buccaneer who tells his own story. Vanity, and his prejudices, without any intention to deceive, lead him to magnify his own exploits ; and the reader naturally makes allowances.

The men whose enterprises are to be related were natives of different European nations, but chiefly of Great Britain and France, and most of them seafaring people, who, being disappointed by accidents or the enmity of the Spaniards in their more sober pursuits in the West Indies, and also instigated by thirst for plunder as much as by desire for vengeance, enrolled themselves, under different leaders of their own choosing, to make predatory war upon the Spaniards. These men the Spaniards naturally treated as pirates ;

but some peculiar circumstances which provoked their first enterprises, and a general feeling of enmity against that nation on account of their American conquests, procured them the connivance of the rest of the maritime states of Europe, and to be distinguished first by the softened appellations of freebooters and adventurers, and afterwards by that of buccaneers.

Spain, or, more strictly speaking, Castile, on the merit of a first discovery, claimed an exclusive right to the possession of the whole of America, with the exception of the Brazils, which were conceded to the Portuguese. These claims and this division the Pope sanctioned by an instrument, entitled a " Bull of Donation," which was granted at a time when all the maritime powers of Europe were under the spiritual dominion of the see of Rome. The Spaniards, however, did not flatter themselves that they should be left in the sole and undisputed enjoyment of so large a portion of the newly-discovered countries ; but they were principally anxious to preserve wholly to themselves the West Indies : and such was the monopolising spirit of the Castilians, that during the life of the Queen Ysabel of Castile, who was regarded as the patroness of Columbus's discovery, it was difficult even for Spaniards, not born subjects of the crown of Castile, to gain access to this new world, prohibitions being repeatedly published against the admission of all other persons into the ships bound thither. Ferdinand, king of Arragon, the husband of Ysabel, had refused to contribute towards the outfit of Columbus's first voyage, having no opinion of the probability that it would produce him an adequate return; and the undertaking being at the expense of Castile, the countries discovered were considered as appendages to the crown of Castile.

If such jealousy was entertained by the Spaniards of each other, what must not have been their feelings respecting other European nations? " Whoever," says Hakluyt, "is conversant with the Portugal and Spanish writers, shall find that they account all other nations for pirates, rovers, and thieves, which visit any heathen coast that they have sailed by or looked on."

Spain considered the New World as what in our law books is called "treasure-trove," of which she became lawfully and exclusively entitled to take possession, as fully as if it had been found without any owner or proprietor. Spain has not been singular in her maxims respecting the rights of dis-coverers. Our books of voyages abound in instances of the same disregard shown to the rights of the native inhabitants, the only rightful proprietors, by the navigators of other European nations, who, with a solemnity due only to offices of a religious nature, have continually put in practice the form of taking possession of countries which to them were new discoveries, their being inhabited or desert making no difference. Not unfrequently has the ceremony been performed in the presence, but not within the understanding, of the wondering natives; and on this formality is grounded a claim to usurp the actual possession, in preference to other Europeans.

Nothing can be more opposed to common-sense, than that strangers should pretend to acquire by discovery a title to countries they find with inhabitants: as if in those very inhabitants the right of prior discovery was not inherent. On some occasions, however, Europeans have thought it expedient to acknowledge the rights of the natives, as when, in disputing each other's claims, a title by gift from the natives has been pretended.

In uninhabited lands, a right of occupancy results from the discovery; but actual and *bonâ fide* possession is requisite to perfect appropriation. If real possession be not taken, or, if taken, shall not be retained, the right acquired by the mere discovery is not indefinite and a perpetual bar of exclusion to all others; for that would amount to discovery giving a right equivalent to annihilation. Movable effects may be hoarded and kept out of use, or be destroyed, and it will not always be easy to prove whether with injury or benefit to mankind: but the necessities of human life will not admit, unless under the strong hand of power, that a right should be pretended to keep extensive and fertile countries waste and secluded from their use, without other reason than the will of a proprietor or claimant.

Particular local circumstances have created objections to the occupancy of territory: for instance, between the confines of the Russian and Chinese empires, large tracts of country are left waste, it being held that their being occupied by the subjects of either empire would affect the security of the other. Several similar instances might be mentioned.

There is in many cases difficulty in settling what constitutes occupancy. On a small island, any first settlement is acknowledged an occupancy of the whole; and sometimes, the occupancy of a single island of a group is supposed to comprehend an exclusive title to the possession of the remainder of the group. In the West Indies the Spaniards regarded their making settlements on a few islands to be an actual taking possession of the whole, as far as European pretensions were concerned.

The first discovery of Columbus set in activity the curiosity and speculative dispositions of all the European maritime powers. King Henry VII. of England, as soon as he was certified of the existence of countries in the western hemisphere, sent ships thither whereby Newfoundland, and parts of the continent of North America, were first discovered. South America was also visited very early, both by the English and the French; "which nations," the historian of Brazil remarks, "had neglected to ask a share of the undiscovered world, when pope Alexander VI. partitioned it, who would as willingly have drawn two lines as one; and, because they derived no advantage from that partition, refused to admit its validity". The West Indies, however, which doubtless was the part most coveted by all, seem to have been considered as more particularly the discovery and right of the Spaniards; and, either from respect to their pretensions, or from the opinion entertained of their force in those parts, they remained many years undisturbed by intruders in the West Indian Seas. But their homeward-bound ships, and also those of the Portuguese from the East Indies, did not escape being molested by pirates: sometimes by those of their own, as well as of other nations.

CHAPTER II.

*Review of the dominion of the Spaniards in Hayti
or Hispaniola.*

THE first settlement formed by the Castilians in their newly-discovered world was on the island by the native inhabitants named Hayti; but to which the Spaniards gave the name of Española or Hispaniola. And in process of time it came to pass, that this same island became the great place of resort and nursery of the European adventurers, who have been so conspicuous under the denomination of the buccaneers of America.

The native inhabitants found in Hayti have been described as a people of gentle, compassionate dispositions, of too frail a constitution, both of body and mind, either to resist oppression or to support themselves under its weight; and to the indolence, luxury, and avarice of the discoverers, their freedom and happiness in the first instance, and finally their existence, fell a sacrifice.

Queen Ysabel, the patroness of the discovery, believed it her duty, and was earnestly disposed, to be their protectress; but she wanted resolution to second her inclination. The island abounded in gold mines. The natives were by degrees more and more heavily tasked to work them; and it was the great misfortune of Columbus, after achieving an enterprise, the glory of which was not exceeded by any action of his contemporaries, to make an ungrateful use of the success Heaven had favoured him with, and to be the foremost in the destruction of the nations his discovery first made known to Europe.

The population of Hayti, according to the lowest estimation made, amounted to a million of souls. The first visit of Columbus was passed in a continual reciprocation of kind offices between them and the Spaniards. One of the Spanish ships was wrecked upon the coast, and the natives gave every assistance in their power towards saving the crew, and their effects to them. When Columbus departed to return to Europe, he left behind him thirty-eight Spaniards, with the consent of the chief or sovereign of the part of the island where he had been so hospitably received. He had erected a fort for their security, and the declared purpose of their remaining was to protect the chief against all his enemies. Several of the native islanders voluntarily embarked in the ships to go to Spain, among whom was a relation of the Hayti chief; and with them were taken gold and various samples of the productions of the New World.

Columbus, on his return, was received by the court of Spain with the honours due to his heroic achievement, indeed with honours little short of adoration. He was declared admiral, governor, and viceroy of the countries that he had discovered, and also of those which he should afterwards discover: he was ordered to assume the style and title of nobility, and was furnished with a larger fleet to prosecute farther the discovery, and to make conquest of the new lands. The instructions for his second expedition contained the following direction : " Forasmuch as you, Christopher Columbus, are going by our command, with our vessels and our men, to discover and subdue certain islands and continent, our will is, that you shall be our admiral, viceroy, and governor in them ". This was the first step in the iniquitous usurpations which the more cultivated nations of the world have practised upon their weaker brethren, the natives of America.

Thus provided and instructed, Columbus sailed on his second voyage. On arriving at Hayti, the first news he learnt was, that the natives had demolished the fort which he had built, and destroyed the garrison, who, it appeared, had given great provocation by their rapacity and licentious conduct. War did not immediately follow. Columbus accepted presents of gold from the chief; he landed a number of colonists, and built a town on the north side of Hayti, which he named after the patroness, Ysabel, and fortified. A second fort was soon built, new Spaniards arrived, and the natives began to understand that it was the intention of their visitors to stay, and be lords of the country. The chiefs held meetings, to confer on the means to rid themselves of such unwelcome guests, and there was appearance of preparation making to that end. The Spaniards had as yet no farther asserted dominion than in taking land for their town and forts, and helping themselves to provisions when the natives neglected to bring supplies voluntarily. The histories of these transactions affect a tone of apprehension on account of the extreme danger in which the Spaniards were from the multitude of the heathen inhabitants; but all the facts show that they perfectly understood the helpless character of the natives. A Spanish officer, named Pedro Margarit, was blamed, not altogether reasonably, for disorderly conduct to the natives, which happened in the following manner. He was ordered, with a large body of troops, to make a progress through the island in different parts, and was strictly enjoined to restrain his men from committing any violence against the natives, or from giving them any cause for complaint. But the troops were sent on their journey without provisions, and the natives were not disposed to furnish them. The troops recurred to violence, which they did not limit to the obtaining of food. If Columbus could spare a detachment strong enough to make such a visitation through the land, he could have entertained no doubt of his ability to subdue it. But before he risked engaging in open war with the natives, he thought it prudent to weaken their means of resisting by what he called stratagem. Hayti was divided into five provinces, or small kingdoms, under the separate dominion of as many princes or caciques. One of these, Coanabo, the cacique of Maguana, Columbus believed to be more resolute and more dangerous to his purpose than any other of the chiefs. To Coanabo, therefore, he sent an officer to propose an accommodation on terms which appeared so reasonable that the Indian chief assented to them. Afterwards, relying on the good faith of the Spaniards, not, as some authors have meanly represented, through credulous and childish

simplicity, but with the natural confidence which generally prevails, and which ought to prevail, among mankind in their mutual engagements, he gave opportunity
for Columbus to get possession of his person, who
caused him to be seized, and embarked in a ship then
ready to sail for Spain. The ship foundered in the
passage. The story of Coanabo, and the contempt
with which he treated Columbus for his treachery,
form one of the most striking circumstances in the
history of the perfidious dealings of the Spaniards in
America. On the seizure of this chief the islanders
rose in arms. Columbus took the field with two hundred foot armed with musketry and cross-bows, with
twenty troopers mounted on horses, and with twenty
large dogs ! *

It is not to be urged in exculpation of the Spaniards
that the natives were the aggressors, by their killing
the garrison left at Hayti. Columbus had terminated
his first visit in friendship ; and, without the knowledge
that any breach had happened between the Spaniards
left behind and the natives, sentence of subjugation
had been pronounced against them. This was not to
avenge injury, for the Spaniards knew not of any committed. Columbus was commissioned to execute this
sentence, and for that end, besides a force of armed
men, he took with him from Spain a number of blood-
hounds, to prosecute a most unrighteous purpose by
the most inhuman means.

Many things are justifiable in defence, which in
offensive war are regarded by the generality of

* *Lebreles de pressa.*

mankind with detestation. All are agreed in the use of dogs, as faithful guards to our persons as well as to our dwellings; but to hunt men with dogs seems to have been till then unheard of, and is nothing less offensive to humanity than cannibalism or feasting on our enemies. Neither jagged shot, poisoned darts, springing of mines, nor any species of destruction can be objected to, if this is allowed in honourable war, or admitted not to be a disgraceful practice in any war.

It was scarcely possible for the Indians, or indeed for any people naked and undisciplined, however numerous, to stand their ground against a force so calculated to excite dread. The islanders were naturally a timid people, and they regarded fire-arms as engines of more than mortal contrivance. Don Ferdinand, the son of Columbus, who wrote a history of his father's actions, relates an instance, which happened before the war, of above 400 Indians running away from a single Spanish horseman. So little was attack, or valiant opposition, apprehended from the natives, that Columbus divided his force into several squadrons, to charge them at different points. "These faint-hearted creatures," says Don Ferdinand, "fled at the first onset; and our men, pursuing and killing them, made such havoc, that in a short time they obtained a complete victory." The policy adopted by Columbus was to confirm the natives in their dread of European arms by a terrible execution. The victors, both dogs and men, used their ascendency like furies. The dogs flew at the throats of the Indians, and strangled or tore them in pieces ; whilst the Spaniards, with the eagerness of hunters, pursued and mowed down the unresisting fugitives Some thousands of the islanders were slaughtered, and those taken prisoners were consigned to servitude. If the fact were not extant, it would not be conceivable that anyone could be so blind to the infamy of such a proceeding as to extol the courage of the Spaniards on this occasion, instead of execrating their cruelty. Three hundred of the natives were shipped for Spain as slaves, and the whole island, with the exception of a small part towards the western coast, which has since been named the *Cul de Sac*, was subdued. Columbus made a leisurely progress through the island, which occupied him nine or ten months, and imposed a tribute generally upon all the natives above the age of fourteen, requiring each of them to pay quarterly a certain quantity of gold, or 25 lbs. of cotton. Those natives who were discovered to have been active against the Spaniards were taxed higher. To prevent evasion, rings or tokens, to be produced in the nature of receipts, were given to the islanders on their paying the tribute, and any islander found without such a mark in his possession was deemed not to have paid, and proceeded against.

Queen Ysabel showed her disapprobation of Columbus's proceedings by liberating and sending back the captive islanders to their own country ; and she moreover added her positive commands that none of the natives should be made slaves. This order was accompanied with others intended for their protection ; but the Spanish colonists, following the example of their governor, contrived means to evade them.

In the meantime, the islanders could not furnish the tribute, and Columbus was rigorous in the collection. It is said in palliation, that he was embarrassed in consequence of the magnificent descriptions he had given to Ferdinand and Ysabel of the riches of Hispaniola, by which he had taught them to expect much, and that the fear of disappointing them and losing their favour prompted him to act more oppressively to the Indians than his disposition otherwise inclined him to do. Distresses of this kind press upon all men ; but only in very ordinary minds do they outweigh solemn considerations. Setting aside the dictates of religion and moral duty, as doubtless was done, and looking only to worldly advantages, if Columbus had properly estimated his situation he would have been resolute not to descend from the eminence he had attained. The dilemma in which he was placed was simply, whether he would risk some diminution of the favour he was in at court, by being the protector of these islanders, who, by circumstances peculiarly calculated to engage his interest, were entitled in an especial manner to have been regarded as his clients ; or, to preserve that favour, would oppress them to their destruction, and to the ruin of his own fame.

The islanders, finding their inability to oppose the invaders, took the desperate resolution to desist from the cultivation of their lands, to abandon their houses, and to withdraw themselves to the mountains ; hoping thereby that want of subsistence would force their oppressors to quit the island. The Spaniards had many resources ; the sea-coast supplied them with fish, and their vessels brought provisions from other islands.

As to the natives of Hayti, one-third part of them, it is said, perished in the course of a few months by famine and by suicide. The rest returned to their dwellings, and submitted. All these events took place within three years after the discovery; so active is rapacity.

Some among the Spaniards (authors of that time say the enemies of Columbus, as if sentiments of humanity were not capable of such an effort,) wrote memorials to their Catholic Majesties, representing the disastrous condition to which the natives were reduced. Commissioners were sent to examine into the fact, and Columbus found it necessary to go to Spain to defend his administration.

So great was the veneration and respect entertained for him, that on his arrival at court accusation was not allowed to be produced against him : and, without instituting enquiry, it was arranged that he should return to his government with a large reinforcement of Spaniards, and with authority to grant lands to whomsoever he chose to think capable of cultivating them. Various accidents delayed his departure from Spain on his third voyage till 1498.

He had left two of his brothers to govern in Hispaniola during his absence; the eldest, Bartolomé, with the title of Adelantado; in whose time (A.D. 1496) was traced, on the south side of the island, the plan of a new town intended for the capital, the land in the neighbourhood of the town of Ysabel, before built, being poor and little productive. The name first given to the new town was Nueva Ysabel; this in a short time gave place to that of Santo Domingo, a name which was not imposed by authority, but adopted, and became in time established by common usage, of which the original cause is not now known.*

Under the Adelantado's government, the parts of the island which till then had held out in their refusal to receive the Spanish yoke were reduced to subjection, and the conqueror gratified his vanity with the public execution of one of the Hayti kings.

Columbus, whilst he was in Spain, received mortification in two instances, of neither of which he had any right to complain. In October, 1496, three hundred natives of Hayti (made prisoners by the Adelantado) were landed at Cadiz, being sent to Spain as slaves. At this act of disobedience the king and queen strongly expressed their displeasure, and said, if the islanders made war against the Castilians, they must have been constrained to do it by hard treatment. Columbus thought proper to blame, and to disavow what his brother had done. The other instance of his receiving mortification was an act of kindness done him, and so intended, and it was the only shadow of anything like reproof offered to him. In the instructions which he now received, it was earnestly recommended to him to prefer conciliation to severity on all occasions which would admit it without prejudice to justice or to his honour.

It was in the third voyage of Columbus that he first saw the continent of South America, in August,

* The name Saint Domingo was afterwards applied to the whole island by the French, who, whilst they contested the possession with the Spaniards, were desirous to supersede the use of the name Espanola or Hispaniola.

1498, which he then took to be an island, and named
Isla Santa. He arrived on the 22nd of the same
month at the city of San Domingo.

The short remainder of Columbus's government in
Hayti was occupied with disputes among the Spaniards
themselves. A strong party was in a state of revolt
against the government of the Columbuses, and accommodation was kept at a distance by neither party daring
to place trust in the other. Columbus would have
had recourse to arms to recover his authority, but some
of his troops deserted to the disaffected, and others refused to be employed against their countrymen. In
this state, the parties engaged in a treaty on some
points, and each sent memorials to the court. The
admiral in his despatches represented that necessity
had made him consent to certain conditions, to avoid
endangering the colony; but that it would be highly
prejudicial to the interests of their Majesties to ratify
the treaty he had been forced to subscribe.

The admiral now made grants of lands to Spanish
colonists, and accompanied them with requisitions to
the neighbouring caciques, to furnish the new proprietors with labourers to cultivate the soil. This was
the beginning of the *repartimientos*, or distributions
of the Indians, which confirmed them slaves, and contributed, more than all former oppressions, to their extermination. Notwithstanding the earnest and express
order of the king and queen to the contrary, the practice of transporting the natives of Hayti to Spain as
slaves was connived at and continued; and this being
discovered lost Columbus the confidence, but not
wholly the support, of Queen Ysabel.

The dissensions in the colony increased, as did the unpopularity of the admiral; and in the year 1500 a new governor-general of the Indies, Francisco de Bovadilla, was sent from Spain, with a commission empowering him to examine into the accusations against the admiral ; and he was particularly enjoined by the queen to declare all the native inhabitants free, and to take measures to secure to them that they should be treated as a free people. How a man so grossly ignorant and intemperate as Bovadilla should have been chosen to an office of such high trust is not a little extraordinary. His first display of authority was to send the Columbuses home prisoners, with the indignity to their persons of confining them in chains. He courted popularity in his government by showing favour to all who had been disaffected to the government or measures of the admiral and his brothers, the natives excepted, for whose relief he had been especially appointed governor. To encourage the Spaniards to work the mines, he reduced the duties payable to the crown on the produce, and trusted to an increase in the quantity of gold extracted for preserving the revenue from diminution. This was to be effected by increasing the labour of the natives ; and that these miserable people might not evade their servitude, he caused muster-rolls to be made of all the inhabitants, divided them into classes, and made distribution of them according to the value of the mines, or to his desire to gratify particular persons. The Spanish colonists believed that the same facilities to enrich themselves would not last long, and made all the haste in their power to profit by the present opportunity.

By these means Bovadilla drew from the mines in a few months so great a quantity of gold, that one fleet, which he sent home, carried a freight more than sufficient to reimburse Spain all the expenses which had been incurred in the discovery and conquest. The procuring these riches was attended with so great a mortality among the natives as to threaten their utter extinction.

Nothing could exceed the surprise and indignation of the queen on receiving information of these proceedings. The bad government of Bovadilla was a kind of palliation which had the effect of lessening the reproach upon the preceding government, and, joined to the disgraceful manner in which Columbus had been sent home, produced a revolution of sentiment in his favour. The good Queen Ysabel wished to compensate him for the hard treatment he had received, at the same time that she had the sincerity to make him understand she would not again commit the Indian natives to his care. All his other offices and dignities were restored to him.

For a successor to Bovadilla in the office of governor-general, Don Nicolas Ovando, a cavalero of the order of Alcantara, was chosen : a man esteemed capable and just, and who entered on his government with apparent mildness and consideration. But in a short time he proved the most execrable of all the tyrants, "as if," says an historian, "tyranny was inherent and contagious in the office, so as to change good men to bad, for the destruction of these unfortunate Indians".

In obedience to his instructions, Ovando, on

arriving at his government, called a general assembly
of all the caciques or principal persons among the
natives, to whom he declared, that their Catholic
Majesties took the islanders under their royal protection ; that no exaction should be made on them,
other than the tribute which had been heretofore
imposed ; and that no person should be employed
to work in the mines, except on the footing of voluntary labourers for wages.

On the promulgation of the royal pleasure all
working in the mines immediately ceased.   The
impression made by their past sufferings was too
strong for any offer of pay or reward to prevail on
them to continue in that work.   [The same thing
happened, many years afterwards, between the Chilese
and the Spaniards.]   A few mines had been allowed
to remain in possession of some of the caciques of
Hayti, on the condition of rendering up half the
produce ; but now, instead of working them, they
sold their implements.   In consequence of this defection, it was judged expedient to lower the royal
duties on the produce of the mines, which produced
some effect.

Ovando, however, was intent on having the
mines worked as heretofore, but proceeded with caution.   In his despatches to the council of the Indies,
he represented in strong colours the natural levity and
inconstancy of the Indians, and their idle and disorderly
manner of living ; on which account, he said, it would
be for their improvement and benefit to find them
occupation in moderate labour ; that there would be
no injustice in so doing, as they would receive wages

for their work, and they would thereby be enabled to pay the tribute which otherwise, from their habitual idleness, many would not be able to satisfy. He added, moreover, that the Indians, being left entirely their own masters, kept at a distance from the Spanish habitations, which rendered it impossible to instruct them in the principles of Christianity.

This reasoning and the proposal to furnish the natives with employment were approved by the council of the Indies; and the court, from the opinion entertained of the justice and moderation of Ovando, acquiesced so far as to trust making the experiment to his discretion. In reply to his representations, he received instructions recommending, "That if it was necessary to oblige the Indians to work, it should be done in the most gentle and moderate manner; that the caciques should be invited to send their people in regular turns; and that the employers should treat them well, and pay them wages, according to the quality of the person and nature of the labour; that care should be taken for their regular attendance at religious service and instruction; and that it should be remembered they were a free people, to be governed with mildness, and on no account to be treated as slaves".

These directions, notwithstanding the expressions of care for the natives contained in them, released the governor-general from all restriction. This man had recently been appointed Grand Master of the order of Calatrava, and thenceforward he was most generally distinguished by the appellation or title of the Grand Commander.

A transaction of a shocking nature, which took place during Bovadilla's government, caused an insurrection of the natives, which did not, however, break out till after the removal of Bovadilla. A Spanish vessel had put into a port of the province of Higuey (the most eastern part of Hayti) to procure a lading of cassava, a root which is used as bread. The Spaniards landed, having with them a large dog held by a cord. Whilst the natives were helping them to what they wanted, one of the Spaniards in wanton insolence pointed to a cacique, and called to the dog in manner of setting him on. The Spaniard who held the cord—it is doubtful whether purposely or by accident—suffered it to slip out of his hand, and the dog instantly tore out the unfortunate cacique's entrails. The people of Higuey sent a deputation to complain to Bovadilla ; but those who went could not obtain attention. In the beginning of Ovando's government, some other Spaniards landed at the same port of Higuey, and the natives, in revenge for what had happened, fell upon them and killed them ; after which they took to arms. This insurrection was quelled with so great a slaughter that the province, from having been well peopled, was rendered almost a desert.

Ovando, on obtaining his new instructions, followed the model set by his predecessors. He enrolled and classed the natives in divisions, called *repartimientos :* from these he assigned to the Spanish proprietors a specified number of labourers, by grants, which, with most detestable hypocrisy, were denominated *enco-miendas.* The word *encomienda* signifies recommendation, and the employer to whom the Indian was consigned was to have the reputation of being his patron. The *encomienda* was conceived in the following terms : " I recommend to A. B. such and such Indians (listed by name), the subjects of such cacique ; and he is to take care to have them instructed in the principles of our holy faith ".

Under the enforcement of the *encomiendas*, the natives were again dragged to the mines ; and many of these unfortunate wretches were kept by their hard employers under ground for six months together. With the labour, and grief at being again doomed to slavery, they sank so rapidly that it suggested to the murderous proprietors of the mines the having recourse to Africa for slaves. Ovando, after small experience of this practice, endeavoured to oppose it as dangerous, the Africans frequently escaping from their masters and finding concealment among the natives, in whom they excited some spirit of resistance.

The ill use made by the Grand Commander of the powers with which he had been trusted appears to have reached the court early, for in 1503 he received fresh orders, enjoining him not to allow, on any pretext, the natives to be employed in labour against their own will, either in the mines or elsewhere. Ovando, however, trusted to being supported by the Spanish proprietors of the mines within his government, who grew rich by the *encomiendas*, and with their assistance he found pretences for not restraining himself to the orders of the court.

In parts of the island the caciques still enjoyed a degree of authority over the natives which rested almost wholly on habitual custom and voluntary attachment. To loosen this band, Ovando, assuming the character of a protector, published ordinances to release the lower classes from the oppressions of the caciques; but from those of their European taskmasters he gave them no relief.

Some of the principal among the native inhabitants of Xaragua, the south-western province of Hayti, had the hardiness openly to express their discontent at the tyranny exercised by the Spaniards established in that province. The person at this time regarded as cacique or chief of Xaragua was a female, sister to the last cacique, who had died without issue. The Spanish histories call her queen of Xaragua. This princess had shown symptoms of something like abhorrence of the Spaniards near her, and they did not fail to send representations to the Grand Commander, with the addition that there appeared indications of an intention in the Xaraguans to revolt. On receiving this notice, Ovando determined that Xaragua, as Higuey had before, should feel the weight of his displeasure. Putting himself at the head of 370 Spanish troops, part of them cavalry, he departed from the city of San Domingo for the devoted province, giving out publicly that his intention was to make a progress into the West to collect the tribute and to visit the queen of Xaragua. He was received by the princess and her people with honours, feastings, and all the demonstrations of joy usually acted by terrified people with the hopes of soothing tyranny, and the troops were regaled with profusion of victuals, with dancing, and shows. After some days thus spent, Ovando invited

the princess, her friends and attendants, to an entertainment which he promised them, after the manner of
Spain.   A large open public building was the chosen
place for holding this festival, and all the Spanish
settlers in the province were required to attend.   A
great concourse of Indians, besides the bidden guests,
crowded round, to enjoy the spectacle.   As the appointed time approached, the Spanish infantry gradually appeared, and took possession of all the avenues ;
which being secured, this Grand Commander himself
appeared, mounted at the head of his cavalry ; and on
his making a signal which had been previously concerted, which was laying his hand on the cross of his
order, the whole of these diabolical conquerors fell
upon the defenceless multitude, who were so hemmed
in that thousands were slaughtered, and it was scarcely
possible for any to escape unwounded.   Some of the
principal Indians or caciques, it is said, were by the
Commander's order fastened to the pillars of the building, where they were questioned, and made to confess
themselves in a conspiracy against the Spanish government ; after which confession the building was set on
fire, and they perished in the flames.   The massacre
did not stop here.   Detachments of troops, with dogs,
were sent to hunt and destroy the natives in different
parts of the province, and some were pursued over to
the island Gonave.   The princess was carried bound
to the city of San Domingo, and, with the forms of law,
was tried, condemned and put to death.

The purposes, besides that of gratifying his revenge
for the hatred shown to his government, which were
sufficient to move Ovando to this bloody act, were,

the plunder of the province, and the reduction of the islanders to a more manageable number, and to the most unlimited submission. Some of the Indians fled to the mountains. " But," say the Spanish chronicles of these events, " in a short time their chiefs were taken and punished, and at the end of six months there was not a native living on the island who had not submitted to the dominion of the Spaniards."

Queen Ysabel died in November, 1504, much and universally lamented. This princess bore a large share in the usurpations practised in the New World; but it is evident she was carried away, contrary to her real principles and disposition—which were just and benevolent—and to her own happiness, by the powerful stream of general opinion.

In Europe, political principles, or maxims of policy, have been in continual change, fashioned by the nature of the passing events, no less than dress has been by caprice : causes which have led one to deviate from plain rectitude, as the other from convenience. One principle, covetousness of the attainment of power, has nevertheless constantly predominated, and has derided and endeavoured to stigmatise as weakness and imbecility the stopping short of great acquisitions, territorial especially, for moral considerations. Queen Ysabel lived surrounded by a world of such politicians, who were, moreover, stimulated to avarice by the prospect of American gold; a passion which yet more than ambition is apt to steel the heart of man against the calls of justice and the distresses of his fellow-creatures. If Ysabel had been endued with more than mortal fortitude, she might have refused her sanction to the usurpations, but could not have prevented them. On her death-bed she earnestly recommended to King Ferdinand to recall Ovando. Ovando, however, sent home much gold, and Ferdinand referred to a distant time the fulfilment of her dying request.

Upon news of the death of Queen Ysabel, the small wages which had been paid the Indians for their labour, amounting to about half a piastre per month, were withheld, as being too grievous a burthen on the Spanish colonists, and the hours of labour were no longer limited. In the province of Higuey, the tyranny and licentiousness of the military again threw the poor natives into a frenzy of rage and despair, and they once more revolted, burnt the fort, and killed the soldiers. Ovando resolved to put it out of the power of the people of Higuey ever again to be troublesome. A strong body of troops was marched into the province, the cacique of Higuey (the last of the Hayti kings) was taken prisoner and executed, and the province pacified.

The pecuniary value of grants of land in Hayti with *encomiendas* became so considerable as to cause them to be coveted and solicited for by many of the grandees and favourites of the court in Spain, who, on obtaining them, sent out agents to turn them to account. The agent was to make his own fortune by his employment, and to satisfy his principal. In no instance were the natives spared through any interference of the Grand Commander. It was a maxim with this bad man always to keep well with the powerful; and every-

thing respecting the natives was yielded to their
accommodation. Care, however, was taken that the
Indians should be baptised, and that a head tax should
be paid to the crown, and, these particulars being
complied with, the rest was left to the patron of the
encomienda. Punishments and tortures of every kind
were practised, to wring labour out of men who were
dying through despair. Some of the accounts, which
are corroborated by circumstances, relate that the
natives were frequently coupled and harnessed like
cattle, and driven with whips. If they fell under their
load, they were flogged up. To prevent their taking
refuge in the woods or mountains, an officer, under the
title of *alguazil del campo*, was constantly on the
watch with a pack of hounds; and many Indians, in
endeavouring to escape, were torn in pieces. The
settlers on the island, the great men at home, their
agents, and the royal revenue, were all to be enriched
at the expense of the destruction of the natives. It
was as if the discovery of America had changed the
religion of the Spaniards from Christianity to the
worship of gold with human sacrifices. If power were
entitled to dominion between man and man, as between
man and other animals, the Spaniards would remain
chargeable with the most outrageous abuse of their
advantages. In enslaving the inhabitants of Hayti, if
they had been satisfied with reducing them to the state
of cattle, it would have been merciful comparatively
with what was done. The labour imposed by mankind
upon their cattle is in general so regulated as not to
exceed what is compatible with their full enjoyment of
health; but the main consideration with the Spanish

proprietors was, by what means they should obtain the
greatest quantity of gold from the labour of the natives
in the shortest time.   By an enumeration made in the
year 1507, the number of the natives in the whole
island Hayti was reckoned at 60,000, the remains of
a population which fifteen years before exceeded a
million.   The insatiate colonists did not stop here:
many of the mines lay unproductive for want of
labourers, and they bent their efforts to the supplying this defect.

The islands of the West Indies have been classed
into three divisions, which chiefly regard their situations ; but they are distinguished also by other peculiar
circumstances.   The four largest islands—Cuba, Hayti,
Jamaica, and Porto Rico—have been called the Grand
Antilles.   When first discovered by Europeans, they
were inhabited by people whose similarity of language,
of customs and character, bespoke them the offspring
of one common stock.   The second division is a chain
of small islands eastward of these, and extending
south to the coast of Paria on the continent of South
America.   They have been called sometimes the Small
Antilles ; sometimes, after the native inhabitants, the
Caribbee Islands ; and not less frequently, by a sub-
division, the Windward and Leeward Islands.   The
inhabitants on these islands were a different race from
the inhabitants of the Grand Antilles.   They spoke a
different language, were robust in person ; and in
disposition fierce, active, and warlike.   Some have
conjectured them to be of Tartar extraction, which
corresponds with the belief that they emigrated from
North America to the West Indies.   It is supposed

they drove out the original inhabitants from the Small Antilles, to establish themselves there; but they had not gained footing in the large islands. The third division of the islands is the cluster which is situated to the north of Cuba, and near East Florida, and are called the Lucayas, of whose inhabitants mention will shortly be made.

The Spanish government participated largely in the wickedness practised to procure labourers for the mines of Hispaniola. Pretending great concern for the cause of humanity, they declared it legal, and gave general licence, for any individual to make war against, and enslave, people who were cannibals; under which pretext every nation, both of the American continent and of the islands, was exposed to their enterprises. Spanish adventurers made attempts to take people from the Small Antilles, sometimes with success; but they were not obtained without danger, and in several expeditions of the kind the Spaniards were repulsed with loss. This made them turn their attention to the Lucayas Islands.

The inhabitants of the Lucayas, an unsuspicious and credulous people, did not escape the snares laid for them. Ovando, in his despatches to Spain, represented the benefit it would be to the holy faith to have the inhabitants of the Lucayas instructed in the Christian religion; for which purpose he said "it would be necessary they should be transported to Hispaniola, as missionaries could not be spared to every place, and there was no other way in which this abandoned people could be converted". King Ferdinand and the council of the Indies were themselves so abandoned and destitute of all goodness, as to pretend to give credit to Ovando's representation, and lent him their authority to sacrifice the Lucayans, under the pretext of advancing religion. Spanish ships were sent to the islands on this business, and the natives were at first inveigled on board by the foulest hypocrisy and treachery. Among the artifices used by the Spaniards, they pretended that they came from a delicious country, where rested the souls of the deceased fathers, kinsmen and friends, of the Lucayans, who had sent to invite them. The innocent islanders so seduced to follow the Spaniards, when, on arriving at Hispaniola, they found how much they had been abused, died in great numbers of chagrin and grief. Afterwards, when these impious pretences of the Spaniards were no longer believed, they dragged away the natives by force, as long as any could be found, till they wholly unpeopled the Lucayas Islands. The buccaneers of America, whose adventures and misdeeds are about to be related, may be esteemed saints in comparison with the men whose names have been celebrated as the conquerors of the New World.

In the same manner as at the Lucayas, other islands of the West Indies, and different parts of the continent, were resorted to for recruits. A pearl fishery was established, in which the Indians were not more spared as divers than on the land as miners.

Porto Rico was conquered at this time. Ore had been brought thence, which was not so pure as that of Hayti; but it was of sufficient value to determine Ovando to the conquest of the island. The islanders were terrified by the carnage which the Spaniards with their dogs made in the commencement of the war, and from the fear of irritating them by further resistance they yielded wholly at discretion and were immediately sent to the mines, where in a short time they all perished. In the same year with Porto Rico, the island of Jamaica was taken possession of by the Spaniards.

Ovando was at length recalled, and was succeeded in the government of Hispaniola by Don Diego Columbus, the eldest son and inheritor of the rights and titles of the admiral Christopher. To conclude with Ovando, it is related that he was regretted by his countrymen in the Indies, and was well received at court.

Don Diego did not make any alteration in the *repartimientos*, except that some of them changed hands in favour of his own adherents. During his government some fathers of the Dominican order had the courage to inveigh from the pulpit against the enormity of the *repartimientos*, and were so persevering in their representations that the court of Spain found it necessary, to avoid scandal, to order an enquiry into the condition of the Indians. In this enquiry it was seriously disputed whether it was just or unjust to make them slaves.

The histories of Hispaniola first notice about this time a great increase in the number of cattle in the island. As the human race disappeared, less and less land was occupied in husbandry, till almost the whole country became pasturage for cattle, by far the greater part of which were wild. An ordinance issued in the year 1511 specified that, as beasts of burthen were so much multiplied, the Indians should not be made to carry or drag heavy loads.

In 1511 the conquest of Cuba was undertaken and completed. The terror conceived of the Spaniards is not to be expressed. The story of the conquest is related in a Spanish history in the following terms: "A leader was chosen, who had acquitted himself in high employments with fortune and good conduct. He had in other respects amiable qualities, and was esteemed a man of honour and rectitude. He went from San Domingo with regular troops and above 300 volunteers. He landed in Cuba, not without opposition from the natives. In a few days he surprised and took the principal cacique, named Hatuey, prisoner, and made him expiate in the flames the fault he had been guilty of in not submitting with a good grace to the conqueror." This cacique when at the stake, being importuned by a Spanish priest to become a Christian, that he might go to heaven, replied, that if any Spaniard was to be met in heaven, he hoped not to go there.

The reader will be detained a very little longer with these irksome scenes. In 1514, the number of the inhabitants of Hayti was reckoned 14,000. A distributor of Indians was appointed, with powers independent of the governor, with intention to save the few remaining natives of Hayti. The new distributor began the exercise of his office by a general revocation of all the *encomiendas*, except those which had been granted by the king; and almost immediately afterwards, in the most open and shameless manner, he made new grants, and sold them to the highest bidder.

He was speedily recalled; and another (the licentiate
Ybarra) was sent to supply his place, who had a high
character for probity and resolution; but he died immediately on his arrival at San Domingo, and not
without suspicion that he was poisoned.

The endeavours of the Dominican friars in behalf
of the natives were seconded by the licentiate Bartolomeo de las Casas, and by Cardinal Ximenes when
he became prime minister of Spain; and, to their
great honour, they were both resolute to exert all their
power to preserve the natives of America. The Cardinal sent commissioners, and with them Las Casas,
with the title of Protector of the Indians. But the
Cardinal died in 1517; after which all the exertions of
Las Casas and the Dominicans could not shake the
repartimientos.

At length, among the native islanders there sprang
up one who had the courage to put himself at the head
of a number of his countrymen, and the address to
withdraw with them from the grip of the Spaniards,
and to find refuge among the mountains. This man
was the son, and according to the laws of inheritance
should have been the successor, of one of the principal
caciques. He had been christened by the name of
Henriquez, and, in consequence of a regulation made
by the late Queen Ysabel of Castile, he had been edu-
cated, on account of his former rank, in a convent of
the Franciscans. He defended his retreat in the
mountains by skilful management and resolute conduct, and had the good fortune in the commencement
to defeat some parties of Spanish troops sent against
him, which encouraged more of his countrymen, and

as many of the Africans as could escape, to flock to
him ; and under his government, as of a sovereign
prince, they withstood the attempts of the Spaniards
to subdue them.   Fortunately for Henriquez and his
followers, the conquest and settlement of Cuba, and the
invasion of Mexico, which was begun at this time, les-
sened the strength of the Spaniards in Hispaniola, and
enabled the insurgents for many years to keep all the
Spanish settlements in the island in continual alarm,
and to maintain their own independence.

During this time, the question of the propriety of
keeping the islanders in slavery underwent grave
examinations.   It is related that the experiment was
tried, of allowing a number of the natives to build
themselves two villages, to live in them according
to their own customs and liking ; and that the result
was they were found to be so improvident, and so
utterly unable to take care of themselves, that the
encomiendas were pronounced to be necessary for
their preservation.   Such an experiment is a mockery.
Before the conquest, and now under Don Henriquez,
the people of Hayti showed they wanted not the
Spaniards to take care of them.

CHAPTER III.

Ships of different European nations frequent the West Indies. Opposition experienced by them from the Spaniards. Hunting of cattle in Hispaniola.

IN the year 1517, or 1518, some Spaniards in a caravela going from San Domingo to the island Porto Rico, to take in a lading of cassava, were surprised at seeing a ship there of about 250 tons, armed with cannon, which did not appear to belong to the Spanish nation ; and on sending a boat to make enquiry she was found to be English. The account given by the English commander was, that two ships had sailed from England in company, with the intention to discover the country of the Great Cham ; that they were soon separated from each other by a tempest, and that this ship was afterwards in a sea almost covered with ice ; that thence she had sailed southward to Brazil, and, after various adventures, had found the way to Porto Rico. This same English ship, being provided with merchandise, went afterwards to Hispaniola, and anchored near the entrance of the port of San Domingo, where the captain sent on shore to demand leave to sell their goods. The demand was forwarded to the Audiencia, or superior court in San Domingo; but the Castellana, or governor of the castle, Francisco de Tapia, could not endure with patience to see a ship of another nation in that part of the world, and, without waiting for the decision of the Audiencia, ordered the cannon of the fort to be fired against her; on which she took up her anchor and returned to Porto Rico, where she purchased provisions, paying for what she got with wrought iron, and afterwards departed for Europe.* When this visit of an English ship to the West Indies was known in Spain, it caused there great inquietude; and the governor of the castle of San Domingo, it is said, was much blamed, because he had not, instead of forcing the ship to depart by firing his cannon, contrived to seize her, so that no one might have returned to teach others of their nation the route to the Spanish Indies.

The English were not the only people of whom the Spaniards had cause to be jealous, nor those from whom the most mischief was to be apprehended. The French, as already noticed, had very early made expeditions to Brazil, and they now began to look at the West Indies, so that in a short time the sight of other European ships than those of Spain became no novelty there. Hakluyt mentions a Thomas Tyson, an Englishman, who went to the West Indies in 1526, as factor to some English merchants. When the Spaniards met any of these intruders, if able to master them, they made prisoners of them, and many they

---

* *Historia General de las Indias*, por Gonç. Hernandez de Oviedo, lib. 19, cap. 13. Also Hakluyt, vol. iii. p. 499, edit. 1600.

treated as pirates. The new comers soon began to
retaliate. In 1529, the governor and council at San
Domingo drew up the plan of a regulation for the
security of their ships against the increasing dangers
from pirates in the West Indies. In this, they recommended that a central port of commerce should be
established in the West Indies, to which every ship
from Spain should be obliged to go first, as to a
general rendezvous, and thence be despatched, as
might suit circumstances, to her farther destination;
also, that all their ships homeward bound, from whatsoever part of the West Indies, should first rendezvous
at the same port; by which regulation their ships,
both outward and homeward bound, would form
escorts to each other, and have the benefit of
mutual support; and they proposed that some port
in Hispaniola should be appointed for the purpose,
as most conveniently situated. This plan appears to
have been approved by the council of the Indies;
but, from indolence, or some other cause, no farther
measures were taken for its adoption.

The attention of the Spaniards was at this time
almost wholly engrossed by the conquest and plunder
of the American continent, which it might have been
supposed would have sufficed them, according to the
opinion of Francisco Preciado, a Spanish discoverer,
who observed, that there was country enough to
conquer for a thousand years. The continental pursuits caused much diminution in the importance of
the West India Islands to the Spaniards. The mines
of the islands were not comparable in richness with
those of the continent, and, for want of labourers,

many were left unworked. The colonists in Hispaniola, however, had applied themselves to the
cultivation of the sugar-cane, and to manufacture
sugar; also to hunting cattle, which was found a
profitable employment, the skins and the suet turning
to good account. The Spaniards denominated their
hunters *matadores*, which in the Spanish language
signifies "killers" or "slaughterers".

That the English, French and Hollanders, in their
early voyages to the West Indies, went in expectation
of meeting hostility from the Spaniards, and with a
determination, therefore, to commit hostility if they
could do so with advantage, appears by an ingenious
phrase of the French adventurers, who, if the first
opportunity was in their favour, termed their profit-
ing by it "*se dedomager par avance*".

Much of Hispaniola had become desert. There
were long ranges of coast, with good ports, that were
unfrequented by any inhabitant whatever, and the
land in every part abounded with cattle. These were
such great conveniences to the ships of the interlopers,
that the western coast, which was the most distant
part from the Spanish capital, became a place of
common resort to them when in want of provisions.
Another great attraction to them was the encouragement they received from Spanish settlers along the
coast, who, from the contracted and monopolising
spirit of their government in the management of
their colonies, had at all times been eager to have
communication with foreigners, that they might obtain
supplies of European goods on terms less exorbitant
than those which the royal regulations of Spain

imposed. The government at San Domingo employed
armed ships to prevent clandestine trade, and to clear
the coasts of Hispaniola of interlopers, which ships
were called *guarda costas;* and it is said their commanders were instructed not to take prisoners. On
the other hand, the intruders formed combinations,
came in collected numbers, and made descents on
different parts of the coast, ravaging the Spanish
towns and settlements.

In the customary course, such transactions would
have come under the cognisance of the governments
in Europe; but matters here took a different turn.
The Spaniards, when they had the upper hand, did
not fail to deal out their own pleasure for law; and, in
like manner, the English, French and Dutch, when
masters, determined their own measure of retaliation.
The different European governments were glad to
avoid being involved in the settlement of disorders
they had no inclination to repress. In answer to representations made by Spain, they said, "that the
people complained against had acted entirely on their
own authority, not as the subjects of any prince, and
that the king of Spain was at liberty to proceed against
them according to his own pleasure" Queen Elizabeth of England, with more open asperity, answered a
complaint made by the Spanish ambassador, of Spanish
ships being plundered by the English in the West
Indies, "that the Spaniards had drawn these incon-
veniencies upon themselves, by their severe and unjust
dealings in their American commerce; for she did not
understand why either her subjects, or those of any
other European prince, should be debarred from traffic

in the Indies. That, as she did not acknowledge the Spaniards to have any title by the donation of the Bishop of Rome, so she knew no right they had to any places other than those they were in actual possession of; for that their having touched only here and there upon a coast, and given names to a few rivers or capes, were such insignificant things as could no ways entitle them to a propriety further than in the parts where they actually settled, and continued to inhabit." * A warfare was thus established between Europeans in the West Indies, local and confined, which had no dependence upon transactions in Europe. All Europeans not Spaniards, whether it was war or peace between their nations in Europe, on their meeting in the West Indies, regarded each other as friends and allies, knowing then no other enemy than the Spaniards; and, as a kind of public avowal of this confederation, they called themselves "Brethren of the Coast".

The first European intruders upon the Spaniards in the West Indies were accordingly mariners, the greater number of whom, it is supposed, were French, and next to them the English. Their first hunting of cattle in Hayti was for provisioning their ships. The time at which they began to form factories or establishments, to hunt cattle for the skins, and to cure the flesh as an article of traffic, is not certain, but it may be concluded that these occupations were begun by the crews of wrecked vessels, or by seamen who had disagreed with their commander, and that the ease, plenty, and freedom from all command and subordination enjoyed in

---

* Camden's *Elizabeth*, A.D. 1680.

such a life soon drew others to quit their ships and
join in the same occupations. The ships that touched
on the coast supplied the hunters with European commodities, for which they received in return hides, tallow,
and cured meat. The appellation of boucanier or
buccaneer was not invented, or at least not applied to
these adventurers, till long after their first footing in
Hayti. At the time of Oxnam's expedition across the
Isthmus of America to the South Sea, A.D. 1575, it
does not appear to have been known.

There is no particular account of the events which
took place on the coasts of Hispaniola in the early
part of the contest between the Spaniards and the new
settlers. It is, however, certain that it was a war of
the severest retaliation; and in this disorderly state
was continued the intercourse of the English, French
and Dutch with the West Indies, carried on by individuals neither authorised nor controlled by their governments for more than a century.

In 1586, the English captain, Francis Drake,
plundered the city of San Domingo; and the numbers
of the English and French in the West Indies increased
so much, that shortly afterwards the Spaniards found
themselves necessitated to abandon all the western and
north-western parts of Hispaniola.

CHAPTER IV.

Iniquitous settlement of the island St. Christopher by the English and French. Tortuga seized by the hunters. Origin of the name buccaneer. The name flibustier. Customs attributed to the buccaneers.

THE increase of trade of the English and French to the West Indies, and the growing importance of the freebooters or adventurers concerned in it, who, unassisted except by each other, had begun to acquire territory and to form establishments in spite of all opposition from the Spaniards, attracted the attention of the British and French governments, and suggested to them a scheme of confederacy, in which some of the principal adventurers were consulted. The project adopted by them was, to plant a royal colony of each nation on some one island and at the same time, by which a constant mutual support would be secured. In as far as regarded the concerns of Europeans with each other, this plan was unimpeachable.

The island chosen by the projectors, as the best suited to their purpose, was one of the Small Antilles or Caribbee Islands, known by the name of St. Christopher, which is in length about seven leagues, and in breadth two and a half.

Thus the governments of Great Britain and France, like friendly fellow-travellers, and not like rivals who were to contend in a race, began their West Indian career by joint consent at the same point both in time and place. In the year 1625, and on the same day, a colony of British and a colony of French, in the names and on the behalf of their respective nations, landed on this small island, the division of which had been settled by previous agreement.

The island St. Christopher was at that time inhabited by Caribbee Indians. The Spaniards had never possessed a settlement on it, but their ships had been accustomed to stop there, to traffic for provisions and refreshments. The French and English who came to take possession landed without obtaining the consent of the native Caribbee inhabitants; and, because danger was apprehended from their discontent, under pretence that the Caribbs were friends to the Spaniards, these new colonists fell upon them by surprise in the night, killed their principal leaders, and forced the rest to quit the island and seek another home. De Rochefort, in his *Histoire Morale des Isles Antilles* (p. 284), mentions the English and French killing the Caribb chiefs, in the following terms : " *Ils se defirent en une nuit de tous les plus factieux de cette nation !* " Thus in usurpation and barbarity was founded the first colony established under the authority of the British and French governments in the West Indies ; which colony was the parent of our African slave trade. When accounts of the conquest and of the proceedings at St. Christopher were transmitted to Europe, they were approved ; West India companies were established, and licences granted to take out colonists. De Rochefort has oddly enough remarked, that the French, English and Dutch, in their first establishments in the West Indies, did not follow the cruel maxims of the Spaniards. True it is, however, that they only copied in part. In their usurpations their aim went no farther than to dispossess, and they did not seek to make slaves of the people whom they deprived of their land.

The English and French in a short time had disagreements, and began to make complaints of each other. The English took possession of the small island Nevis, which is separated only by a narrow channel from the south end of St. Christopher. P. Charlevoix says : " The ambition of the English disturbed the good understanding between the colonists of the two nations; but M. de Cusac arriving with a squadron of the French king's ships, by taking and sinking some British ships lying there, brought the English governor to reason, and to confine himself to the treaty of partition ". After effecting this amicable adjustment, De Cusac sailed from St. Christopher, and was scarcely clear of the island when a powerful fleet, consisting of thirty-nine large ships, arrived from Spain, and anchored in the roads. Almost without opposition the Spaniards became masters of the island, although the English and French, if they had cordially joined, could have mustered a force of twelve hundred men. Intelligence that the Spaniards intended this attack had been duly received in France, and M. de Cusac's squadron had in consequence been despatched to assist in the defence of St. Christopher; but the Spaniards

being slow in their preparations, their fleet did not
arrive at the time expected, and De Cusac, hearing no
news of them, presumed that they had given up their
design against St. Christopher. Without strengthening
the joint colony, he gave the English a lesson on
moderation little calculated to incline them to co-
operate heartily with the French in defence of the
island, and sailed on a cruise to the Gulf of Mexico.
Shortly after his departure, towards the end of the
year 1629, the Spanish fleet arrived. The colonists
almost immediately despaired of being able to oppose
so great a force. Many of the French embarked in
their ships in time to effect their escape, and to take
refuge among the islands northward. The remainder,
with the English, lay at the disposal of the Spanish
commander, Don Frederic de Toledo. At this time
Spain was at war with England, France and Holland ;
and this armament was designed ultimately to act
against the Hollanders in Brazil, but was ordered by
the way to drive the English and the French from the
island of St. Christopher. Don Frederic would not
weaken his force by leaving a garrison there, and was
in haste to prosecute his voyage to Brazil. As the
settlement of St. Christopher had been established
on regular government authorities, the settlers were
treated as prisoners of war. To clear the island in
the most speedy manner, Don Frederic took many of
the English on board his own fleet, and made as many
of the other colonists embark as could be crowded in
any vessels which could be found for them. He saw
them get under sail and leave the island ; and from
those who remained he required their parole, that they

would depart by the earliest opportunity which should
present itself, warning them, at the same time, that if,
on his return from Brazil, he found any Englishmen or
Frenchmen at St. Christopher, they should be put
to the sword. After this he sailed for Brazil. As
soon, however, as it was known that the Spanish fleet
had left the West Indian sea, the colonists, both English
and French, returned to St. Christopher, and repos-
sessed themselves of their old quarters.

The settlement of the island St. Christopher gave
great encouragement to the hunters on the west coast
of Hispaniola. Their manufactories for the curing
of meat, and for drying the skins, multiplied, and as
the value of them increased they began to think it
of consequence to provide for their security. To this
end they took possession of the small island Tortuga,
near the north-west end of Hispaniola, where the
Spaniards had placed a garrison, but which was too
small to make opposition. There was a road for shipping, with good anchorage, at Tortuga; and its separation from the mainland of Hispaniola seemed to be a
good guarantee from sudden and unexpected attack.
They built magazines there, for the lodgment of their
goods, and regarded this island as their headquarters,
or place of general rendezvous, to which to repair in
times of danger. They elected no chief, erected no
fortification, set up no authorities, nor fettered themselves by any engagement. All was voluntary; and
they were negligently contented at having done so
much towards their security.

About the time of their taking possession of Tortuga, they began to be known by the name of " bucca-

neers," of which appellation it will be proper to speak at some length.

The flesh of the cattle killed by the hunters was cured to keep good for use, after a manner learnt from the Caribbee Indians, which was as follows : The meat was laid to be dried upon a wooden grate or hurdle (*grille de bois*) which the Indians called *barbecu*, placed at a good distance over a slow fire. The meat when cured was called *boucan*, and the same name was given to the place of their cookery. Père Labat describes *viande boucannée* to be, *viande sechée à petit feu et à la fumée.* The Caribbees are said to have sometimes served their prisoners after this fashion : "*Ils les mangent après les avoir bien boucanné, c'est à dire, rôtis bien sec* ".* The boucan was a very favourite method of cooking among these Indians. A Caribbee has been known, on returning home from fishing fatigued and pressed with hunger, to have had the patience to wait the roasting of a fish on a wooden grate fixed two feet above the ground, over a fire so small as sometimes to require the whole day to dress it. †

The flesh of the cattle was in general dried in the smoke, without being salted. The *Dictionnaire de Trevoux* explains *boucaner* to be "*faire sorer sans sel,*" to dry red without salt. But the flesh of wild hogs, and also of the beeves, when intended for keeping a length of time, was first salted. The same thing was practised among the Brazilians. It was remarked in one of the earliest visits of the Portuguese to Brazil,

---

* *Hist. des Antilles*, par P. du Tertre, Paris, 1667. Tom. i. p. 415.
† La Rochefort, *Sur le Repas des Carribees.*

that the natives (who were cannibals) kept human flesh salted and smoked hanging up in their houses.* It is probable the meat cured by the buccaneers to sell to shipping for sea-store was all salted. The process is thus described: "The bones being taken out, the flesh was cut into convenient pieces and salted, and the next day was taken to the boucan". Sometimes, to give a peculiar relish to the meat, the skin of the animal was cast into the fire under it. The meat thus cured was of a fine red colour, and of excellent flavour; but in six months after it was boucanned it had little taste left, except of salt. The boucanned hog's flesh continued good a much longer time than the flesh of the beeves, if kept in dry places.

From adopting the boucan of the Carribees, the hunters in Hispaniola, the Spaniards excepted, came to be called *boucaniers*, but afterwards, according to a pronunciation more in favour with the English, buccaneers.† Many of the French hunters were natives of Normandy; whence it became proverbial in some of the seaports of Normandy to say of a smoky house, *c'est un vrai boucan*.

The French buccaneers and adventurers were also called flibustiers, and more frequently by that than by any other name. The word flibustier is merely the French mariner's mode of pronouncing the English word "freebooter," a name which long

* *History of Brazil*, by Robert Southey, p. 17.

† In some of the English accounts the name is written *bucanier*; but uniformity in spelling was not much attended to at that time. Dampier wrote *buccaneer*, which agrees with the present manner of pronouncing the word, and he is to be esteemed the best authority.

preceded that of boucanier or buccaneer, as the occupation of cruising against the Spaniards preceded that of hunting and curing meat. Some authors have given a derivation to the name flibustier from the word "flyboat" because, say they, the French hunters in Hispaniola bought vessels of the Dutch, called flyboats, to cruise upon the Spaniards. There are two objections to this derivation. First, the word "flyboat" is only an English translation of the Dutch word "fluyt," which is the proper denomination of the vessel intended by it. Secondly, it would not very readily occur to anyone to purchase Dutch fluyts, or flyboats, for chasing vessels.

Some have understood the boucanier and flibustier to be distinct both in person and character.* This was probably the case with a few, after the settlement of Tortuga ; but before, and very generally afterwards, the occupations were joined, making one of amphibious character. Ships from all parts of the West Indies frequented Tortuga, and it continually happened that some among the crews quitted their ships to turn buccaneers; whilst among the buccaneers some would be desirous to quit their hunting employment to go on a cruise, to make a voyage, or to return to Europe. The two occupations of hunting

---

* The French account says, that after taking possession of Tortuga, the adventurers divided into three classes : that those who occupied themselves in the chase took the name of boucaniers ; those who went on cruises, the name of flibustiers ; and a third class, who cultivated the soil, called themselves *habitans* (inhabitants). See *Histoire des Avanturiers qui se sont signalez dans les Indes*, par Alex. Ol. Oexmelin ; Paris, 1688. Vol. i. p. 22.

and cruising being so common to the same person, caused the names flibustier and buccaneer to be esteemed synonymous, signifying always and principally the being at war with the Spaniards. The buccaneer and flibustier, therefore, as long as they continued in a state of independence, are to be considered as the same character, exercising sometimes one, sometimes the other employment; and either name was taken by them indifferently, whether they were employed on the sea or on the land. But a fanciful kind of inversion took place, through the different caprices of the French and English adventurers. The greater part of the first cattle hunters were French, and the greater number of the first cruisers against the Spaniards were English. The French adventurers, nevertheless, had a partiality for the name of flibustier; whilst the English showed a like preference for the name of buccaneer, which, as will be seen, was assumed by many hundred seamen of their nation, who were never employed either in hunting or in the boucan.

A propensity to make things which are extraordinary appear more so has caused many peculiar customs to be attributed to the buccaneers, which, it is pretended, were observed as strictly as if they had been established laws. It is said that every buccaneer had his chosen and declared comrade, between whom property was in common, and, if one died, the survivor was inheritor of the whole. This was called by the French *matelotage*. It is, however acknowledged, that the *matelotage* was not a compulsory regulation, and that the buccaneers sometimes bequeathed by will. A general

right of participation in some things, among which was
meat for present consumption, was acknowledged
among them, and it is said that bolts, locks, and every
species of fastening were prohibited, it being held that
the use of such securities would have impeached the
honour of their vocation. Yet, on commencing buccaneer it was customary with those who were of
respectable lineage to relinquish their family name,
and assume some other, as a *nom de guerre*. Their
dress, which was uniformly slovenly when engaged in
the business of hunting or of the boucan, is mentioned
as a prescribed costume, but it doubtless was prescribed
only by their own negligence and indolence; in particular, that they wore an unwashed shirt and panta-
loons dyed in the blood of the animals they had
killed. Other distinctions, equally capricious, and to
little purpose, are related, which have no connection
with their history. Some curious anecdotes are produced, to show the great respect some among them
entertained for religion and for morality. A certain
flibustier captain, named Daniel, shot one of his crew
in the church, for behaving irreverently during the
performance of Mass. Raveneau de Lussen (whose
adventures will be frequently mentioned) took the
occupation of a buccaneer because he was in debt, and
wished, as every honest man should do, to have where-
withal to satisfy his creditors.

In their sea enterprises, they followed most of the
customs which are generally observed in private ships
of war, and sometimes were held together by a subscribed written agreement, by the English called
"charter-party," by the French, *chasse-partie*—which

might in this case be construed "a chasing agreement". Whenever it happened that Spain was at open and declared war with any of the maritime nations of Europe, the buccaneers who were natives of the country at war with her obtained commissions, which rendered the vessels in which they cruised regular privateers.

The English adventurers sometimes, as is seen in Dampier, called themselves "privateers," applying the term to persons in the same manner we now apply it to private ships of war. The Dutch, whose terms are generally faithful to the meaning intended, called the adventurers *zee roovers;* the word *roover* in the Dutch language comprising the joint sense of the two English words "rover" and "robber".

CHAPTER V.

Treaty made by the Spaniards with Don Henriquez. Increase of English and French in the West Indies. Tortuga surprised by the Spaniards. Policy of the English and French governments with respect to the buccaneers. Mansvelt: his attempt to form an independent buccaneer establishment. French West India Company. Morgan succeeds Mansvelt as chief of the buccaneers.

THE Spanish government at length began to think it necessary to relax from their large pretensions, and in the year 1630 entered into treaties with other European nations for mutual security of their West India possessions. In a treaty concluded that year with Great Britain it was declared that peace, amity and friendship should be observed between their respective subjects in all parts of the world. But this general specification was not sufficient to produce effect in the West Indies.

In Hispaniola, in the year 1633, the government at San Domingo concluded a treaty with Don Henriquez, which was the more readily accorded to him because it was apprehended the revolted natives would league with the Brethren of the Coast. By this treaty all the followers of Don Henriquez who could claim descent from the original natives, in number four thousand persons, were declared free and under his protection, and lands were marked out for them. But, what is revolting to all generous hopes of human nature, the negroes were abandoned to the Spaniards. Magnanimity was not to be expected of the natives of Hayti ; yet they had shown themselves capable of exertion for their own relief, and a small degree more of firmness would have included these, their most able champions, in the treaty. This weak and wicked defection from friends confederated with them in one common and righteous cause seems to have wrought its own punishment. The vigilance and vigour of mind of the negro might have guarded against encroachments upon the independence obtained ; instead of which, the wretched Haytians in a short time fell again wholly into the grinding hands of the Spaniards, and in the early part of the eighteenth century it was reckoned that the whole number living, of the descendants of the party of Don Henriquez, did not quite amount to one hundred persons.

The settlement of the buccaneers at Tortuga drew many Europeans there, as well settlers as others, to join in their adventures and occupations. They began to clear and cultivate the grounds, which were before overgrown with woods, and made plantations of tobacco, which proved to be of extraordinary good quality.

More Europeans, not Spaniards, consequently allies of the buccaneers, continued to pour into the West Indies, and formed settlements on their own accounts on some of the islands of the Small Antilles. These

settlements were not composed of mixtures of different
people, but were most of them all English or all
French; and as they grew into prosperity, they were
taken possession of for the crowns of England or of
France by the respective governments. Under the
government authorities new colonists were sent out,
royal governors were appointed, and codes of law
established, which combined with the security of the
colony the interests of the mother-country. But at
the same time these benefits were conferred, grants of
land were made under royal authority, which dispos-
sessed many persons who by labour and perilous
adventure, and some who at considerable expense, had
achieved establishments for themselves, in favour of
men till then no way concerned in any of the under-
takings. In some cases, grants of whole islands were
obtained by purchase or favour; and the first settlers,
who had long before gained possession, and who had
cleared and brought the ground into a state of cultivation, were rendered dependent upon the new pro-
prietary governors, to whose terms they were obliged
to submit, or to relinquish their tenure. Such were
the hard accompaniments to the protection afforded by
the governments of France and Great Britain to
colonies, which, before they were acknowledged legiti-
mate offsprings of the mother-country, had grown into
consideration through their own exertions; and, only
because they were found worth adopting, were now
received into the parent family. The discontents
created by this rapacious conduct of the governments,
and the disregard shown to the claims of the first
settlers, instigated some to resistance and rebellion,

and caused many to join the buccaneers. The Caribbee inhabitants were driven from their lands also with as little ceremony.

The buccaneer colony at Tortuga had not been beheld with indifference by the Spaniards. The buccaneers, with the carelessness natural to men in their loose condition of life, under neither command nor guidance, continued to trust to the supineness of the enemy for their safety, and neglected all precaution. In the year 1638, the Spaniards with a large force fell unexpectedly upon Tortuga, at a time when the greater number of the settlers were absent in Hispaniola on the chase; and those who were on the island, having neither fortress nor government, became an easy prey to the Spaniards, who made a general massacre of all who fell into their hands—not only of those they surprised in the beginning, but many who afterwards came in from the woods to implore their lives on condition of returning to Europe, they hanged. A few kept themselves concealed till they found an opportunity to cross over to their brethren in Hispaniola.

It happened not to suit the convenience of the Spaniards to keep a garrison at Tortuga, and they were persuaded the buccaneers would not speedily again expose themselves to a repetition of such treatment as they had just experienced; therefore, they contented themselves with destroying the buildings, and as much as they could of the plantations; after which they returned to San Domingo. In a short time after their departure, the remnant of the hunters collected to the number of three hundred, again fixed themselves at Tortuga, and, for the first time, elected a commander.

As the hostility of the buccaneers had constantly and solely been directed against the Spaniards, all other Europeans in the West Indies regarded them as champions in the common cause, and the severities which had been exercised against them created less of dread than of a spirit of vengeance. The numbers of the buccaneers were quickly recruited by volunteers of English, French and Dutch from all parts; and both the occupations of hunting and cruising were pursued with more than usual eagerness. The French and English governors in the West Indies, influenced by the like feelings, either openly or by connivance, gave constant encouragement to the buccaneers. The French governor at St. Christopher, who was also governor-general for the French West India Islands, was most ready to send assistance to the buccaneers. This governor, Monsieur de Poincy, an enterprising and capable man, had formed a design to take possession of the island Tortuga for the crown of France; which he managed to put in execution three years after, having by that time predisposed some of the principal French buccaneers to receive a garrison of the French king's troops. This appropriation was made in 1641; and De Poincy, thinking his acquisition would be more secure to France by the absence of the English, forced all the English buccaneers to quit the island. The French writers say that, before the interposition of the French governor, the English buccaneers took advantage of their numbers, and domineered in Tortuga. The English governors in the West Indies could not at this time show the same tender regard for the English buccaneers, as the report they received from home was very precarious, owing to the disputes which then subsisted in England between King Charles and the English Parliament, which engrossed so much of the public attention as to leave little to colonial concerns.

The French commander De Poincy pushed his success. In his appointment of a governor to Tortuga, he added the title of governor of the west coast of Hispaniola, and by degrees he introduced French garrisons. This was the first footing obtained by the government of France in Hispaniola. The same policy was observed there respecting the English as at Tortuga, by which means was effected a separation of the English buccaneers from the French. After this time, it was only occasionally, and from accidental circumstances, or by special agreement, that they acted in concert. The English adventurers, thus elbowed out of Hispaniola and Tortuga, lost the occupation of hunting cattle and of the boucan, but they continued to be distinguished by the appellation of buccaneers, and when not cruising most generally harboured at the islands possessed by the British.

Hitherto it had rested in the power of the buccaneers to have formed themselves into an independent state. Being composed of people of different nations, the admission of a governor from any one might easily have been resisted. Now, they were considered in a kind of middle state, between that of buccaneers and of men returned to their native allegiance. It seemed now in the power of the English and French governments to put a stop to their cruisings, and to

furnish them with more honest employment; but
politics of a different cast prevailed. The buccaneers
were regarded as profitable to the colonies, on account
of the prizes they brought in, and even vanity had a
share in their being countenanced. The French
authors call them *nos braves*, and the English speak of
their "unparalleled exploits". The policy both of
England and of France with respect to the buccaneers
seems to have been well described in the following
sentence: "On laissoit faire des avanturiers, qu'on pou-
voit toujours desavouer, mais dont les succes pouvoient
etre utiles": *i.e.*, "they connived at the actions of these
adventurers, which could always be disavowed, and
whose successes might be serviceable". This was not
esteemed *friponnerie*, but a maxim of sound state
policy.　In the character given of a good French
West India governor, he is praised for that, "besides
encouraging the cultivation of lands, he never neglected
to encourage the flibustiers. It was a certain means
of improving the colony, by attracting thither the
young and enterprising. He would scarcely receive a
slight portion of what he was entitled to from his right
of bestowing commissions in time of war.* And when
we were at peace, and our flibustiers, for want of
other employment, would go cruising, and would carry
their prizes to the English islands, he was at the pains
of procuring them commissions from Portugal, which
country was then at war with Spain; in virtue of which
our flibustiers continued to make themselves redoubt-
able to the Spaniards, and to spread riches and abun-

---

*The governor or admiral who granted the commission
claimed one tenth of all prizes made under its authority.

dance in our colonies." This panegyric was bestowed by Père Labat, who seems to have had more of national than of moral or religious feeling on this head.

It was a powerful consideration with the French and English governments to have at their occasional disposal, without trouble or expense, a well-trained military force, always at hand, and willing to be employed upon emergency, who required no pay nor other recompense for their services and constant readiness than their share of plunder, and that their piracies upon the Spaniards should pass unnoticed.

Towards the end of 1644, a new governor-general for the French West India possessions was appointed by the French regency (during the minority of Louis XIV.); but the commander De Poincy did not choose to resign, and the colonists were inclined to support him. Great discontents prevailed in the French colonies, which rendered them liable to being shaken by civil wars, and the apprehensions of the regency on this head enabled De Poincy to stand his ground. He remained governor-general over the French colonies not only for the time, but was continued in that office, by succeeding administrations, many years.

About the year 1654, a large party of buccaneers, French and English, joined in an expedition on the continent. They ascended a river of the Mosquito shore, a small distance on the south side of Cape Gracias a Dios, in canoes, and, after labouring nearly a month against a strong stream and waterfalls, they left their canoes and marched to the town of Nueva Segovia, which they plundered, and then returned down the river.

In the same year, the Spaniards took Tortuga from the French.

In the year following, 1655, England being at war with Spain, a large force was sent from England to attempt the conquest of the island Hispaniola. In this attempt they failed; but they afterwards fell upon Jamaica, of which island they made themselves masters, and kept possession. In the conquest of Jamaica, the English were greatly assisted by the buccaneers, and a few years after, with their assistance also, the French regained possession of Tortuga.

On the recovery of Tortuga, the French buccaneers greatly increased in the northern and western parts of Hispaniola. Spain also sent large reinforcements from Europe, and for some years war was carried on with great spirit and animosity on both sides. During the heat of this contest, the French buccaneers followed more the occupation of hunting, and less that of cruising, than at any other period of their history.

The Spaniards, finding they could not expel the French from Hispaniola, determined to join their efforts to those of the French hunters, for the destruction of the cattle and wild hogs on the island, so as to render the business of hunting unproductive. But the French had begun to plant, and the depriving them of the employment of hunting drove them to other occupations not less contrary to the interest and wishes of the Spaniards. The less profit they found in the chase, the more they became cultivators and cruisers.

The buccaneer histories of this period abound with relations of daring actions performed by them, many ɔf which are chiefly remarkable for the ferocious cruelty of the leaders by whom they were conducted. Pierre, a native of Dieppe, for his success received to his name the addition of *le grand*, and is mentioned as one of the first flibustiers who obtained much notoriety. In a boat, with a crew of twenty-eight men, he surprised and took the ship of the vice-admiral of the Spanish galeons, as she was sailing homeward-bound with a rich freight. He set the Spanish crew on shore at Cape Tiburon, the west end of Hispaniola, and sailed in his prize to France. A Frenchman named Alexandre, also in a small vessel, took a Spanish ship of war.

It is related of another Frenchman, a native of Languedoc, named Montbars, that on reading a history of the cruelty of the Spaniards to the Americans, he conceived such an implacable hatred against the Spaniards, that he determined on going to the West Indies to join the buccaneers ; and that he there pursued his vengeance with so much ardour as to acquire the surname of the " Exterminator".

One buccaneer of some note was a native of Portugal, known by the name of Bartolomeo Portuguez, who, however, was more renowned for his wonderful escapes, both in battle and from the gallows, than for his other actions.

But no one of the buccaneers hitherto named arrived at so great a degree of notoriety as a Frenchman, called François l'Olonnois, a native of part of the French coast which is near the sands of Olonne, but whose real name is not known. This man and Michel le Basque, both buccaneer commanders, at the head of 650 men took the towns of Maracaibo and Gibraltar in the Gulf of Venezuela, on the *tierra firma.* The booty they obtained by the plunder and ransom of these places was estimated at 400,000 crowns. The barbarities practised on the prisoners could not be exceeded. Olonnois was possessed with an ambition to make himself renowned for being terrible. At one time, it is said, he put the whole crew of a Spanish ship, ninety men, to death, performing himself the office of executioner, by beheading them. He caused the crews of four other vessels to be thrown into the sea, and more than once, in his frenzies, he tore out the hearts of his victims and devoured them. Yet this man had his encomiasts ; so much will loose notions concerning glory, aided by a little partiality, mislead even sensible men. Père Charlevoix says: " Celui de tous, dont les grandes actions illustrerent davantage les premieres années du gouvernement de M. d'Ogeron, fut l'Olonnois. Ses premiers succès furent suivis de quelques malheurs, qui ne servirent qu'à donner un nouveau lustre à sa gloire." The career of this savage was terminated by the Indians of the coast of Darien, on which he had landed.

The buccaneers now went in such formidable numbers that several Spanish towns, both on the continent and among the islands of the West Indies, submitted to pay them contribution ; and at this time a buccaneer commander, named Mansvelt, more provident and more ambitious in his views than any who preceded him, formed a project for founding an independent buccaneer establishment. Of what country Mansvelt was native does not appear, but he was so

popular among the buccaneers, that both French and
English were glad to have him for their leader. The
greater number of his followers in his attempt to form
a settlement were probably English, as he fitted out in
Jamaica. A Welshman, named Henry Morgan, who
had made some successful cruises as a buccaneer, went
with him as second in command. The place designed
by them for their establishment was an island named
Santa Katalina, or Providence, situated in latitude
13° 24′ north, about 40 leagues to the eastward of the
Mosquito shore. This island is scarcely more than
two leagues in its greatest extent, but has a harbour
capable of being easily fortified against an enemy, and
very near to its north end is a much smaller island.
The late charts assign the name of Santa Katalina to
the small island, and give to the larger island that of
Old Providence, the epithet " old " having been added
to distinguish this from the Providence of the Bahama
Islands. At the time Mansvelt undertook his scheme
of settlement this Santa Katalina, or Providence
Island, was occupied by the Spaniards, who had a fort
and good garrison there. Some time in or near the
year 1664, Mansvelt sailed thither from Jamaica with
fifteen vessels and 500 men. He assaulted and took
the fort, which he garrisoned with one hundred
buccaneers and all the slaves he had taken, and left
the command to a Frenchman named Le Sieur Simon.
At the end of his cruise he returned to Jamaica,
intending to procure there recruits for his settlement
of Santa Katalina ; but the governor of Jamaica,
however friendly to the buccaneers whilst they made
Jamaica their home, saw many reasons for disliking

Mansvelt's plan, and would not consent to his raising men.

Not being able to overcome the governor's unwillingness, Mansvelt sailed for Tortuga to try what assistance he could procure there, but in the passage he was suddenly taken ill and died. For a length of time after, Simon remained at Santa Katalina with his garrison, in continual expectation of seeing or hearing from Mansvelt; instead of which, a large Spanish force arrived and besieged his fort, when, learning of Mansvelt's death and seeing no prospect of receiving reinforcement or relief, he found himself obliged to surrender.

The government in France had appointed commissioners on behalf of the French West India Company to take all the Islands called the French Antilles out of the hands of individuals, subjects of France, who had before obtained possession, and to put them into the possession of the said company, to be governed according to such provisions as they should think proper. In February, 1665, M. d'Ogeron was appointed governor of Tortuga, and of the French settlements in Hispaniola, or St. Domingo, as the island was now more commonly called. On his arrival at Tortuga the French adventurers, both there and in Hispaniola, declared that if he came to govern in the name of the king of France he should find faithful and obedient subjects; but they would not submit themselves to any company, and in no case would they consent to the prohibiting their trade with the Hollanders, "with whom," said the buccaneers, "we have been in the constant habit of trading, and were so before it was known in France that there was a single Frenchman in Tortuga, or on the coast of St. Domingo ".

M. d'Ogeron had recourse to dissimulation to allay these discontents. He yielded consent to the condition respecting the commerce with the Dutch, fully resolved not to observe it longer than till his authority should be sufficiently established for him to break it with safety, and to secure the commerce within his government exclusively to the French West India Company, who, when rid of all competitors, would be able to fix their own prices. It was not long before M. d'Ogeron judged the opportunity was arrived for effecting this revocation without danger; but it caused a revolt of the French settlers in St. Domingo, which did not terminate without bloodshed and an execution; and so partial as well as defective in principle were the historians who have related the fact, that they have at the same time commended M. d'Ogeron for his probity and simple manners. In the end he prevailed in establishing a monopoly for the Company, to the injury of his old companions, the French buccaneers, with whom he had at a former period associated, and who had been his benefactors in a time of distress.

On the death of Mansvelt, Morgan was regarded as the most capable and most fortunate leader of any of the Jamaica buccaneers. With a body of several hundred men who placed themselves under his command he took and plundered the town of Puerto del Principe in Cuba. A quarrel happened at this place among the buccaneers, in which a Frenchman was treacherously slain by an Englishman. The French

took to arms to revenge the death of their countryman ; but Morgan pacified them by putting the
murderer in irons, and promising he should be
delivered up to justice on their return to Jamaica :
which was done, and the criminal was hanged. But
in some other respects the French were not so well
satisfied with Morgan for their commander as they
had been with Mansvelt. Morgan was a great rogue,
and little respected the old proverb of "honour among
thieves" : this had been made manifest to the French,
and almost all of them separated from him.

Maracaibo was now a second time pillaged by the
French buccaneers, under Michel le Basque.

Morgan's next undertaking was against Porto Bello,
one of the principal and best-fortified ports belonging
to the Spaniards in the West Indies. He had under
his command only 460 men ; but, not having revealed
his design to any person, he came on the town by
surprise, and found it unprepared. Shocking cruelties
are related to have been committed in this expedition.
Among many others, that a castle having made more
resistance than had been expected, Morgan after its
surrendering shut up the garrison in it, and caused
fire to be set to the magazine, destroying thereby the
castle and the garrison together. In the attack on
another fort he compelled a number of religious
persons, both male and female, whom he had taken
prisoners, to carry and plant scaling ladders against
the walls, and many of them were killed by those who
defended the fort. The buccaneers in the end became
masters of the place, and the use they made of their
victory corresponded with their actions in obtaining it.

Many prisoners died under tortures inflicted on them
to make them discover concealed treasures, whether
they knew of any or not. A large ransom was also
extorted for the town and prisoners.

This success attracted other buccaneers, among
them the French, to again join Morgan, and by a
kind of circular notice they rendezvoused in large force
under his command at the Isla de la Vaca (by the
French called Isle Avache), near the south-western part of Hispaniola.

A large French buccaneer ship was lying at La
Vaca, which was not of this combination, the commander and crew of which refused to join with
Morgan though much solicited. Morgan was angry,
but dissembled, and with a show of cordiality invited
the French captain and his officers to an entertainment on board his own ship. When they were his
guests they found themselves his prisoners, and their
ship being left without officers was taken without
resistance. The men put by Morgan in charge of
the ship fell to drinking, and, whether from their
drunkenness and negligence or from the revenge of
any of the prisoners cannot be known, she suddenly
blew up, by which 350 English buccaneers and all
the Frenchmen on board her perished. *The History
of the Buccaneers of America*, in which the event is
related, adds by way of remark: "Thus was this
unjust action of Captain Morgan's soon followed by
divine justice; for this ship, the largest in his fleet,
was blown up in the air with 350 Englishmen and
all the French prisoners". This comment seems to
have suggested to Voltaire the ridicule he has thrown

on the indiscriminate manner in which men sometimes
pronounce misfortune to be a peculiar judgment of
God, in the dialogue he put into the mouths of
Candide and Martin on the wicked Dutch skipper
being drowned.

From Isla de la Vaca Morgan sailed with his fleet
to Maracaibo and Gibraltar, which unfortunate towns
were again sacked. It was a frequent practice with
these desperadoes to secure their prisoners by shutting
them up in churches, where it was easy to keep guard
over them. This was done by Morgan at Maracaibo
and Gibraltar, and with so little care for their subsistence that many of the prisoners were actually starved
to death whilst their merciless victors were rioting in
the plunder of their houses.

Morgan remained so long at Gibraltar that the
Spaniards had time to repair and put in order a castle
at the entrance of the Lagune of Maracaibo; and
three large Spanish ships of war arrived and took
stations near the castle, by which they hoped to cut
off the retreat of the pirates. The buccaneer histories give Morgan much credit here for his management in extricating his fleet and prizes from their
difficult situation, which is related to have been in the
following manner : he converted one of his vessels
into a fire-ship, but so fitted up as to preserve the
appearance of a ship intended for fighting, and clumps
of wood were stuck up in her, dressed with hats on
to resemble men. By means of this ship, the rest of
his fleet following close at hand, he took one of the
Spanish ships, and destroyed the two others. Still
there remained the castle to be passed, which he

effected without loss by a stratagem which deceived the Spaniards from their guard. During the day, and in sight of the castle, he filled his boats with armed men, and they rowed from the ships to a part of the shore which was well concealed by thickets. After waiting as long as might be supposed to be occupied in the landing, all the men lay down close in the bottom of the boats, except two in each, who rowed them back, going to the sides of the ships which were farthest from the castle. This being repeated several times caused the Spaniards to believe that the buccaneers intended an assault by land with their whole force, and they made disposition with their cannon accordingly, leaving the side of the castle towards the sea unprovided. When it was night, and the ebb tide began to make, Morgan's fleet took up their anchors and, without setting sail, it being moonlight, they fell down the river, unperceived, till they were nigh the castle. They then set their sails and fired upon the castle, and before the Spaniards could bring their guns back to return the fire the ships were past. The value of the booty made in this expedition was 250,000 pieces of eight.

Some minor actions of the buccaneers are omitted here, not being of sufficient consequence to excuse detaining the reader, to whom will next be related one of their most remarkable exploits.

CHAPTER VI.

Treaty of America. Expedition of the buccaneers against Panama. Exquemelin's History of the American Sea Rovers. Misconduct of the European governors in the West Indies.

IN July, 1670, was concluded a treaty between Great Britain and Spain, made expressly with the intention of terminating the buccaneer war and of settling all disputes between the subjects of the two countries in America. It has been with this especial signification entitled the Treaty of America, and is the first which appears to have been dictated by a mutual disposition to establish peace in the West Indies. The articles particularly directed to this end are the following :—

Art. II. There shall be an universal peace and sincere friendship, as well in America as in other parts, between the kings of Great Britain and Spain, their heirs and successors, their kingdoms, plantations, &c.

III. That all hostilities, depredations, &c., shall cease between the subjects of the said kings.

IV. The two kings shall take care that their subjects forbear all acts of hostility, and shall call in all commissions, letters of marque and reprisals, and punish all offenders, obliging them to make reparation.

VII. All past injuries on both sides shall be buried in oblivion.

VIII. The king of Great Britain shall hold and enjoy all the lands, countries, &c., he is now possessed of in America.

IX. The subjects on each side shall forbear trading or sailing to any places whatsoever under the dominion of the other without particular licence.

XIV. Particular offences shall be repaired in the common course of justice, and no reprisals made unless justice be denied or unreasonably retarded.

When notice of this treaty was received in the West Indies the buccaneers immediately as of one accord resolved to undertake some grand expedition. Many occurrences had given rise to jealousies between the English and the French in the West Indies, but Morgan's reputation as a commander was so high that adventurers from all parts signified their readiness to join him, and he appointed Cape Tiburon on the west of Hispaniola for the place of general rendezvous. In consequence of this summons, in the beginning of December, 1670, a fleet was there collected under his command, consisting of no less than thirty-seven vessels of different sizes carrying above 2000 men. Having so large a force he held council with the principal commanders, and proposed for their determination which they should attempt of the three places—Carthagena, Vera Cruz, or Panama. Panama was believed to be the richest, and on that city the lot fell.

A century before, when the name of buccaneer was not known, roving adventurers had crossed the Isthmus of America from the West Indies to the South Sea; but the fate of Oxnam and his companions deterred others from the like attempt until the time of the buccaneers, who, as they increased in numbers, extended their enterprises, urged by a kind of necessity, the West Indies not furnishing plunder sufficient to satisfy so many men whose modes of expenditure were not less profligate than their means of obtaining were violent and iniquitous.

The rendezvous appointed by Morgan for meeting his confederates was distant from any authority which could prevent or impede their operations; and, whilst they remained on the coast of Hispaniola, he employed men to hunt cattle and cure meat. He also sent vessels to collect maize at the settlements on the *tierra firma*. Specific articles of agreement were drawn up and subscribed to for the distribution of plunder. Morgan as commander-in-chief was to receive one hundredth part; each captain was to have eight shares; provision was stipulated for the maimed and wounded, and rewards for those who should particularly distinguish themselves. These matters being settled, on the 16th December the whole fleet sailed from Cape Tiburon; on the 20th they arrived at the island Santa Katalina, then occupied by the Spaniards, who had garrisoned it chiefly with criminals sentenced to serve there by way of punishment. Morgan had fully entered into the project of Mansvelt for forming an establishment at Santa Katalina, and he was not the less inclined to it now that he considered himself as the head of the buccaneers. The island surrendered upon summons. It is related that at the request of the governor, in which Morgan indulged him, a military farce was performed, Morgan causing cannon charged only with powder to be fired at the fort, which returned the like fire for a decent time, and then lowered their flag.

Morgan judged it would contribute to the success of the proposed expedition against Panama to make himself master of the fort or castle of San Lorenzo at the entrance of the river Chagre. For this purpose he sent a detachment of 400 men under the command of an old buccaneer named Brodely, and in the meantime remained himself with the main body of his forces at Santa Katalina, to avoid giving the Spaniards cause to suspect his further designs.

The castle of Chagre was strong, both in its works and in situation, being built on the summit of a steep hill. It was valiantly assaulted and no less valiantly defended. The buccaneers were once forced to retreat. They returned to the attack and were nearly a second time driven back, when a powder magazine in the fort blew up, and the mischief and confusion thereby occasioned gave the buccaneers opportunity to force entrance through the breaches they had made. The governor of the castle refused to take quarter, which was offered him by the buccaneers, as did also some of the Spanish soldiers. More than 200 men of 314 which composed the garrison were killed. The loss on the side of the buccaneers was above 100 men killed outright and 70 wounded.

On receiving intelligence of the castle being taken, Morgan repaired with the rest of his men from Santa Katalina. He set the prisoners to work to repair the castle of San Lorenzo, in which he stationed a garrison of 500 men ; he also appointed 150 men to take care of the ships, and on the 18th January, 1671,* he set forward at the head of 1200 men for Panama. One party with artillery and stores embarked in canoes to mount the river Chagre, the course of which is extremely serpentine. At the end of the second day, however, they quitted the canoes on account of the many obstructions from trees which had fallen in the river, and because the river was at this time in many places almost dry ; but the way by land was also found so difficult for the carriage of stores that the canoes were again resorted to. On the sixth day, when they had expended great part of their travelling store of provisions, they had the good fortune to discover a barn full of maize. They saw many native Indians, who all kept at a distance, and it was in vain that they endeavoured to overtake some.

On the seventh day they came to a village called Cruz, the inhabitants of which had set fire to their houses and fled. They found there, however, fifteen jars of Peruvian wine and a sack of bread. The village of Cruz is at the highest part of the river Chagre which boats or canoes can reach. It

* It is proper to mention that an erroneously printed date in the English edition of the *Buccaneers of America* occasioned a mistake to be made in the account given of Narbrough's Voyage, respecting the time the buccaneers kept possession of Panama. See vol. iii. of *Voyages and Discoveries in the South Sea*, p. 374.

was reckoned to be eight leagues distant from Panama.

On the ninth day of their journey they came in sight of the South Sea ; and here they were among fields in which cattle grazed. Towards evening they had sight of the steeples of Panama. In the course of their march thus far from the castle of Chagre they had lost, by being fired at from concealed places, ten men killed, and as many more were wounded.

Panama had not the defence of regular fortifications. Some works had been raised, but in parts the city lay open, and had to be won or defended by plain fighting. According to the buccaneer account, the Spaniards had about 2000 infantry and 400 horse, which force, it is supposed, was in part composed of inhabitants and slaves.

January the 27th, early in the morning, the buccaneers resumed their march towards the city. The Spaniards came out to meet them. In this battle the Spaniards made use of wild bulls, which they drove upon the buccaneers to disorder their ranks; but it does not appear to have had much effect. In the end the Spaniards gave way, and before night the buccaneers were masters of the city. All that day the buccaneers gave no quarter, either during the battle or afterwards. Six hundred Spaniards fell. The buccaneers lost many men but the number is not specified.

One of the first precautions taken by Morgan after his victory was to prevent drunkenness among his men ; to which end he contrived to have it reported to him that all the wine in the city had been poisoned by the inhabitants; and on the ground of this intelligence he strictly prohibited everyone, under severe penalties, from tasting wine. Before they had well fixed their quarters in Panama several parts of the city burst out in flames, which spread so rapidly that in a short time many magnificent edifices built with cedar and a great part of the city were burnt to the ground. Whether this was done designedly or happened accidentally, owing to the consternation of the inhabitants during the assault, has been disputed. Morgan is accused of having directed some of his people to commit this mischief, but no motive is assigned that could induce him to an act which cut off his future prospect of ransom. Morgan charged it upon the Spaniards; and it is acknowledged the buccaneers gave all the assistance they were able to those of the inhabitants who endeavoured to stop the progress of the fire, which nevertheless continued to burn near four weeks before it was quite extinguished. Among the buildings destroyed was a factory-house belonging to the Genoese, who then carried on the trade of supplying the Spaniards with slaves from Africa.

The rapacity, licentiousness and cruelty of the buccaneers in their pillage of Panama had no bounds. "They spared," says the narrative of a buccaneer named Exquemelin, "in these their cruelties no sex nor condition whatsoever. As to religious persons and priests, they granted them less quarter than others, unless they procured a considerable sum of money for their ransom." Morgan sent detachments to scour the country for plunder, and to bring in prisoners from whom ransom might be extorted. Many of the inhabitants escaped with their effects by sea and went for shelter to the islands in the Bay of Panama. Morgan found a large boat lying aground in the port, which he caused to be launched and manned with a numerous crew, and sent her to cruise among the islands. A galleon on board which the women of a convent had taken refuge, and in which money, plate, and other valuable effects had been lodged, very narrowly escaped falling into their hands. They made prizes of several vessels, one of which was well adapted for cruising. This opened a new prospect, and some of the buccaneers began to consult how they might quit Morgan, and seek their fortunes on the South Sea, whence they proposed to sail, with the plunder they should obtain, by the East Indies to Europe. But Morgan received notice of their design before it could be put in execution, and, to prevent such a diminution of his force, he ordered the masts of the ship to be cut away, and all the boats or vessels lying at Panama which could suit their purpose to be burnt.

The old city of Panama is said to have contained 7000 houses, many of which were magnificent edifices built with cedar. On the 24th of February Morgan and his men departed from its ruins, taking with them 175 mules laden with spoil, and 600 prisoners, some of them carrying burthens, and others for whose release ransom was expected. Among the latter were many women and children. These poor creatures were designedly caused to suffer extreme hunger and thirst, and kept under apprehensions of being carried to Jamaica to be sold as slaves, that they might the more earnestly endeavour to procure money to be brought for their ransom. When some of the women upon their knees and in tears begged of Morgan to let them return to their families, his answer to them was that "he came not there to listen to cries and lamentations, but to seek money". Morgan's thirst for money was not restrained to seeking it among his foes. He had a hand equally ready for that of his friends. Neither did he think his friends people to be trusted; for in the middle of the march back to Chagre he drew up his men and caused them to be sworn that they had not reserved or concealed any plunder, but had delivered all fairly into the common stock. This ceremony, it seems, was not uncustomary. "But Captain Morgan having had experience that those loose fellows would not much stickle to swear falsely in such a case, he commanded everyone to be searched; and that it might not be esteemed an affront he permitted himself to be first searched, even to the very soles of his shoes. The French buccaneers who had engaged on this expedition with Morgan were not well satisfied with this new custom of searching, but, their number being less than that of the English, they were forced to submit." On arriving at Chagre a division was made. The narrative says: "every person received his portion, or rather what part thereof Captain Morgan was pleased to give him. For so it was that his companions, even those of his own nation, complained of his proceedings; for they judged it impossible that, of so many valuable robberies, no greater share should belong to them than 200 pieces of eight per head.

But Captain Morgan was deaf to these and to many other complaints of the same kind."

As Morgan was not disposed to allay the discontents of his men by coming to a more open reckoning with them, to avoid having the matter pressed upon him he determined to withdraw from his command, "which he did without calling any council, or bidding any one adieu; but went secretly on board his own ship, and put out to sea without giving notice, being followed only by three or four vessels of the whole fleet, who it is believed went shares with him in the greatest part of the spoil".

The rest of the buccaneer vessels soon separated. Morgan went to Jamaica, and had begun to levy men to go with him to the island Santa Katalina, which he purposed to hold as his own, and to make it a common place of refuge for pirates, when the arrival of a new governor at Jamaica, Lord John Vaughan, with orders to enforce the late treaty with Spain, obliged him to relinquish his plan.

The foregoing account of the destruction of Panama by Morgan is taken from a history of the buccaneers of America, written originally in the Dutch language by a buccaneer named Exquemelin, and published at Amsterdam in 1678, with the title of *De Americænsche Zee Roovers*. Exquemelin's book contains only partial accounts of the actions of some of the principal among the buccaneers. He has set forth the valour displayed by them in the most advantageous light; but, generally, what he has related is credible. His history has been translated into all the European languages, but with various additions and alterations by the translators, each of whom has endeavoured to maintain the military reputation of his own nation. The Spanish translation is entitled *Piratas*, and has the following short complimentary poem prefixed, addressed to the Spanish editor and emendator :—

De Agamenôn cantó la vida Homero
Y Virgilio de Eneas lo piadoso
Camoës de Gama el curso presurosso
Gongora el brio de Colon Velero.

Tu, O Alonso! mas docto y verdadoro,
Descrives del America ingenioso
Lo que assalta el Pirata codicioso :
Lo que defiende el Español Guerrero.

The French translation is entitled *Les Avanturiers qui se sont signalez dans les Indes*, and contains actions of the French flibustiers which are not in Exquemelin. The like has been done in the English translation, which has for title *The Bucaniers of America*. The English translator, speaking of the sacking of Panama, has expressed himself with a strange mixture of boasting and compunctious feeling. This account, he says, contains the unparalleled and bold exploits of Sir Henry Morgan, written by one of the buccaneers who was present at those tragedies.

It has been remarked that the Treaty of America furnishes an apology for the enterprises of the buccaneers previous to its notification, it being so worded as to admit an inference that the English and Spaniards were antecedently engaged in a continual war in America.

The new governor of Jamaica was authorised and instructed to proclaim a general pardon and indemnity from prosecution for all piratical offences committed to that time, and to grant thirty-five acres of land to every buccaneer who should claim the benefit of the proclamation, and would promise to apply himself to planting : a measure from which the most beneficial effects might have been expected, not to the British colonists only, but to all around, in turning a number of able men from destructive occupations to useful and productive pursuits, if it had not been made subservient to sordid views. The author of the *History of Jamaica* says : " This offer was intended as a lure to engage the buccaneers to come into port with their effects, that the governor might—and which he was directed to do—take from them the tenths and fifteenths of their booty as the dues of the crown (and of the colonial government) for granting them commissions". Those who had neglected to obtain commissions would of course have to make their peace by an increased com-position. In consequence of this scandalous procedure, the Jamaica buccaneers, to avoid being so taxed, kept aloof from Jamaica, and were provoked to continue their old occupations. Most of them joined the French flibustiers at Tortuga. Some were afterwards appre-hended at Jamaica, where they were brought to trial, condemned as pirates, and executed.

A war which was entered into by Great Britain and France against Holland furnished for a time employ-ment for the buccaneers and flibustiers, and procured the Spaniards a short respite.

In 1673 the French made an attempt to take the island of Curaçao from the Dutch, and failed. M. d'Ogeron, the governor of Tortuga, intended to have joined in this expedition, for which purpose he sailed in a ship named " L'Ecueil," manned with three hundred flibustiers ; but in the night of the 25th of February she ran aground among some small islands and rocks near the north side of the island Porto Rico. The people got safe to land, but were made close prisoners by the Spaniards. After some months' imprisonment M. d'Ogeron with three others made their escape in a canoe and got back to Tortuga. The governor-general over the French West India Islands at that time was a M. de Baas, who sent to Porto Rico to demand the deliverance of the French detained there as prisoners. The Spanish governor of Porto Rico required 3000 pieces of eight to be paid for expenses incurred. De Baas was unwilling to comply with the demand, and sent an agent to negotiate for an abatement in the sum; but they came to no agreement. M. d'Ogeron in the meantime collected five hundred men in Tortuga and Hispaniola, with whom he embarked in a number of small vessels to pass over to Porto Rico, to endeavour the release of his shipwrecked companions ; but by repeated tempests several of his flotilla were forced back, and he reached Porto Rico with only three hundred men.

On their landing, the Spanish governor put to death all his French prisoners except seventeen of the officers. Afterwards, in an engagement with the Spaniards, D'Ogeron lost seventeen men, and found his strength not sufficient to force the Spaniards to terms; upon which he withdrew from Porto Rico, and returned to Tortuga. The seventeen French officers that were spared in the massacre of the prisoners the governor of Porto Rico put on board a vessel bound for the *tierra firma*, with the intention of transporting them to Peru; but from that fate they were delivered by meeting at sea with an English buccaneer cruiser. Thus, by the French governor-general disputing about a trifling balance, three hundred of the French buccaneers, whilst employed for the French king's service under one of his officers, were sacrificed.

CHAPTER VII.

Thomas Peche. Attempt of La Sound to cross the Isthmus of America. Voyage of Antonio de Vea to the Strait of Magalhanes. Various adventures of the buccaneers in the West Indies to the year 1679.

IN 1673 Thomas Peche, an Englishman, fitted out a ship in England for a piratical voyage to the South Sea against the Spaniards. Previous to this, Peche had been many years a buccaneer in the West Indies, and therefore his voyage to the South Sea is mentioned as a buccaneer expedition; but it was in no manner connected with any enterprise in or from the West Indies. The only information we have of Peche's voyage is from a Spanish author, Seixas y Lovera, and by that it may be conjectured that Peche sailed to the Aleutian Isles.*

About this time the French West India Company was suppressed; but another company was at the same time erected in its stead, and under the unpromising title of *Compagnie des Fermiers du domaine d'Occident.*

Since the plundering of Panama the imaginations

---

* *Theatro Naval Hydrographico,* cap. xi. See also of Peche in vol. iii. of *South Sea Voyages and Discoveries,* p. 392.

of the buccaneers had been continually running on expeditions to the South Sea. This was well known to the Spaniards, and produced many forebodings and prophecies, in Spain as well as in Peru, of great invasions both by sea and land. The alarm was increased by an attempt of a French buccaneer named La Sound, with a small body of men, to cross over land to the South Sea. La Sound got no farther than the town of Cheapo, and was driven back. Dampier relates: " Before my going to the South Seas, I being then on board a privateer off Portobel, we took a packet from Carthagena. We opened a great many of the merchants' letters, several of which informed their correspondents of a certain prophecy that went about Spain that year, the tenor of which was, that the English privateers in the West Indies would that year open a door into the South Seas."

In 1675 it was reported and believed in Peru that strange ships, supposed to be pirates, had been seen on the coast of Chili, and it was apprehended that they designed to form an establishment there. In consequence of this information or rumour the viceroy sent a ship from Peru, under the command of Don Antonio de Vea, accompanied with small barques as tenders, to reconnoitre the Gulf de la Santissima Trinidada, and to proceed thence to the west entrance of the Strait of Magalhanes. De Vea made examination at those places, and was convinced, from the poverty of the land, that no settlement of Europeans could be maintained there. One of the Spanish barques, with a crew of sixteen men, was wrecked on the small islands called Evangelists, at the west entrance of the strait. De Vea returned to Callao in April, 1676.*

The cattle in Hispaniola had again multiplied so much as to revive the business of hunting and the boucan. In 1679, some French who had habitations in the Peninsula of Samana (the north-east part of Hispaniola) made incursions on the Spaniards, and plundered one of their villages. Not long afterwards the Spaniards learnt that in Samana there were only women and children, the men being all absent on the chase, and that it would be easy to surprise not only the habitations but the hunters also, who had a boucan at a place called the Round Mountain. This the Spaniards executed, and with such full indulgence to their wish to extirpate the French in Hispaniola that they put to the sword everyone they found at both the places. The French, in consequence of this misfortune, strengthened their fortifications at Cape François, and made it their principal establishment in the island.

In 1678 the French again undertook an expedition against the Dutch island Curaçao, with a large fleet of the French king's ships, under the command of Admiral the Count d'Etrées. The French court were so earnest for the conquest of Curaçao, to wipe off the disgrace of the former failure, that the governor of Tortuga was ordered to raise 1200 men to join the Admiral d'Etrées. The king's troops within his government did not exceed 300 men; nevertheless, the governor collected the number required, the

---

* *Not. de las Exp. Magal.*, p. 268, of Ult. Viage al Estrecho.

flibustiers willingly engaging in the expedition. Part of them embarked on board the king's ships, and part in their own cruising vessels. By mistake in the navigation, d'Etrées ran ashore in the middle of the night on some small isles to the east of Curaçao, called De Aves, which are surrounded with breakers, and eighteen of his ships, besides some of the flibustier vessels, were wrecked. The crews were saved, excepting about 300 men.

The Curaçao expedition being thus terminated, the flibustiers who had engaged in it, after saving as much as they could from the wrecks, went on expeditions of their own planning, to seek compensation for their disappointment and loss. Some landed on Cuba, and pillaged Puerto del Principe. One party, under Granmont, a leader noted for the success of his enterprises, went to the Gulf of Venezuela, and the ill-fated towns Maracaibo and Gibraltar were again plundered ; but what the buccaneers obtained was not of much value. In August this year France concluded a treaty with Spain and Holland.

The government in Jamaica had by this time relapsed to its former propensities, and again encouraged the buccaneers, and shared in their gains. One crew of buccaneers carried there a vessel taken from the Spaniards, the cargo of which produced, for each man's share, to the value of £400. After disposing of the cargo, they burnt the vessel ; and "having paid the governor his duties, they embarked for England, where," added the author, "some of them live in good reputation to this day ".*

* Buccaneers of America, part iii. ch. xi.

As long as the war had lasted between France and Spain the French buccaneers had the advantage of being lawful privateers. An English buccaneer relates : "We met a French private ship of war, mounting eight guns, who kept in our company some days. Her commission was only for three months. We showed them our commission, which was for three years to come. This we had purchased at a cheap rate, having given for it only ten pieces of eight ; but the truth of the thing was that our commission was made out at first only for three months, the same date as the Frenchman's, whereas among ourselves we contrived to make it that it should serve for three years, for with this we were resolved to seek our fortunes." Whenever Spain was at war with another European power, adventurers of any country found no difficulty in the West Indies in procuring commissions to war against the Spaniards; with which commission, and carrying aloft the flag of the nation hostile to Spain, they assumed that they were lawful enemies. Such pretensions did them small service if they fell into the hands of the Spaniards; but they were allowed in the ports of neutral nations, which benefited by being made the mart of the buccaneer prize goods ; and the buccaneers thought themselves well recompensed in having a ready market and the security of the port.

The enterprises of the buccaneers on the *tierra firma* and other parts of the American Continent brought them into frequent intercourse with the natives of those parts, and produced friendships, and sometimes alliances, against the Spaniards, with whom each were alike at constant enmity. But there sometimes happened disagreements between them and the natives. The buccaneers, if they wanted provisions or assistance from the Indians, had no objection to pay for it when they had the means; nor had the natives any objection to supply them on that condition, and occasionally out of pure goodwill. The buccaneers nevertheless did not always refrain from helping themselves, with no other leave than their own. Sometime before Morgan's expedition to Panama they had given the Indians of Darien much offence ; but shortly after that expedition they were reconciled, in consequence of which the Darien Indians had assisted La Sound. In 1678 they gave assistance to another party of flibustiers which went against Cheapo, under a French captain named Bournano, and offered to conduct them to a place called Tocamoro, where they said the Spaniards had much gold. Bournano did not think his force sufficient to take advantage of their offer, but promised he would come again and be better provided.

In 1679 three buccaneer vessels (two of them English and one French) joined in an attempt to plunder Porto Bello. They landed 200 men at such a distance from the town that it occupied them three nights in travelling, for during the day they lay concealed in the woods before they reached it. Just as they came to the town they were discovered by a negro, who ran before to give intelligence of their coming; but the buccaneers followed so quickly after him that they got possession of the town before the inhabitants could take any step for their defence, and, being unacquainted with the strength of the enemy, they all fled.   The buccaneers remained in the town collecting plunder two days and two nights, all the time in apprehension that the Spaniards would "pour in the country" upon their small force or intercept their retreat.   They got back, however, to their ships unmolested, and, on a division of the booty, shared 160 pieces of eight to each man.

CHAPTER VIII.

Meeting of buccaneers at the Samballas and Golden Island. Party formed by the English buccaneers to cross the isthmus. Some account of the native inhabitants of the Mosquito shore.

I MMEDIATELY after the plundering of Porto Bello a number of buccaneer vessels, both English and French, on the report which had been made by Captain Bournano, assembled at the Samballas, or Isles of San Blas, near the coast of Darien. One of these vessels was commanded by Bournano. The Indians of Darien received them as friends and allies, but they now disapproved the project of going to Tocamoro. The way thither, they said, was mountainous and through a long tract of uninhabited country in which it would be difficult to find subsistence, and, instead of Tocamoro, they advised going against the city of Panama. Their representation caused the design upon Tocamoro to be given up. The English buccaneers were for attacking Panama; but the French objected to the length of the march; and on this difference the English and French separated, the English buccaneers going to an island called by them Golden Island, which is the most eastern of the Samballas, if not more properly to be said to the eastward of all the Samballas.

Without the assistance of the French, Panama was too great an undertaking. They were bent, however, on crossing the isthmus; and, at the recommendation of their Darien friends, they determined to visit a Spanish town named Santa Maria, situated on the banks of a river that ran into the South Sea. The Spaniards kept a good garrison at Santa Maria, on account of gold which was collected from mountains in its neighbourhood.

The buccaneers who engaged in this expedition were the crews of seven vessels, of force as in the following list :—

	Guns.		Men.		
A vessel of	8	and	97	commanded by	John Coxon.
,,	25	,,	107	,,	Peter Harris.
,,	1	,,	35	,,	Richard Sawkins.
,,	2	,,	40	,,	Bart. Sharp.
,,	0	,,	43	,,	Edmond Cook.
,,	0	,,	24	,,	Robert Alleston.
,,	0	,,	20	,,	—— Macket.

It was settled that Alleston and Macket, with thirty-five men, themselves included, should be left to guard the vessels during the absence of those who went on the expedition, which was not expected to be of long continuance. These matters were arranged at Golden Island, and agreement made with the Darien Indians to furnish them with subsistence during the march.

William Dampier, a seaman at that time of no celebrity, but of good observation and experience, was among these buccaneers, and of the party to cross the isthmus, as was Lionel Wafer—since well known for his *Description of the Isthmus of Darien*—who had engaged with them as surgeon.

In this party of buccaneers were also some native Americans, of a small tribe called Mosquito Indians, who inhabited the sea coast on each side of Cape Gracias a Dios, one way towards the river San Juan de Nicaragua, the other towards the Gulf of Honduras, which is called the Mosquito shore. If Europeans had any plea in justification of their hostility against the Spaniards in the West Indies, much more had the native Americans. The Mosquito Indians, moreover, had long been, and were at the time of these occurrences, in an extraordinary degree attached to the English, insomuch that voluntarily of their own choice they acknowledged the king of Great Britain for their sovereign. They were an extremely ingenious people, and were greatly esteemed by the European seamen in the West Indies on account of their great expertness in the use of the harpoon and in taking turtle. The following character of them is given by Dampier : "These Mosquito Indians," he says, "are tall, well made, strong, and nimble of foot; long visaged, lank black hair, look stern, and are of a dark copper complexion. They are but a small nation or family. They are very ingenious in throwing the lance or harpoon. They have extraordinarily good eyes, and will descry a sail at sea farther than we. For these things they are esteemed and coveted by all privateers ; for one or two of them in a ship will sometimes maintain a hundred men. When they come among privateers they learn the use of guns, and prove very good marksmen. They behave themselves bold in fight, and are never seen to flinch or hang back, for they think that the white men with whom they are always know better than they do when it is best to fight; and, be the disadvantage never so great, they do not give back while any of their party stand. These Mosquito men are in general very kind to the English, of whom they receive a great deal of respect, both on board their ships and on shore, either in Jamaica or elsewhere. We always humour them, letting them go anywhere as they will, and return to their country in any vessel bound that way, if they please. They will have the management of themselves in their striking fish, and will go in their own little canoe, nor will they then let any white man come in their canoe: all which we allow them. For should we cross them, though they should see shoals of fish or turtle or the like, they will purposely strike their harpoons and turtle-irons aside, or so glance them as to kill nothing. They acknowledge the king of England for their sovereign, learn our language, and take the governor of Jamaica to be one of the greatest princes in the world. While they are among the English they wear good clothes, and take delight to go neat and tight; but when they return to their own country they put by all their clothes and go after their own country fashion."

In Dampier's time it was the custom among the Mosquito Indians, when their chief died, for his successor to obtain a commission, appointing him chief, from the governor of Jamaica; and till he received his commission he was not acknowledged in form by his countrymen.*

How would Dampier have been grieved if he could have foreseen that this simple and honest people, whilst their attachment to the English had suffered no diminution, would be delivered by the British government into the hands of the Spaniards; which, from all experience of what had happened, was delivering them to certain destruction.

Before this unhappy transaction took place, and after the time Dampier wrote, the British government took actual possession of the Mosquito country by erecting a fort and stationing there a garrison of British troops. British merchants settled among the Mosquito natives, and magistrates were appointed with authority to administer justice. Mosquito men were taken into British pay to serve as soldiers, of which the following story is related in Long's *History of Jamaica:* "In the year 1738 the government of Jamaica took into their pay two hundred Mosquito Indians to assist in the suppression of the maroons or

---

* "They never forfeit their word. The king has his commission from the governor of Jamaica, and at every new governor's arrival they come over to know his pleasure. The king of the Mosquitos was received by his Grace the Duke of Portland (governor of Jamaica, A.D. 1722-3) with that courtesy which was natural to him, and with more ceremony than seemed to be due to a monarch who held his sovereignty by commission." "The Mosquito Indians had a victory over the Spanish Indians about thirty years ago, and cut off a number, but gave a negro who was with them his life purely on account of his speaking English." *History of Jamaica.* London, 1774. Bk. i. ch. xii. And *British Empire in America*, vol. ii. pp. 367 and 371.

wild negroes.   During a march on this service one
of their white conductors shot a wild hog.   The
Mosquito men told him that was not the way to surprise the negroes, but to put them on their guard ; and
if he wanted provisions, they would kill the game
equally well with their arrows.   They effected considerable service on this occasion, and were well
rewarded for their good conduct ; and, when a pacifica-
tion took place with the maroons, they were sent well
satisfied to their own country."

In the year 1770 there resided in the Mosquito
country of British settlers, between 200 and 300
whites, as many of mixed blood, and 900 slaves.
On the breaking out of the war between Great
Britain and Spain, in 1779, when the Spaniards
drove the British logwood cutters from their settlements in the Bay of Honduras, the Mosquito men
armed and assisted the British troops of the line in the
recovery of the logwood settlements.   They behaved
on that occasion, and on others in which they served
against the Spaniards, with their accustomed fidelity.
An English officer who was in the West Indies during
that war has given a description of the Mosquito
men, which exactly agrees with what Dampier has
said ; and all that is related of them whilst with the
buccaneers gives the most favourable impression of
their dispositions and character.   It was natural to the
Spaniards to be eagerly desirous to get the Mosquito
country and people into their power ; but it was not
natural that such a proposition should be listened to
by the British.   Nevertheless, the matter did so
happen.

When notice was received in the West Indies that a negotiation was on foot for the delivery of the Mosquito shore to Spain, the council at Jamaica drew up a report and remonstrance against it, in which it was stated that "the number of the Mosquito Indians, so justly remarkable for their fixed hereditary hatred to the Spaniards and attachment to us, was from seven to ten thousand". Afterwards, in continuation, the memorial says : "We beg leave to state the nature of His Majesty's territorial right, perceiving with alarm, from papers submitted to our inspection, that endeavours have been made to create doubts as to His Majesty's just claims to the sovereignty of this valuable and delightful country. The native Indians of this country have never submitted to the Spanish government. The Spaniards never had any settlement amongst them. During the course of 150 years they have maintained a strict and uninterrupted alliance with the subjects of Great Britain. They made a free and formal cession of the dominion of their country to His Majesty's predecessors, acknowledging the king of Great Britain for the sovereign, long before the American treaty concluded at Madrid in 1670; and, consequently, by the eighth article of that treaty, our right was declared." * In one memorial and remonstrance which was presented to the British Ministry on the final ratification (in 1786) of the treaty, it is complained that thereby His Majesty had given up to the king of Spain "the Indian people and country

* *Case of His Majesty's Subjects upon the Mosquito Shore, most humbly submitted*, &c.   London, 1789.

of the Mosquito shore, which formed the most secure
West Indian province possessed by Great Britain, and
which we held by the most pure and perfect title of
sovereignty ".   Much of this is digression ; but the
subject unavoidably came into notice, and could not
be hastily quitted.

Some mercantile arrangement, said to be advantageous to Great Britain, but which has been disputed,
was the publicly assigned motive to this act.   It has
been conjectured that a desire to show civility to the
prime minister of Spain was the real motive.   Only
blindness or want of information could give either of
these considerations such fatal influence.

The making over or transferring inhabited territory from the dominion and jurisdiction of one state to
that of another has been practised not always with
regard to propriety.   It has been done sometimes
unavoidably, sometimes justly, and sometimes inex-
cusably.   Unavoidably, when a weaker state is necessitated to submit to the exactions of a stronger.
Justly, when the inhabitants of the territory it is
proposed to transfer are consulted, and give their
consent.   Also, it may be reckoned just to exercise
the power of transferring a conquered territory, the
inhabitants of which have not been received and
adopted as fellow-subjects with the subjects of the
state under whose power it had fallen.

The inhabitants of a territory who with their lands
are transferred to the dominion of a new state without
their inclinations being consulted are placed in the
condition of a conquered people.

The connection of the Mosquito people with Great

Britain was formed in friendship, and was on each side a voluntary engagement. That it was an engagement should be no question. In equity and honour, whoever permits it to be believed that he has entered into an engagement, thereby becomes engaged. The Mosquito people were known to believe, and had been allowed to continue in the belief, that they were permanently united to the British. The governors of Jamaica giving commissions for the instalment of their chief, the building a fort, and placing a garrison in the country, show both acceptance of their submission and exercise of sovereignty.

Vattel has described this case. He says: "When a nation has not sufficient strength of itself, and is not in a condition to resist its enemies, it may lawfully submit to a more powerful nation on certain conditions upon which they shall come to an agreement; and the pact or treaty of submission will be afterwards the measure and rule of the rights of each. For that which submits, resigning a right it possessed, and conveying it to another, has an absolute power to make this conveyance upon what conditions it pleases; and the other, by accepting the submission on this footing, engages to observe religiously all the clauses in the treaty.

"When a nation has placed itself under the protection of another that is more powerful, or has submitted to it with a view of protection; if this last does not effectually grant its protection when wanted, it is manifest that by failing in its engagements it loses the rights it had acquired."

The rights lost or relinquished by Great Britain

might possibly be of small import to her; but the loss
of our protection was of infinite consequence to the
Mosquito people.   Advantages, supposed or real,
gained to Great Britain are not to be pleaded in excuse
or palliation for withdrawing her protection; for that
would seem to imply that an engagement is more or
less binding according to the greater or less interest
there may be in observing it.   But if there had been
no engagement, the length and steadiness of their
attachment to Great Britain would have entitled them
to her protection, and the nature of the case rendered
the obligation sacred; for, be it repeated, that experience had shown the delivering them up to the dominion of the Spaniards was delivering them to certain
slavery and death.   These considerations possibly
might not occur, for there seems to have been a want
of information on the subject in the British Ministry,
and also a want of attention to the remonstrances
made.   The Mosquito country and the native inhabitants, the best affected and most constant of all the
friends the British ever had, were abandoned in the
summer of 1787 to the Spaniards, the known exter-
minators of millions of the native Americans, and who
were, moreover, incensed against the Mosquito men
for the part they had always taken with the British,
by whom they were thus forsaken.   The British
settlers in that country found it necessary to withdraw
as speedily as they had opportunity with their effects.

If the business had been fully understood, and the
safety of Great Britain had depended upon abandon-
ing the Mosquito people to their merciless enemies,
it would have been thought disgraceful by the nation

to have done it ; but the national interest being trivial,
and the public in general being uninformed in the
matter, the transaction took place without attracting
much notice. A motion, however, was made in the
British House of Lords, " that the terms of the Convention with Spain, signed in July, 1786, did not meet
the favourable opinion of this House " ; and the noble
mover objected to that part of the Convention which
related to the surrender of the British possessions on
the Mosquito shore, that it was a humiliation, and
derogating from the rights of Great Britain. The
first article of the treaty of 1786 says : " His Brit-
annic Majesty's subjects, and the other colonists who
have hitherto enjoyed the protection of England, shall
evacuate the country of the Mosquitos, as well as the
continent in general and the islands adjacent, without
exception, situated beyond the line hereafter described,
as what ought to be the extent of territory granted by
his Catholic Majesty to the English ".

In the debate rights were asserted for Spain, not
only to what she then possessed on the continent of
America, but to parts she had never possessed. Was
this want of information or want of consideration ?
The word " granted " was improperly introduced. In
truth and justice, the claims of Spain to America are
not to be acknowledged rights. They were founded
in usurpation, and prosecuted by the extermination of
the lawful and natural proprietors. It is an offence to
morality and to humanity to pretend that Spain had so
clear and just a title to any part of her possessions on
the continent of America as Great Britain had to the
Mosquito country. The rights of the Mosquito people,

and their claims to the friendship of Great Britain, were not sufficiently made known, and the motion was negatived. It might have been of service in this debate to have quoted Dampier.

In conclusion, the case of the Mosquito people deserves and demands the reconsideration of Great Britain. If, on examination, it shall be proved that they have been ungenerously and unjustly treated, it may not be too late to seek to make reparation, which ought to be done as far as circumstances will yet admit. The first step towards this would be to institute enquiry if there are living any of our forsaken friends, or of their posterity, and what is their present condition. If the Mosquito people have been humanely and justly governed since their separation from Great Britain, the enquiry will give the Spaniards cause for triumph, and the British cause to rejoice that evil has not resulted from their act. On the other hand, should it be found that they have shared in the common calamities heaped upon the natives of America by the Spaniards, then, if there yet exist enough of their tribe to form a nation, it would be right to restore them, if practicable, to the country and situation of which their fathers were deprived, or to find them an equivalent; and, at any price or pains, to deliver them from oppression. If only few remain, those few should be freed from their bondage, and be liberally provided with lands and maintenance in our own West India Islands.

CHAPTER IX.

Journey of the buccaneers across the Isthmus of America.

ON the 5th of April, 1680, three hundred and
thirty-one buccaneers, most of them English,
passed over from Golden Island and landed in Darien,
"each man provided with four cakes of bread called
dough-boys, with a fusil, a pistol, and a hanger".
They began their journey marshalled in divisions,
with distinguishing flags, under their several commanders, Bartholomew Sharp and his men taking the
lead. Many Darien Indians kept them company as
their confederates, and supplied them with plantains,
fruit, and venison, for which payment was made in
axes, hatchets, knives, needles, beads, and trinkets;
all which the buccaneers had taken care to come well
provided with. Among the Darien Indians in company were two chiefs, who went by the names of
Captain Andreas and Captain Antonio.

The commencement of their march was through
the skirt of a wood, which having passed, they proceeded about a league by the side of a bay, and
afterwards about two leagues directly up a woody
valley, where was an Indian house and plantation by
the side of a river. Here they took up their lodging
for the night, those who could not be received in the

house building huts. The Indians were earnest in cautioning them against sleeping in the grass, on account of adders. This first day's journey discouraged four of the buccaneers, and they returned to the ships. Stones were found in the river, which, on being broken, shone with sparks of gold. These stones, they were told, were driven down from the neighbouring mountains by torrents during the rainy season.*

The next morning, at sunrise, they proceeded in their journey, labouring up a steep hill, which they surmounted about three in the afternoon ; and at the foot on the other side they rested on the bank of a river, which Captain Andreas told them ran into the South Sea, and was the same by which the town of Santa Maria was situated. They marched afterwards about six miles farther, over another steep hill, where the path was so narrow that seldom more than one man could pass at a time. At night they took up their lodging by the side of the river, having marched this day, according to their computation, eighteen miles.

The next day, April the 7th, the march was continued by the river, the course of which was so serpentine that they had to cross it almost at every half mile—sometimes up to their knees, sometimes to their middle—and running with a very swift current. About noon they arrived at some large Indian houses, neatly built, the sides of the wood of the cabbage-tree, and the roofs of cane, thatched over with palmito leaves.

* Narrative by Basil Ringrose, p. 5.

The interior had divisions into rooms, but no upper
storey; and before each house was a large plantain
walk. Continuing their journey, at five in the afternoon they came to a house belonging to a son of
Captain Andreas, who wore a wreath of gold about
his head, for which he was honoured by the Buccaneers with the title of King Golden Cap. They
found their entertainment at King Golden Cap's
house so good that they rested there the whole of the
following day. Bartholomew Sharp, who published
a journal of his expedition, says here: "The inhabitants of Darien are, for the most part, very handsome,
especially the female sex, who are also exceeding
loving and free to the embraces of strangers". This
was calumny. Basil Ringrose, another buccaneer,
whose journal has been published, and who is more
entitled to credit than Sharp, as will be seen, says of
the Darien women: "they are generally well featured,
very free, airy, and brisk; yet withal very modest".
Lionel Wafer also, who lived many months among
the Indians of the Isthmus, speaks highly of the
modesty, kindness of disposition, and innocency of
the Darien women.

On the 9th, after breakfast, they pursued their
journey, accompanied by the Darien chiefs, and about
two hundred Indians, who were armed with bows and
lances. They descended along the river, through
which they had to wade between fifty and sixty times,
and they came to a house "only here and there". At
most of these houses the owner, who had been
apprised of the march of the buccaneers, stood at the
door, and as they passed gave to each man a ripe

plantain, or some sweet cassava root. If the buccaneer desired more, he was expected to purchase. Some of the Indians, to count the number of the buccaneers, for every man that went by dropped a grain of corn. That night they lodged at three large houses, where they found entertainment provided, and also canoes for them to descend the river, which began here to be navigable.

The next morning, as they were preparing to depart, two of the buccaneer commanders, John Coxon and Peter Harris, had some disagreement, and Coxon fired his musket at Harris, who was about to fire in return, but other buccaneers interposed, and effected a reconciliation. Seventy of the buccaneers embarked in fourteen canoes, in each of which two Indians also went, who best knew how to manage and guide them down the stream : the rest prosecuted their march by land. The men in the canoes found that mode of travelling quite as wearisome as marching, for at almost every furlong they were constrained to quit their boats to launch them over rocks, or over trees that had fallen athwart the river, and sometimes over necks of land. At night they stopped and made themselves huts on a green bank by the river's side. Here they shot wild-fowl.

The next day the canoes continued to descend the river, having the same kind of impediments to overcome as on the preceding day ; and at night they lodged again on the green bank of the river. The land party had not kept up with them. Bartholomew Sharp says : "Our supper entertainment was a very good sort of a wild beast called a 'warre,' which is much like to our English hog, and altogether as good. There are store of them in this part of the world : I observed that the navels of these animals grew upon their backs." Wafer calls this species of the wild hog "pecary".* In the night a small tiger came, and, after looking at them some time, went away. The buccaneers did not fire at him, lest the noise of their muskets should give alarm to the Spaniards at Santa Maria.

The next day the water party again embarked, but under some anxiety at being so long without having any communication with the party marching by land. Captain Andreas, perceiving their uneasiness, sent a canoe back up the river, which returned before sunset with some of the land party, and intelligence that the rest were near at hand.

Tuesday the 13th, early in the day, the buccaneers arrived at a beachy point of land, where another stream from the uplands joined the river. This place had sometimes been the rendezvous of the Darien Indians, when they collected for attack or defence against the Spaniards ; and here the whole party now made a halt to rest themselves, and to clean and prepare their arms. They also made paddles and oars to row with ; for thus far down the river the canoes had been carried by the stream, and guided with poles : but here the river was broad and deep.

On the 14th the whole party, buccaneers and

---

* De Rochfort describes this animal under the name "javaris". *Hist. Nat. des Isles Antilles*, p. 138, edit. 1665. It is also described by Pennant, in his *Synopsis of Quadrupeds*, Art. "Mexican Wild Hog".

Indians, making nearly six hundred men, embarked in
sixty-eight canoes which the Indians had provided.
At midnight they put to land, within half-a-mile of the
town of Santa Maria.   In the morning, at the break
of day, they heard muskets fired by the guard in the
town, and a "drum beating *à travailler*".* The buccaneers put themselves in motion, and by seven in the
morning came to the open ground before the fort, when
the Spaniards began firing upon them.   The fort was
formed simply with palisadoes, without brickwork, so
that, after pulling down two or three of the palisadoes,
the buccaneers entered without farther opposition and
without the loss of a man ; nevertheless, they acted with
so little moderation or mercy, that twenty-six Spaniards
were killed and sixteen wounded.   After the surrender, the Indians took many of the Spaniards into the
adjoining woods, where they killed them with lances ;
and if they had not been discovered in their amuse-
ment and prevented, not a Spaniard would have been
left alive.   It is said in a buccaneer account that they
found here the eldest daughter of the king of Darien,
Captain Andreas, who had been forced from her
father's house by one of the garrison, and was with
child by him ; which greatly incensed the father
against the Spaniards.

The buccaneers were much disappointed in their

---

* Ringrose, *Buccaneers of America*, part iv. p. 10.   The early
morning drum has in our time been called the *reveiller*.   Either
that or *à travailler* seems applicable ; for, according to Boyer, *travailler* signifies to trouble, or disturb, as well as to work ; and it is
probable, from the age of the authority above cited, that the original
term was *à travailler*.

expectations of plunder, for the Spaniards had by some means received notice of their intended visit in time to send away almost all that was of value. A buccaneer says: "though we examined our prisoners severely, the whole that we could pillage, either in the town or fort, amounted only to twenty pounds' weight of gold and a small quantity of silver; whereas, three days sooner, we should have found three hundred pounds' weight in gold in the fort".

The majority of the buccaneers were desirous to proceed in their canoes to the South Sea, to seek compensation for their disappointment at Santa Maria. John Coxon and his followers were for returning; on which account, and not from an opinion of his capability, those who were for the South Sea offered Coxon the post of general, provided he and his men would join in their scheme, which offer was accepted.

It was then determined to descend with the stream of the river to the Gulf de San Miguel, which is on the east side of the Bay of Panama. The greater part of the Darien Indians, however, separated from them at Santa Maria, and returned to their homes. The Darien chief, Andreas, and his son, Golden Cap, with some followers, continued with the buccaneers.

Among the people of Darien were remarked some white, "fairer than any people in Europe, who had hair like unto the finest flax; and it was reported of them that they could see farther in the dark than in the light".*

The river of Santa Maria is the largest of several

* Narrative by Basil Ringrose, p. 3.

rivers which fall into the Gulf de San Miguel. Abreast where the town stood, it was reckoned to be twice as broad as the river Thames is at London. The rise and fall of the tide there was two fathoms and a half.*

April the 17th, the buccaneers and their remaining allies embarked from Santa Maria in canoes and a small barque which was found at anchor before the town. About thirty Spaniards who had been made prisoners earnestly entreated that they should not be left behind to fall into the hands of the Indians. "We had much ado," say the buccaneers, "to find boats enough for ourselves ; the Spaniards, however, found or made bark logs, and, it being for their lives, made shift to come along with us." At ten that night it was low water, and they stopped on account of the flood tide. The next morning they pursued their course to the sea.

* Ringrose, p. 11.

CHAPTER X.

First buccaneer expedition in the South Sea.

ON the 19th of April the buccaneers, under the command of John Coxon, entered the Bay of Panama, and the same day, at one of the islands in the bay, they captured a Spanish vessel of 30 tons, on board of which 130 of the buccaneers immediately placed themselves, glad to be relieved from the cramped and crowded state they had endured in the canoes. The next day another small barque was taken The pursuit of these vessels, and seeking among the islands for provisions, had separated the buccaneers, but they had agreed to rendezvous at the island Chepillo, near the entrance of the river Cheapo. Sharp, however, and some others, wanting fresh water, went to the Pearl Islands. The rest got to Chepillo on the 22nd, where they found good provision of plantains, fresh water, and hogs ; and at four o'clock that same afternoon they rowed from the island towards Panama.

By this time intelligence of their being in the bay had reached the city. Eight vessels were lying in the road, three of which the Spaniards hastily equipped, manning them with the crews of all the vessels, and the addition of men from the shore ; the whole, according to the buccaneer accounts, not exceeding

230 men, and not more than one-third of them being Europeans ; the rest were mulattoes and negroes.

On the 23rd, before sunrise, the buccaneers came in sight of the city, and as soon as they were descried the three armed Spanish ships got under sail and stood towards them. The conflict was severe, and lasted the greater part of the day, when it terminated in the defeat of the Spaniards, two of their vessels being carried by boarding, and the third being obliged to save herself by flight. The Spanish commander fell, with many of his people. Of the buccaneers, eighteen were killed and above thirty wounded. Peter Harris, one of their captains, was among the wounded, and died two days after.

One buccaneer account says : " we were in all sixty-eight men that were engaged in the fight of that day ". Another buccaneer relates : " we had sent away the Spanish barque to seek fresh water, and had put on board her above one hundred of our best men ; so that we had only canoes for this fight, and in them not above two hundred fighting men ". The Spanish ships fought with great bravery, but were overmatched, being manned with motley and untaught crews, whereas the buccaneers had been in constant training to the use of their arms, and their being in canoes was no great disadvantage, as they had a smooth sea to fight in. The valour of Richard Sawkins, who, after being three times repulsed, succeeded in boarding and capturing one of the Spanish ships, was principally instrumental in gaining the victory to the buccaneers. It gained him also their confidence, and the more fully as some among them were thought to have shown backwardness, of which number John Coxon, their elected commander, appears to have been one. The Darien chiefs were in the heat of the battle.

Immediately after the victory the buccaneers stood towards Panama, then a new city and on a different site from the old, being four miles westward of the ruins of the city burnt by Morgan. The old city had yet some inhabitants. The present adventurers did not judge their strength sufficient for landing, and they contented themselves with capturing the vessels that were at anchor near the small islands of Perico, in the road before the city. One of these vessels was a ship named the "Trinidad," of four hundred tons' burthen, in good condition, a fast sailer, and had on board a cargo principally consisting of wine, sugar, and sweetmeats, and, moreover, a considerable sum of money. The Spanish crew, before they left her, had both scuttled and set her on fire, but the buccaneers took possession in time to extinguish the flames, and to stop the leaks. In the other prizes they found flour and ammunition; and two of them, besides the "Trinidad," they fitted up for cruising. Two prize vessels, and a quantity of goods which were of no use to them, as iron, skins, and soap, which the Spaniards at Panama refused to ransom, they destroyed. Besides these, they captured among the islands some small vessels laden with poultry. Thus, in less than a week after their arrival across the isthmus to the coast of the South Sea, they were provided with a small fleet, not ill equipped, with which they now formed an actual and close blockade by sea of Panama, stationing themselves at anchor in front of the city.

This new city was already considerably larger than old Panama had ever been, its extent being in length full a mile and a half, and in breadth above a mile. The churches (eight in number) were not yet finished. The cathedral church at the old town was still in use, "the beautiful building whereof," says Ringrose, "maketh a fair show at a distance, like unto the church of St. Paul's at London. Round the city for the space of seven leagues, more or less, all the adjacent country is what they call in the Spanish language *savana*—that is to say, plain and level ground, as smooth as a sheet; only here and there is to be seen a small spot of woody land. And everywhere this level ground is full of *vacadas*, where whole droves of cows and oxen are kept. But the ground whereon the city standeth is damp and moist, and of bad repute for health. The sea is also very full of worms, much prejudicial to shipping, for which reason the king's ships are always kept near Lima. We found here in one night after our arrival worms of three quarters of an inch in length, both in our bed-clothes and other apparel."

Within two or three days after the battle with the Spanish *armadilla* discord broke out among the buccaneers. The reflections made upon the behaviour of Coxon and some of his followers determined him and seventy men to return by the river of Santa Maria over the isthmus to the North Sea. Two of the small prize vessels were given them for this purpose, and at the same time the Darien chiefs, Captain Andreas and Captain Antonio, with most of their people, departed to return to their homes. Andreas showed his goodwill towards the buccaneers

who remained in the South Sea by leaving with them
a son and one of his nephews.

On the departure of Coxon, Richard Sawkins was
chosen general or chief commander. They continued ten days in the road before Panama, at the
end of which they retired to an island named Taboga,
more distant, but whence they could see vessels going
to, or coming from, Panama. At Taboga they stopped
nearly a fortnight, having had notice that a rich ship
from Lima was shortly expected; but she came not
within that time. Some other vessels, however, fell
into their hands, by which they obtained in specie
between 50,000 and 60,000 dollars, 1200 packs
of flour, 2000 jars of wine, a quantity of brandy, sugar,
sweetmeats, poultry, and other provisions, some gunpowder and shot, besides various other articles of
merchandise. Among their prisoners were a number
of negro slaves, which was a temptation to the merchants of Panama to go to the ships whilst they lay
at Taboga, who purchased part of the prize goods and
as many of the negroes as the buccaneers would part
with, giving for a negro 200 pieces of eight; and
they also sold to the buccaneers such stores and
commodities as they were in need of. Ringrose
relates that, in the course of this communication,
a message was delivered to their chief from the
governor of Panama, demanding "why, during a
time of peace between England and Spain, Englishmen should come into those seas to commit injury,
and from whom they had their commission so to do".
To which message Sawkins returned answer that "he
and his companions came to assist their friend the

king of Darien, who was the rightful lord of Panama
and all the country thereabouts.   That, as they had
come so far it was reasonable they should receive
some satisfaction for their trouble ; and, if the governor
would send to them 500 pieces of eight for each man,
and 1000 for each commander, and would promise not
any farther to annoy the Darien Indians, their allies,
that then the buccaneers would desist from hostilities
and go quietly about their business."

By the Spaniards who traded with them, Sawkins
learnt that the bishop of Panama was a person whom
he had formerly taken prisoner in the West Indies,
and sent him a small present as a token of regard ; the
bishop sent a gold ring in return.

Sawkins would have waited longer for the rich
ship expected from Peru, but all the live stock within
reach had been consumed, and his men became
impatient for fresh provisions.   " This Taboga," says
Sharp, " is an exceeding pleasant island, abounding in
fruits, such as pine-apples, oranges, lemons, pears,
mammees, cocoa-nuts, and others ; with a small, but
brave, commodious fresh river running in it.   The
anchorage is also clear and good."

On the 15th of May they sailed to the island
Otoque, at which place they found hogs and poultry ;
and the same day, or the day following, they departed
with three ships and two small barques from the Bay of
Panama, steering westward for a Spanish town named
Pueblo Nuevo.

In this short distance they had much blowing
weather and contrary winds, by which both the small
barques—one with fifteen men, the other with seven

men—were separated from the ships, and did not join them again. The crew of one of these barques returned over the isthmus with Coxon's party. The other barque was taken by the Spaniards.

About the 21st the ships anchored near the island Quibo, from the north part of which, to the town of Pueblo Nuevo on the mainland, was reckoned eight leagues. Sawkins, with sixty men, embarked on board the smallest ship, and sailed to the entrance of a river which leads to the town. He there left the ship with a few men to follow him, and proceeded with the rest in canoes up the river by night, having a negro prisoner for pilot. Those left with the care of the ship " entered the river, keeping close by the east shore, on which there is a round hill. Within two stones' cast of the shore there was four fathoms' depth; and within the point a very fine and large river opens. But, being strangers to the place, the ship was run aground nigh a rock which lieth by the westward shore; for the true channel of this river is nearer to the east than to the west shore. The island Quibo is south south-east from the mouth of this river." *

The canoes met with much obstruction from trees which the Spaniards had felled across the river, but they arrived before the town during the night. The Spaniards had erected some works, on which account the buccaneers waited in their canoes till daylight and then landed, when Richard Sawkins, advancing with the foremost of his men towards a breastwork, was killed, as were two of his followers. Sharp was the

* Ringrose, chap. iv.

next in command, but he was disheartened by so unfortunate a beginning and ordered a retreat. Three buccaneers were wounded in the re-embarkation.

In the narrative which Sharp himself published, he says : " we landed at a *stockado* built by the Spaniards, where we had a small rencounter with the enemy, who killed us three men, whereof the brave Captain Sawkins was one, and wounded four or five more ; besides which we got nothing, so that we found it our best way to retreat down the river again ".

The death of Sawkins was a great misfortune to the buccaneers, and was felt by them as such. One buccaneer relates : " Captain Sawkins, landing at Pueblo Nuevo before the rest, as being a man of undaunted courage, and running up with a small party to a breastwork, was unfortunately killed. And this disaster occasioned a mutiny amongst our men, for our commanders were not thought to be leaders fit for such hard enterprises. Now Captain Sharp was left in chief, and he was censured by many, and the con-, test grew to that degree that they divided into parties, and about seventy of our men fell off from us."

Ringrose was not in England when his narrative was published, and advantage was taken of his absence to interpolate in it some impudent passages in commendation of Sharp's valour. In the printed narrative attributed to Ringrose he is made to say : " Captain Sawkins, in running up to the breastwork at the head of a few men, was killed ; a man as valiant and courageous as any could be, and, next unto Captain Sharp, the best loved of all our company, or the most part thereof ".

Ringrose's manuscript journal has been preserved in the Sloane Collection at the British Museum (No. 3820 * of Ayscough's catalogue), wherein, with natural expression of affection and regard, he says : "Captain Sawkins was a valiant and generous-spirited man, and beloved above any other we ever had among us, which he well deserved".

In their retreat down the river of Pueblo Nuevo the buccaneers took a ship laden with indigo, butter, and pitch, and burnt two other vessels. When returned to Quibo they could not agree in the choice of a commander. Bartholomew Sharp had a greater number of voices than any other pretender, which he obtained by boasting that he would take them a cruise whereby he did not at all doubt they would return home with not less than a thousand pounds to each man. Sharp was elected by but a small majority. Between sixty and seventy men, who had remained after Coxon quitted the command, from attachment to Captain Sawkins, would not stay to be commanded by Sharp, and departed from Quibo in one of the prize vessels to return over the isthmus to the West Indies, where they safely arrived. All the Darien Indians also returned to the isthmus. One hundred and forty-six buccaneers remained with Bartholomew Sharp.

"On the south-east side of the island Quibo is a shoal, or spit of sand, which stretches out a quarter of a league into the sea." † Just within this shoal, in

---

* No. 48 in the same collection is a manuscript copy of Ringrose's journal, but varied in the same manner from the original as the printed narrative.

† Ringrose, p. 44.

fourteen fathoms' depth, the buccaneer ships lay at
anchor. ˗ The island abounded in fresh rivers, this
being the rainy season.   They caught red deer, turtle
and oysters.   Ringrose says : "here were oysters so
large that we were forced to cut them into four pieces,
each quarter being a good mouthful".   Here were also
oysters of a smaller kind, from which the Spaniards
collected pearls.   They killed alligators at Quibo, some
above twenty feet in length ; "they were very fearful,
and tried to escape from those who hunted them".
Ringrose relates that he stood under a manchineal
tree to shelter himself from the rain, but some drops
fell on his skin from the tree, which caused him to break
out all over in red spots, and he was not well for a week
afterwards.

June the sixth, Sharp and his followers, in two
ships, sailed from Quibo southward for the coast of
Peru, intending to stop by the way at the Galapagos
Islands ; but the winds prevented them.   On the
seventeenth they anchored on the south side of the
island Gorgona, near the mouth of a river.   "Gorgona
is a high, mountainous island, about four leagues in
circuit, and is distant about four leagues from the continent.   The anchorage is within a pistol-shot of the
shore, in depth from fifteen to twenty fathoms.   At
the south-west of Gorgona is a smaller island, and
without the same stands a small rock." *   There were
at this time streams of fresh water on every side of the
island.

Gorgona, being uninhabited, was thought to be a
good place of concealment.   The island supplied

* Ringrose and Sharp.

rabbits, monkeys, turtle, oysters and birds; which provision was inducement to the Buccaneers, notwithstanding the rains, to remain there, indulging in idleness, till near the end of July, when the weather began to be dry. They killed a snake at Gorgona, eleven feet long, and fourteen inches in circumference.

July the twenty-fifth they put to sea. Sharp had expressed an intention to attack Guayaquil; but he was now of opinion that their long stay at Gorgona must have occasioned their being discovered by the Spaniards, "notwithstanding that he himself had persuaded them to stay"; their plan was therefore changed for the attack of places more southward, where they would be less expected. The winds were from the southward, and it was not till the 13th August that they got as far as the island Plata.

The only landing at Plata at this time was on the north-east side, near a deep valley, where the ships anchored in twelve fathoms. Goats were on this island in such numbers that they killed above a hundred in a day with little labour, and salted what they did not want for present use. Turtle and fish were in plenty. They found only one small spring of fresh water, which was near the landing-place, and did not yield them more than twenty gallons in the twenty-four hours. There were no trees on any part of the island.

From Plata they proceeded southward. On the 25th, near Cape St. Elena, they met a Spanish ship from Guayaquil, bound to Panama, which they took after a short action in which one buccaneer was killed and two others were wounded. In this prize they found three thousand dollars. They learnt from their pri-

soners that one of the small buccaneer tenders, which
had been separated from Sawkins in sailing from the
Bay of Panama, had been taken by the Spaniards,
after losing six men out of seven which composed her
crew. Their adventure was as follows. Not being
able to join their commander, Sawkins, at Quibo, they
sailed to the island Gallo near the continent (in about
2° north), where they found a party of Spaniards, from
whom they took three white women. A few days
afterwards they put in at another small island four
leagues distant from Gallo, where they proposed to
remain on the look-out, in hopes of seeing some of
their friends come that way, as Sawkins had declared
it his intention to go to the coast of Peru. Whilst
they were waiting in this expectation, a Spaniard whom
they had kept prisoner made his escape from them,
and got over to the mainland. This small buccaneer
crew had the imprudence, nevertheless, to remain in
the same quarters long enough to give time for a party
of Spaniards to pass over from the mainland, which
they did without being perceived, and placed themselves in ambuscade with so much advantage that at
one volley they killed six buccaneers out of the seven ;
the one remaining became their prisoner.

Sharp and his men divided the small sum of money
taken in their last prize, and sank her. Ringrose
relates : "We also punished a friar and shot him upon
the deck, casting him overboard while he was yet alive.
I abhorred such cruelties, yet was forced to hold my
tongue." It is not said in what manner the friar had
offended, and Sharp does not mention the circumstance
in his journal.

One of the two vessels in which the buccaneers cruised sailed badly, on which account she was abandoned, and they all embarked in the ship named the "Trinidad".

On the 4th of September they took a vessel from Guayaquil bound for Lima, with a lading of timber, chocolate, raw silk, Indian cloth and thread stockings. It appears here to have been a custom among the buccaneers for the first who boarded an enemy, or captured vessel, to be allowed some extra privilege of plunder. Ringrose says: "We cast dice for the first entrance, and the lot fell to the larboard watch, so twenty men belonging to that watch entered her". They took out of this vessel as much of the cargo as they chose, and put some of their prisoners in her; after which they dismissed her with only one mast standing and one sail, that she should not be able to prosecute her voyage southward. Sharp passed Callao at a distance from land, being apprehensive there might be ships of war in the road. On October the 26th he was near the town of Arica when the boats, manned with a large party of buccaneers, departed from the ship with intention to attack the town; but on coming near the shore they found the surf high, and the whole country appeared to be in arms. They returned to the ship, and it was agreed to bear away for Ilo, a small town on the coast, in latitude about 17° 40'. Their stock of fresh water was by this time so reduced that they had come to an allowance of only half a pint for a man for the day; and it is related that a pint of water was sold in the ship for thirty dollars. They succeeded, however, in landing at Ilo, and obtained there fresh water, wine, fruits, flour, oil, chocolate, sugar, and other provisions. The Spaniards would give neither money nor cattle to have their buildings and plantations spared, and the buccaneers committed all the mischief they could.

From Ilo they proceeded southward. December the first, in the night, being in latitude about 31° they found themselves in white water, like banks or breakers, which extended a mile or more in length; but they were relieved from their alarm by discovering that what they had apprehended to be rocks and breakers was a large shoal of anchovies.

December the third they landed at the town of La Serena, which they entered without opposition. Some Spaniards came to negotiate with them to ransom the town from being burnt, for which they agreed to pay ninety-five thousand pieces of eight; but the money came not at the time appointed, and the buccaneers had reason to suspect the Spaniards intended to deceive them. Ringrose relates that a man ventured to come in the night from the shore on a float made of a horse's hide blown up like a bladder. "He being arrived at the ship, went under the stern and crammed oakum and brimstone and other combustible matter between the rudder and the stern-post. Having done this, he fired it with a match, so that in a small time our rudder was on fire, and all the ship in a smoke. Our men, both alarmed and amazed with this smoke, ran up and down the ship, suspecting the prisoners to have fired the vessel, thereby to get their liberty and seek our destruction. At last they found out where the fire was, and had the good fortune to quench it before its going too far. After which we sent the boat ashore, and found both the hide afore-mentioned and the match burning at both ends, whereby we became acquainted with the whole matter."

By the La Serena expedition they obtained five hundred pounds' weight of silver. One of the crew died in consequence of hard drinking whilst on shore. They released all their prisoners here, except a pilot, after which they stood from the continent for Juan Fernandez. In their approach to that island, it is remarked by Ringrose that they saw neither bird nor fish; and this being noticed to the pilot, he made answer, that he had many times sailed by Juan Fernandez, and had never seen either fish or fowl whilst at sea in sight of the island.

On Christmas Day they anchored in a bay at the south part of Juan Fernandez; but finding the winds south-east and southerly they quitted that anchorage and went to a bay on the north side of the island, where they cast anchor in fourteen fathoms, so near to the shore that they fastened the end of another cable from the ship to the trees, being sheltered by the land from east south-east round by the south and west, and as far as north by west.* Their fastenings, however, did not hold the ship against the strong flurries that blew from the land, and she was twice forced to sea, but each time recovered the anchorage without much difficulty.

The shore of this bay was covered with seals and sea lions, whose noise and company were very trouble-

* Sharp's journal, p. 72.

some to the men employed in filling fresh water.　The
seals coveted to lie where streams of fresh water ran
into the sea, which made it necessary to keep people
constantly employed to beat them off.　Fish were
in the greatest plenty, and innumerable sea birds had
their nests near the shore, which makes the remark
of Ringrose on approaching the island the more
extraordinary.　Craw-fish and lobsters were in abundance ; and on the island itself goats were in such
plenty that, besides what they ate during their stay,
they killed about a hundred for salting, and took away
as many alive.

Here new disagreements broke out among the
buccaneers.　Some wished to sail immediately homeward by the Strait of Magalhanes ; others desired to
try their fortune longer in the South Sea.　Sharp was
of the party for returning home ; but in the end the
majority deposed him from the command, and elected
for his successor John Watling, "an old privateer,
and esteemed a stout seaman".　Articles were drawn
up in writing between Watling and the crew, and
subscribed.

One narrative says : "The true occasion of the
grudge against Sharp was, that he had got by these
adventures almost a thousand pounds, whereas many
of our men were scarce worth a groat ; and good
reason there was for their poverty, for at the Isle of
Plate and other places they had lost all their money
to their fellow-buccaneers at dice ; so that some had
a great deal and others just nothing.　Those who
were thrifty sided with Captain Sharp, but the others,
being the greatest number, turned Sharp out of his

command, and Sharp's party were persuaded to have patience, seeing they were the fewest, and had money to lose, which the other party had not." Dampier says Sharp was displaced by general consent, the company not being satisfied either with his courage or his conduct.

Watling began his command by ordering the observance of the Sabbath. "This day, the 9th January," says Ringrose, "was the first Sunday that ever we kept by command since the loss and death of our valiant commander Captain Sawkins, who once threw the dice overboard, finding them in use on the said day."

The 11th, two boats were sent from the ship to a distant part of the island to catch goats. On the following morning the boats were seen returning in great haste, and firing muskets to give alarm. When arrived on board, they gave information that three sail, which they believed to be Spanish ships of war, were in sight of the island, and were making for the anchorage. In half an hour after this notice the strange ships were seen from the bay; upon which all the men employed on shore in watering, hunting, and other occupations, were called on board with the utmost speed, and, not to lose time, the cable was slipped, and the ship put to sea. It happened in this hurry of quitting the island that one of the Mosquito Indians who had come with the buccaneers, and was by them called William, was absent in the woods hunting goats, and heard nothing of the alarm. No time could be spared for search, and the ship sailed without him. This it seems was not the first instance of a solitary individual being left to inhabit Juan Fernandez. Their Spanish pilot affirmed to them that "many years before a ship had been cast away there, and only one man saved, who lived alone upon the island five years, when another ship coming that way took him off".

The three vessels whose appearance caused them in such haste to quit their anchorage were armed Spanish ships. They remained in sight of the buccaneer ship two days, but no inclination appeared on either side to try the event of a battle. The buccaneers had not a single great gun in their ship, and must have trusted to their musketry and to boarding.

On the evening of the 13th, after dark, they resigned the honour of the field to the Spaniards, and made sail eastward for the American coast with design to attack Arica, which place they had been informed contained great riches.

The 26th, they were close to the small island named Yqueque, about twenty-five leagues to the south of Arica, where they plundered a small Indian village of provisions, and took two old Spaniards and two Indians prisoners. This island was destitute of fresh water, and the inhabitants were obliged to supply themselves from the continent, at a river named De Camarones, eleven Spanish leagues to the north of Yqueque. The people on Yqueque were the servants and slaves of the governor of Arica, and were employed by him to catch and dry fish, which were disposed of to great profit among the inland towns of the continent. The Indians here ate much and often of certain leaves, "which were in taste much like to the bay leaves in England, by the continual use of which their teeth were dyed of a green colour".

On the 27th Watling examined one of the old Spaniards concerning the force at Arica, and, being offended at his answers, ordered him to be shot : which was done. The same morning they took a small barque from the river Camarones laden with fresh water.

In the night of the 28th Watling with one hundred men departed from the ship in the small prize barque and boats for Arica. They put ashore on the mainland, about five leagues to the south of Arica, before it was light, and remained concealed among rocks all day. At night they again proceeded, and at daylight (on the 30th) Watling landed with ninety-two men four miles from the town, to which they marched and gained entrance, with the loss of three men killed and two wounded. There was a castle or fort which, for their own security, they ought immediately to have attacked ; but Watling was only intent on making prisoners, until he was incommoded with more than could be well guarded. This gave the inhabitants who had fled time to recover from their alarm, and they collected in the fort. To complete the mistake, Watling at length advanced to attack the fort, where he found more resistance than he expected. Watling put in practice the expedient of placing his prisoners in front of his own men, but the defenders of the fort were not a whit deterred thereby from firing on the buccaneers, who were twice repulsed. The Spaniards without, in the meantime, began to make head from all parts, and in a little time the buccaneers, from

being the assailants, found themselves obliged to look
to their defence. Watling, their chief, was killed, as
were two quarter-masters, the boatswain, and some
others of their best men; and the rest thought it
necessary to retreat to their boats, which, though
harassed the whole way by a distant firing from the
Spaniards, they effected in tolerable order, and embarked.

In this attack the buccaneers lost, in killed and
taken prisoners by the Spaniards, twenty-eight men,
and of those who got back to the ship eighteen were
wounded. Among the men taken by the Spaniards
were two surgeons, to whose care the wounded had
been committed. "We could have brought off our
doctors," says Ringrose, "but they got to drinking
whilst we were assaulting the fort, and when we called
them they would not come with us." The Spaniards
gave quarter to the surgeons, "they being able to do
them good service in that country; but as to the
wounded men taken prisoners, they were all knocked
on the head".

The whole party that landed at Arica narrowly
escaped destruction, for the Spaniards learnt, from the
prisoners they took, the signals which had been agreed
upon with the men left in charge of the boats; of
which information they made such use that the boats
had quitted their station and set sail to run down to
the town, but some buccaneers, who had been most
speedy in the retreat, arrived at the sea-side just in
time to call them back.

This miscarriage so much disheartened the whole
buccaneer crew that they made no attempt to take

three ships which were at anchor in the road before
Arica. Sharp was reinstated in the command because
he was esteemed a leader of safer conduct than any
other ; and every one was willing to quit the South
Sea, which it was now proposed they should do
by recrossing the isthmus. They did not, however,
immediately steer northward, but continued to beat up
against the wind to the southward till the 10th of
March, when they landed at Guasco, or Huasco (in
latitude about 28½°), from which place they carried off
120 sheep, 80 goats, 200 bushels of corn, and filled
their jars with fresh water.

From Huasco they stood to the north. On the
27th they passed Arica. The narrative remarks :
"Our former entertainment had been so very bad
that we were no ways encouraged to stop there
again". They landed at Ylo, of which Wafer says :
"The river Ylo is situated in a valley which is the
finest I have seen in all the coast of Peru, and furnished
with a multitude of vegetables. A great dew falls here
every night."

April the 16th they were near the island Plata. By
this time new opinions and new projects had been formed.
Many of the crew were again willing to try their fortune longer in the South Sea ; but one party would
not continue under the command of Sharp, and others
would not consent to choosing a new commander. As
neither party would yield, it was determined to separate, and agreed upon by all hands "that which party
soever upon polling should be found to have the
majority should keep the ship". The other party was
to have the long boat and the canoes. On coming to

a division, Sharp's party proved the more numerous. The minority consisted of forty-four Europeans, two Mosquito Indians, and a Spanish Indian. On the forenoon of the 17th the party in the boats separated from the ship, and proceeded for the Gulf de San Miguel, where they landed, and returned over the isthmus back to the West Indies. In this party were William Dampier and Lionel Wafer, the surgeon. Dampier afterwards published a brief sketch of the expedition, and an account of his return across the isthmus, both of which are in the first volume of his *Voyages*. Wafer met with an accidental hurt whilst on the isthmus, which disabled him from travelling with his countrymen, and he remained some months living with the Darien Indians, of whom he afterwards published an entertaining description, with a narrative of his own adventures among them.

Sharp and his diminished crew sailed in their ship from the island Plata northward to the Gulf of Nicoya, where they met with no booty, nor with any adventure worth mentioning.

They returned southward to the island Plata, and on the way took three prizes, the first a ship named the "San Pedro," from Guayaquil, bound for Panama, with a lading of cocoa-nuts, and 21,000 pieces of eight in chests, and 16,000 in bags, besides plate. The money in bags and all the loose plunder was divided, each man receiving for his share 234 pieces of eight; whence it may be inferred that their number was reduced to about seventy men. The rest of the money was reserved for a future division. Their second prize was a packet from Panama bound for

Callao, by which they learnt that in Panama it was believed all the buccaneers had returned overland to the West Indies. The third was a ship named the "San Rosario," which did not submit to them without resistance, nor till her captain was killed. She was from Callao, laden with wine, brandy, oil and fruit and had in her as much money as yielded to each buccaneer ninety-four dollars. One narrative says a much greater booty was missed through ignorance. "Besides the lading already mentioned, we found in the "San Rosario" 700 pigs of plate, which we supposed to be tin, and under this mistake they were slighted by us all, especially by the captain, who would not, by persuasions used by some few, be induced to take them into our ship, as we did most of the other things. Thus we left them in the "Rosario," which we turned away loose into the sea. This, it should seem, was plate not thoroughly refined and fitted for coin, which occasioned our being deceived. We took only one pig of the 700 into our ship, thinking to make bullets of it ; and to this effect, or what else our seamen pleased, the greatest part of it was melted and squandered away. Afterwards, when we arrived at Antigua, we gave the remaining part (which was about one-third thereof) to a Bristol man, who knew presently what it was, who brought it to England, and sold it there for £75 sterling. Thus we parted with the richest booty we got in the whole voyage through our own ignorance and laziness." *

The same narrative relates that they took out of

* *Buccaneers of America*, part iii. p. 80.

the "Rosario" "a great book full of sea charts and maps, containing an accurate and exact description of all the ports, soundings, rivers, capes and coasts of the South Sea, and all the navigation usually performed by the Spaniards in that ocean. This book was, for its novelty and curiosity, presented unto His Majesty on the return of some of the buccaneers to England, and was translated into English by His Majesty's order." *

August the 12th they anchored at the island Plata, whence they departed on the 16th, bound southward, intending to return by the Strait of Magalhanes or Strait le Maire to the West Indies.

The 28th they looked in at Paita, but finding the place prepared for defence they stood off from the coast and pursued their course southward, without again coming in sight of land and without the occurrence of anything remarkable till they passed the 50th degree of latitude.

October the 11th they were in latitude 49° 54' south, and estimated their distance from the American coast to be 120 leagues. The wind blew strong from the

---

* Nos. 239 and 44 in the Sloane Collection of manuscripts in the British Museum are probably the charts and translation spoken of above. No. 239 is a book of Spanish charts of the sea-coast of New Spain, Peru, and Chili, each chart containing a small portion of coast on which is drawn a rude likeness of the appearance of the land, making it at the same time both landscape and chart. They are generally without compass, latitude, or divisions of any kind by lines, and with no appearance of correctness, but apparently with knowledge of the coast. No. 44 is a copy of the same, or of similar Spanish charts of the same coast, and is dedicated to King Charles II. by Bartholomew Sharp.

south-west, and they stood to the south-east. On the
morning of the 12th, two hours before day, being in
latitude by account 50° 50′ south, they suddenly found
themselves close to land. The ship was ill prepared
for such an event, the foreyard having been lowered
to ease her on account of the strength of the wind.
" The land was high and towering, and here appeared
many islands scattered up and down." They were so
near, and so entangled, that there was no possibility
of standing off to sea, and, with such light as they had,
they steered as cautiously as they could in between
some islands and along an extensive coast, which,
whether it was a larger island or part of the continent, they could not know. As the day advanced
the land was seen to be mountainous and craggy, and
the tops covered with snow. Sharp says : " We bore
up for a harbour, and steered in northward about
five leagues. On the north side there are plenty of
harbours." * At eleven in the forenoon they came to
an anchor " in a harbour in forty-five fathoms, within
a stone's cast of the shore, where the ship was land-
locked, and in smooth water. As the ship went in,
one of the crew, named Henry Shergall, fell overboard as he was going into the spritsail top, and was
drowned, on which account this was named Shergall's
Harbour."

The bottom was rocky where the ship had anchored ; a boat was therefore sent to look for better
anchorage. They did not, however, shift their berth
that day ; and during the night strong flurries of wind

* Sharp's manuscript journal, British Museum.

from the hills, joined with the sharpness of the rocks at the bottom, cut their cable in two, and they were obliged to set sail.   They ran about a mile to another bay, where they let go another anchor, and moored the ship with a fastening to a tree on shore.

They shot geese and other wild-fowl.   On the shores they found large mussels, cockles like those in England, and limpets : here also were penguins, which were shy and not taken without pursuit ; "they padded on the water with their wings very fast, but their bodies were too heavy to be carried by the said wings".

The first part of the time they lay in this harbour they had almost continual rain.   On the night of the 15th, in a high north wind, the tree to which their cable was fastened gave way, and came up by the root, in consequence of which the stern of the ship took the ground and damaged the rudder.   They secured the ship afresh by fastening the cable to other trees, but were obliged to unhang the rudder to repair.

The 18th was a day of clear weather.   The latitude was observed 50° 40′ south.   The difference of the rise and fall of the tide was seven feet perpendicular : the time of high water is not noted.   The arm of the sea, or gulf, in which they were, they named the English Gulf, and the land forming the harbour the Duke of York's Island ; "more by guess than any-thing else, for whether it were an island or continent was not discovered".   Ringrose says : "I am persuaded that the place where we now are is not so great an island as some hydrographers do lay it down, but rather an archipelago of smaller islands.   Our captain gave to them the name of the Duke of York's

Islands. Our boat which went eastward found several
good bays and harbours, with deep water close to the
shore; but there lay in them several sunken rocks, as
there did also in the harbour where the ship lay.
These rocks are less dangerous to shipping by reason
they have weeds lying about them."

From all the preceding description it appears that
they were at the south part of the island named Madre
de Dios in the Spanish atlas, which island is south of
the channel, or arm of the sea, named the Gulf de la
Sma. Trinidada, and that Sharp's English Gulf is the
Brazo de la Conçepçion of Sarmiento.

Ringrose has drawn a sketch of the Duke of York's
Islands, and one of the English Gulf; but these are
not worth copying, as they have neither compass,
meridian line, scale, nor soundings. He has given
other plans in the same defective manner, on which
account they can be of little use. It is necessary,
however, to remark a difference in the plan which has
been printed of the English Gulf, from the plan in the
manuscript. In the printed copy the shore of the
gulf is drawn as one continued line, admitting no
thoroughfare, whereas in the manuscript plan there
are clear openings, leaving a prospect of channels
through.

Towards the end of October the weather settled
fair. Hitherto they had seen no inhabitants; but on
the 27th a party went from the ship in a boat on an
excursion in search of provisions, and unhappily caught
sight of a small boat belonging to the natives of the
land. The ship's boat rowed in pursuit, and the
natives, a man, a woman and a boy, finding their boat

would be overtaken, all leapt overboard, and swam towards shore. This villainous crew of buccaneers had the barbarity to shoot at them in the water, and they shot the man dead; the woman made her escape to land; the boy, a stout lad about eighteen years of age, was taken, and, with the Indian boat, was carried to the ship.

The poor lad thus made prisoner had only a small covering of sealskin. " He was squint-eyed, and his hair was cut short. The *doree*, or boat, in which he and the other Indians were was built sharp at each end and flat-bottomed : in the middle they had a fire burning for dressing victuals, or other use. They had a net to catch penguins, a club like to our bandies, and wooden darts. This young Indian appeared by his actions to be very innocent and foolish. He could open large mussels with his fingers, which our buccaneers could scarcely manage with their knives. He was very wild, and would eat raw flesh."

By the beginning of November the rudder was repaired and hung. Ringrose says : " We could perceive, now the stormy weather was blown over, much small fry of fish about the ship, whereof before we saw none. The weather began to be warm, or rather hot, and the birds, as thrushes and blackbirds, to sing as sweetly as those in England."

On the 5th of November they sailed out of the English Gulf, taking with them their young Indian prisoner, to whom they gave the name of Orson. As they departed the natives on some of the lands to the eastward made great fires. At six in the evening the ship was without the mouth of the gulf: the wind blew

fresh from north-west, and they stood out south-west
by west, to keep clear of breakers which lie four
leagues without the entrance of the gulf to the south
and south-south-east. Many reefs and rocks were
seen hereabouts, on account of which they kept close to
the wind till they were a good distance clear of the land.

Their navigation from here to the Atlantic was,
more than could have been imagined, like the journey
of travellers by night in a strange country without a
guide. The weather was stormy, and they would not
venture to steer in for the Strait of Magalhanes, which
they had purposed to do for the benefit of the provision
which the shores of the strait afford of fresh water,
fish, vegetables, and wood. They ran to the south to
go round the Tierra del Fuego, having the wind from
the north-west, which was the most favourable for
this navigation; but they frequently lay to, because
the weather was thick. On the 12th they had not
passed the Tierra del Fuego. The latitude according
to observation that day was 55° 25′, and the course
they steered was south-south-east. On the 14th,
Ringrose says: "The latitude was observed 57° 50′
south, and on this day we could perceive land, from
which at noon we were due west". They steered
east by south, and expected that at daylight the next
morning they should be close in with the land; but the
weather became cloudy with much fall of snow, and
nothing more of it was seen. No longitude or meridian
distance is noticed, and it must remain doubtful whether
what they took for land was floating ice, or their
observation for the latitude erroneous, and that they
saw the Isles of Diego Ramirez.

Three days afterwards, in latitude 58° 30′ south, they fell in with ice islands, one of which they reckoned to be two leagues in circumference. A strong current set here southward. They held on their course eastward so far that when at length they did sail northward they saw neither the Tierra del Fuego nor Staten Island.

December the 5th they divided the plunder which had been reserved, each man's share of which amounted to 328 pieces of eight. Their course was now bent for the West Indies.

January the 15th died William Stephens, a seaman, whose death was attributed to his having eaten three manchineal apples six months before, when on the coast of New Spain, "from which time he wasted away till he became a perfect skeleton".

January the 28th, 1682, they made the island of Barbadoes, but learnt that the "Richmond," a British frigate, was lying in the road. Ringrose and his fellow-journalists say: "We, having acted in all our voyage without a commission, dared not be so bold as to put in, lest the said frigate should seize us for pirateering, and strip us of all we had got in the whole voyage". They next sailed to Antigua; but the governor at that island, Colonel Codrington, would not give them leave to enter the harbour, though they endeavoured to soften him by sending a present of jewels to his lady, which, however, was not accepted. Sharp and his crew grew impatient at their uneasy situation, and came to a determination to separate. Some of them landed at Antigua; Sharp and others landed at Nevis, whence they got passage to England. Their ship, which was the "Trinidad" captured in the Bay of Panama, was left to seven men of the company who had lost their money by gaming. The buccaneer journals say nothing of their Patagonian captive, Orson, after the ship sailed from his country, and what became of the ship after Sharp quitted her does not appear.

Bartholomew Sharp and a few others, on their arrival in England, were apprehended, and a court of admiralty was held at the Marshalsea in Southwark, where, at the instance of the Spanish ambassador, they were tried for committing acts of piracy in the South Sea; but, from the defectiveness of the evidence produced, they escaped conviction. One of the principal charges against them was for taking the Spanish ship "Rosario," and killing the captain and another man belonging to her; "but it was proved," says the author of the anonymous narrative, who was one of the men brought to trial, "that the Spaniards fired at us first, and it was judged that we ought to defend ourselves". Three buccaneers of Sharp's crew were also tried at Jamaica, one of whom was condemned and hanged, "who," the narrator says, "was wheedled into an open confession: the other two stood it out, and escaped for want of witnesses to prove the fact against them". Thus terminated what may be called the first expedition of the buccaneers in the South Sea, the boat excursion by Morgan's men in the Bay of Panama being of too little consequence to be so reckoned. They had now made successful experiment of the route both by sea and land, and the Spaniards in the South Sea had reason to apprehend a speedy renewal of their visits.

Carlos Enriquez Clerck, who went from England with Captain Narbrough, was at this time executed at Lima on a charge of holding correspondence with the English of Jamaica ; which act of severity probably is attributable more to the alarm which prevailed in the Government of Peru than to any guilty practices of Clerck.

CHAPTER XI.

Disputes between the French Government and their West India colonies. Morgan becomes deputy-governor of Jamaica. La Vera Cruz surprised by the flibustiers. Other of their enterprises.

WHILST so many of the English buccaneers were seeking plunder in the South Sea, the French flibustiers had not been inactive in the West Indies, notwithstanding that the French government, after the conclusion of the war with Spain, issued orders prohibiting the subjects of France in the West Indies from cruising against the Spaniards. A short time before this order arrived, a cruising commission had been given to Granmont, who had thereupon collected men, and made preparation for an expedition to the *tierra firma;* and they did not choose that so much pains should be taken to no purpose. The French settlers generally were at this time much dissatisfied on account of some regulations imposed upon them by the Company of Farmers, whose privileges and authority extended to fixing the price upon growth, the produce of the soil, and which they exercised upon tobacco—the article then most cultivated by the French in Hispaniola—rigorously requiring the planters to

deliver it to the company at the price so prescribed.
Many of the inhabitants, ill brooking to live under such
a system of robbery, made preparations to withdraw
to the English and Dutch settlements ; but their discontent on this account was much allayed by the
governor writing a remonstrance to the French minister, and promising them his influence towards obtaining a suppression of the farming tobacco. Fresh cause
of discontent soon occurred by a monopoly of the
French African slave trade being put into the hands
of a new company, which was named the Senegal
Company.

Granmont and the flibustiers engaged with him
went to the coast of Cumana, where they did considerable mischief to the Spaniards, with some loss
and little profit to themselves.

In the autumn of this same year the Earl of
Carlisle, who was governor of Jamaica, finding the
climate did not agree with his constitution, returned to
England, and left as his deputy to govern in Jamaica,
Morgan, the plunderer of Panama, but who was now
Sir Henry Morgan. This man had found favour with
King Charles II. or with his ministers, had been
knighted, and appointed a commissioner of the
admiralty court in Jamaica. On becoming deputy-
governor his administration was far from being
favourable to his old associates, some of whom suffered
the extreme hardship of being tried and hanged under
his authority ; and one crew of buccaneers, most of
them Englishmen, who fell into his hands, he sent to
be delivered up (it may be presumed that he sold them)
to the Spaniards at Carthagena. Morgan's authority

as governor was terminated the following year by the
arrival of a governor from England.*

The impositions on planting and commerce in the
French settlements, in the same degree that they discouraged cultivation, encouraged cruising, and the
flibustier party so much increased as to have little
danger to apprehend from any governor's authority.
The matter, however, did not come to an issue, for in
1683 war again broke out between France and Spain.
But before the intelligence arrived in the West Indies
1200 French flibustiers had assembled under Van
Horn (a native of Ostend), Granmont, and another
noted flibustier named Laurent de Graaf, to make an
expedition against the Spaniards.

Van Horn had been a notorious pirate, and for a
number of years had plundered generally, without
showing partiality or favour to ships of one nation
more than to those of another   After amassing great
riches, he began to think plain piracy too dangerous
an occupation, and determined to reform, which he
did by making his peace with the French governor in
Hispaniola, and turning buccaneer or flibustier, into
which fraternity he was admitted on paying entrance.

The expedition which he undertook in conjunction
with Granmont and de Graaf was against La Vera
Cruz in the Gulf of Mexico, a town which might be

---

* Morgan continued in office at Jamaica during the remainder
of the reign of King Charles II., but was suspected by the Spaniards
of connivance with the buccaneers, and in the next reign the court
of Spain had influence to procure his being sent home prisoner from
the West Indies. He was kept three years in prison, but without
charge being brought forward against him.

considered as the magazine for all the merchandise
which passed between New Spain and Old Spain, and
was defended by a fort said to be impregnable. The
flibustiers sailed for this place with a fleet of ten
ships. They had information that two large Spanish
ships, with cargoes of cacao, were expected at La
Vera Cruz from the Caraccas, and, upon this intelligence, they put in practice the following expedient.
They embarked the greater number of their men on
board two of their largest ships, which on arriving
near La Vera Cruz put aloft Spanish colours and
ran with all sail set directly for the port, like ships
chased, the rest of the buccaneer ships appearing at
a distance behind, crowding sail after them. The
inhabitants of La Vera Cruz believed the two head-
most ships to be those which were expected from the
Caraccas, and, as the flibustiers had contrived that
they should not reach the port till after dark, suffered
them to enter without offering them molestation,
and to anchor close to the town, which they did
without being suspected to be enemies.   In the middle
of the night the flibustiers landed and surprised the
fort, which made them masters of the town. The
Spaniards of the garrison, and all the inhabitants who
fell into their hands, they shut up in the churches,
where they were kept three days, and with so little
care for their subsistence that several died from thirst,
and some by drinking immoderately when water was
at length given to them.   With the plunder, and
what was obtained for ransom of the town, it is
said the flibustiers carried away a million of piastres,
besides a number of slaves and prisoners.

Van Horn shortly after died of a wound received
in a quarrel with De Graaf. The ship he had commanded, which mounted fifty guns, was bequeathed by
him to Granmont, who a short time before had lost a
ship of nearly the same force in a gale of wind.

Some quarrels happened at this time between the
French flibustiers and the English buccaneers, which
are differently related by the English and the French
writers. The French account says, that in a Spanish
ship captured by the flibustiers was found a letter
from the governor of Jamaica addressed to the
governor of the Havannah, proposing a union of
their force to drive the French from Hispaniola.
Also, that an English ship of thirty guns came cruising
near Tortuga, and when the governor of Tortuga
sent a sloop to demand of the English captain his
business there, the Englishman insolently replied
that the sea was alike free to all, and he had no
account to render to anyone. For this answer the
governor sent out a ship to take the English ship,
but the governor's vessel was roughly treated, and
obliged to retire into port. Granmont had just
returned from the La Vera Cruz expedition, and
the governor applied to him to go with his fifty-gun
ship to revenge the affront put upon their nation.
"Granmont," says the narrator, "accepted the commission joyfully. Three hundred flibustiers embarked
with him in his ship ; he found the Englishman proud
of his late victory ; he immediately grappled with him
and put all the English crew to the sword, saving only
the captain, whom he carried prisoner to Cape François." On the merit of this service his disobedience to

the royal prohibitory order in attacking La Vera Cruz
was to pass with impunity.   The English were not yet
sufficiently punished.   The account proceeds : "Our
flibustiers would no longer receive them as partakers
in their enterprises, and even confiscated the share
they were entitled to receive for the La Vera Cruz
expedition ".   Thus the French account.

If the story of demolishing the English crew is
true, the fact is not more absurd than the being vain
of such an exploit.   If a fifty-gun ship will determine
to sink a thirty-gun ship, the thirty-gun ship must in
all probability be sunk.   The affront given, if it
deserves to be called an affront, was not worthy being
revenged with a massacre.   The story is found only
in the French histories, the writers of which, it may be
suspected, were moved to make Granmont deal so un-
mercifully with the English crew by the kind of feeling
which so generally prevails between nations who are
near neighbours.   To this it may be attributed that
Père Charlevoix, both a good historian and good
critic, has adopted the story ; but, had it been believed
by him, he would have related it in a more rational
manner, and not with exultation.

English writers mention a disagreement which
happened about this time between Granmont and the
English buccaneers, on account of his taking a sloop
belonging to Jamaica and forcing the crew to serve
under him, but which crew found opportunity to take
advantage of some disorder in his ship and to escape
in the night.*   This seems to have been the whole

* *British Empire in America*, vol. ii. p. 319.

fact ; for an outrage such as is affirmed by the French writers could not have been committed and have been boasted of by one side without incurring reproach from the other.

The French government was highly offended at the insubordination and unmanageableness of the flibustiers in Hispaniola, and no one was more so than the French King, Louis XIV. Towards reducing them to a more orderly state, instructions were sent to the governors in the West Indies to be strict in making them observe port regulations, the principal of which were, that all vessels should register their crew and lading before their departure, and also at their return into port ; that they should abstain from cruising in times of peace, and should take out regular commissions in times of war ; and that they should pay the dues of the crown, one item of which was a tenth of all prizes and plunder.

The number of the French flibustiers in 1684 was estimated to be 3000. The French government desired to convert them into settlers. A letter written in that year from the French minister to the governor-general of the French West India Islands has this remarkable expression : " His Majesty esteems nothing more important than to render these vagabonds good inhabitants of Saint Domingo ". Such being the disposition of the French government, it was an oversight that they did not contribute towards so desirable a purpose by making some abatement in the impositions which oppressed and retarded cultivation, which would have conciliated the colonists and have been an encouragement to the flibustiers to become

planters.   But the colonists still had to struggle
against farming the tobacco, which they had in vain
attempted to get commuted for some other burthen,
and many cultivators of that plant were reduced to
indigence.   The greediness of the French chartered
companies appears in the Senegal Company making it
a subject of complaint that the flibustiers sold the
negroes they took from the Spaniards to whomsoever
they pleased, to the prejudice of the interest of the
company.   It was unreasonable to expect that the
flibustiers would give up their long accustomed modes
of gain, sanctioned as they had hitherto been by the
acquiescence and countenance of the French government, and turn planters under circumstances discourag-
ing to industry.   Their number, likewise, rendered it
necessary to observe mildness and forbearance in the
endeavour to reform them; but both the encouragement
and the forbearance were neglected, and, in consequence of their being made to apprehend rigorous
treatment in their own settlements, many removed to
the British and Dutch islands.

The French flibustiers were unsuccessful at this
time in some enterprises they undertook in the Bay of
Campeachy, where they lost many men ; on the other
hand, three of their ships, commanded by De Graaf,
Michel le Basque, and another flibustier named
Jonqué, engaged and took three Spanish ships which
were sent purposely against them out of Carthagena.

CHAPTER XII.

Circumstances which preceded the second irruption of the buccaneers into the South Sea. Buccaneers under John Cook sail from Virginia; stop at the Cape de Verde Islands; at Sierra Leone. Origin and history of the report concerning the supposed discovery of Pepys Island.

THE prohibitions being enforced determined many, both of the English buccaneers and of the French flibustiers, to seek their fortunes in the South Sea, where they would be at a distance from the control of any established authority. This determination was not a matter generally concerted. The first example was speedily followed, and a trip to the South Sea in a short time became a prevailing fashion among them. Expeditions were undertaken by different bodies of men unconnected with each other, except when accident, or the similarity of their pursuits, brought them together.

Among the buccaneers in the expedition of 1680 to the South Sea, who from dislike to Sharp's command returned across the Isthmus of Darien at the same time with Dampier, was one John Cook, who, on arriving again in the West Indies, entered on board a vessel commanded by a Dutchman of the name of Yanky, which was fitted up as a privateer, and pro-

vided with a French commission to cruise against the
Spaniards.   Cook, being esteemed a capable seaman,
was made quarter-master, by which title, in privateers
as well as in buccaneer vessels, the officer next in
command to the captain was called.   Cook continued
quarter-master with Yanky till they took a Spanish
ship which was thought well adapted for a cruiser.
Cook claimed to have the command of this ship, and,
according to the usage among privateers in such cases,
she was allotted to him, with a crew composed of men
who volunteered to sail with him.   Dampier was of
the number, as were several others who had returned
from the South Sea ; division was made of the prize
goods, and Cook entered on his new command.

This arrangement took place at Isla Vaca, or Isle
à Vache, a small island near the south coast of Hispaniola, which was then much resorted to by both
privateers and buccaneers.   It happened at this time
that besides Yanky's ship some French privateers
having legal commissions were lying at Avache, and
their commanders did not contentedly behold men
without a commission, and who were but buccaneers,
in the possession of a finer ship than any belonging to
themselves who cruised under lawful authority.   The
occasion being so fair, and remembering what Morgan
had done in a somewhat similar case, after short
counsel, they joined together and seized the buccaneer
ship, goods and arms, and turned the crew ashore.   A
fellow-feeling that still existed between the privateers
and buccaneers, and probably a want of hands,
induced a Captain Tristian, who commanded one of
the privateers, to receive into his ship ten of the

buccaneers to be part of his crew. Among these were Cook, and a buccaneer afterwards of greater note, named Edward Davis. Tristian sailed to Petit Guaves, where the ship had not been long at anchor before he himself and the greatest part of his men went on shore. Cook and his companions thought this also a fair occasion, and accordingly they made themselves masters of the ship. Those of Tristian's men who were on board they turned ashore, and immediately taking up the anchors sailed back close in to the Isle à Vache, where, before notice of their exploit reached the governor, they collected and took on board the remainder of their old company and sailed away. They had scarcely left the Isle à Vache when they met and captured two vessels, one of which was a ship from France laden with wines. Thinking it unsafe to continue longer in the West Indies, they directed their course for Virginia, where they arrived with their prizes in April, 1683.

In Virginia they disposed of their prize goods and two vessels, keeping one with which they proposed to make a voyage to the South Sea, and which they named the "Revenge". She mounted eighteen guns, and the number of adventurers who embarked in her were about seventy, the major part of them old buccaneers, some of whose names have since been much noted, as William Dampier, Edward Davis, Lionel Wafer, Ambrose Cowley, and John Cook, their captain. August the 23rd, 1683, they sailed from the Chesapeak.

Dampier and Cowley have both related their piratical adventures, but with some degree of caution, to prevent bringing upon themselves a charge of piracy. Cowley pretended that he was engaged to sail in the "Revenge" to navigate her, but was kept in ignorance of the design of the voyage, and made to believe they were bound for the island Hispaniola; and that it was not revealed to him till after they got out to sea, that, instead of to the West Indies, they were bound to the coast of Guinea, there to seek for a better ship, in which they might sail to the great South Sea. William Dampier, who always shows respect for truth, would not stoop to dissimulation; but he forbears being circumstantial concerning the outset of this voyage, and the particulars of their proceedings whilst in the Atlantic, supplying the chasm in the following general terms: "August the 23rd, 1683, we sailed from Virginia under the command of Captain Cook, bound for the South Seas. I shall not trouble the reader with an account of every day's run, but hasten to the less known parts of the world."

Whilst near the coast of Virginia they met a Dutch ship, out of which they took six casks of wine, and other provisions; also two Dutch seamen, who voluntarily entered with them. Some time in September they anchored at the Isle of Sal, where they procured fish and a few goats, but neither fruits nor good fresh water. Only five men lived on the island, who were all black; but they called themselves Portuguese, and one was styled the governor. These Portuguese exchanged a lump of ambergris, or what was supposed to be ambergris, for old clothes. Dampier says: "Not a man in the ship knew ambergris, but I have since seen it in other places, and am certain this was not the right; it was of a dark colour, like sheep's dung, very soft, but of no smell, and possibly was goat's dung. Some I afterwards saw sold at the Nicobars in the East Indies was of a lighter colour, and very hard; neither had that any smell, and I suppose was also a cheat. Mr. Hill, a surgeon, once showed me a piece of ambergris, and related to me that one Mr. Benjamin Barker, a man I have been long well acquainted with, and know to be a very sober and credible person, told this Mr. Hill that, being in the Bay of Honduras, he found in a sandy bay upon the shore of an island a lump of ambergris so large that when carried to Jamaica it was found to weigh upwards of 100 lbs. When he found it, it lay dry above the mark of the sea at high water, and in it were a great multitude of beetles. It was of a dusky colour, towards black, about the hardness of mellow cheese, and of a very fragrant smell. What Mr. Hill showed me was some of it, which Mr. Barker had given him." *

There were wild-fowl at Sal, and flamingoes, of which, and their manner of building their nests, Dampier has given a description. The flesh of the flamingo is lean and black, yet good meat, "tasting neither fishy nor anyway unsavoury. A dish of flamingoes' tongues is fit for a prince's table; they are large, and have a knob of fat at the root which is an excellent bit. When many of them stand together, at a distance they appear like a brick wall; for their feathers are of the colour of new red brick, and, except when feeding, they commonly stand upright exactly in a row close by each other."

* Dampier, vol. 1. p. 73.

From the Isle of Sal they went to other of the Cape de Verde Islands. At St. Nicholas they watered the ship by digging wells, and at Mayo they procured some provisions. They afterwards sailed to the island St. Jago, but a Dutch ship was lying at anchor in Port Praya, which fired her guns at them as soon as they came within reach of shot, and the buccaneers thought it prudent to stand out again to sea.

They next sailed to the coast of Guinea, which they made in the beginning of November, near Sierra Leone. A large ship was at anchor in the road, which proved to be a Dane. On sight of her, and all the time they were standing into the road, all the buccaneer crew, except a few men to manage the sails, kept under deck ; which gave their ship the appearance of being a weakly manned merchant-vessel. When they drew near the Danish ship, which they did with intention to board her, the buccaneer commander, to prevent suspicion, gave direction in a loud voice to the steersman to put the helm one way, and, according to the plan preconcerted, the steersman put it the contrary, so that their vessel seemed to fall on board the Dane through mistake. By this stratagem they surprised and, with the loss of five men, became masters of a ship mounting thirty-six guns, which was victualled and stored for a long voyage. This achievement is related circumstantially in Cowley's manuscript journal ; * but in his published account he only says : " Near Cape Sierra Leone we alighted on a new ship of forty guns, which we boarded, and carried her away".

* In the Sloane Collection, British Museum.

They went with their prize to a river south of the
Sierra Leone, called the Sherborough, to which they
were safely piloted through channels among shoals, by
one of the crew who had been there before. At the
river Sherborough there was then an English factory,
but distant from where they anchored. Near them
was a large town inhabited by negroes, who traded
freely, selling them rice, fowls, plantains, sugar-canes,
palm-wine and honey. The town was screened from
shipping by a grove of trees.

The buccaneers embarked here all in their new
ship, and named her the " Batchelor's Delight ".
Their old ship they burnt, " that she might tell no
tales," and set their prisoners on shore to shift as well
as they could for themselves.

They sailed from the coast of Guinea in the middle
of November, directing their course across the Atlantic
towards the Strait of Magalhanes. On January 28,
1684, they had sight of the northernmost of the islands
discovered by Captain John Davis in 1592 (since,
among other appellations, called the Sebald de Weert
Islands). From the circumstance of their falling in
with this land originated the extraordinary report of
an island being discovered in the Southern Atlantic
Ocean in latitude 47° south, and by Cowley named
Pepys Island, which was long believed to exist, and has
been sought after by navigators of different European
nations even within our own time. The following are
the particulars which caused so great a deception.

Cowley says in his manuscript journal: " January,
1683 : This month we were in latitude 47° 40', where
we espied an island bearing west of us, and bore

away for it, but being too late we lay by all night. The island seemed very pleasant to the eye, with many woods. I may say the whole island was woods, there being a rock above water to the eastward of it with innumerable fowls. I sailed along that island to the southward, and about the south-west side of the island there seemed to me to be a good place for ships to ride. The wind blew fresh, and they would not put the boat out. Sailing a little further, having twenty-six and twenty-seven fathoms water, we came to a place where we saw the weeds ride, and found only seven fathoms water and all rocky ground, therefore we put the ship about : but the harbour seemed a good place for ships to ride in. There seemed to me harbour for 500 sail of shipping, the going in but narrow, and the north side of the entrance shallow that I could see ; but I think there is water enough on the south side. I would have had them stand upon a wind all night, but they told me they did not come out to go upon discovery. We saw likewise another island by this, which made me to think them the Sibble D'wards." *

The latitude given by Cowley is to be attributed to his ignorance, and to this part of his narrative being composed from memory, which he acknowledges, though it is not so stated in the printed narrative. His describing the land to be covered with wood is sufficiently accounted for by the appearance it makes at a distance, which has in the same manner deceived other voyagers. Pernety, in his Introduction to M. de Bougainville's *Voyage to the Malouines* (by which

* Cowley's manuscript journal, Sloane Collection, No. 54.

name the French voyagers have chosen to call John Davis's Islands), says : " As to wood, we were deceived by appearances in running along the coast of the Malouines ; we thought we saw some, but, on landing, these appearances were discovered to be only tall bulrushes with large flat leaves, such as are called corn flags ". * The editor of Cowley's journal, William Hack, might possibly believe from the latitude mentioned by Cowley that the land seen by him was a new discovery. To give it a less doubtful appearance, he dropped the forty minutes of latitude, and also Cowley's conjecture that the land was the Sebald de Weerts, and with this falsification of the journal he took occasion to compliment the Honourable Mr. Pepys, who was then secretary of the admiralty, by putting his name to the land, giving as Cowley's words : " In the latitude of 47° we saw land, the same being an island not before known. I gave it the name of Pepys Island." Hack embellished this account with a drawing of Pepys Island, in which is introduced an Admiralty Bay and Secretary's Point.

The account which Dampier has given of their falling in with this land would have cleared up the whole matter but for a circumstance which is far more extraordinary than any yet mentioned, which is, that it long escaped notice, and seems never to have been generally understood, that Dampier and Cowley were at this time in the same ship, and their voyage thus far the same.

Dampier says : " January the 28th (1683-4), we

---

* See also Pernety's journal, p. 179, English translation.

made the Sebald de Weerts. They are three rocky, barren islands without any tree, only some bushes growing on them. The two northernmost lie in 51° south, the other in 51° 20' south. We could not come near the two northern islands, but we came close by the southern ; but we could not obtain soundings till within two cables' length of the shore, and there found the bottom to be foul, rocky ground." * In consequence of the inattention or oversight in not perceiving that Dampier and Cowley were speaking of the same land, Hack's ingenious adulation of the secretary of the admiralty flourished a full century undetected, a Pepys Island being all the time admitted in the charts.

Near these islands the variation was observed 23° 10' easterly. They passed through great shoals of small red lobsters, "no bigger than the top of a man's little finger, yet all their claws, both great and small, were like a lobster. I never saw," says Dampier, "any of this sort of fish naturally red, except here."

The winds blew hard from the westward, and they could not fetch the Strait of Magalhanes. On the 6th February they were at the entrance of Strait le Maire when it fell calm, and a strong tide set out of the strait northward, which made a short irregular sea, as in a race, or place where two tides meet, and broke over the waist of the ship, "which was tossed about like an egg-shell". A breeze springing up from the west-north-west, they bore away eastward, and

* Dampier's manuscript journal, No. 3236, Sloane Collection, British Museum.

passed round the east end of Staten Island; after which they saw no other land till they came into the South Sea. They had much rain, and took advantage of it to fill twenty-three casks with fresh water.

March the 17th they were in latitude 36° south, standing for the island Juan Fernandez. Variation 8° east.

CHAPTER XIII.

*Buccaneers under John Cook arrive at Juan Fernandez.
Account of William, a Mosquito Indian, who had
lived there three years. They sail to the Galapagos
Islands; thence to the coast of New Spain. John
Cook dies. Edward Davis chosen commander.*

CONTINUING their course for Juan Fernandez,
on the 19th, in the morning, a strange ship was
seen to the southward standing after them under all
her sail. The buccaneers were in hopes she would
prove to be a Spaniard, and brought to, to wait her
coming up. The people on board the strange vessel
entertained similar expectations, for they also were
English, and were come to the South Sea to pick up
what they could. This ship was named the "Nicholas": her commander, John Eaton. She fitted out
in the river Thames under pretence of a trading, but in
reality with the intention of making a piratical voyage.

The two ships soon joined; and, on its being found
that they had come on the same errand to the South
Sea, Cook and Eaton and their men agreed to keep
company together.

It was learnt from Eaton that another English
ship, named the "Cygnet," commanded by a Captain
Swan, had sailed from London for the South Sea; but

fitted out by reputable merchants and provided with a cargo for a trading voyage, having a licence from the Duke of York, then Lord High Admiral of England. The "Cygnet" and the "Nicholas" had met at the entrance of the Strait of Magalhanes, and they entered the South Sea in company, but had since been separated by bad weather.

March the 22nd, the "Batchelor's Delight" and the "Nicholas" came in sight of the island Juan Fernandez.

The reader may remember that when the buccaneers, under Watling, were at Juan Fernandez in January, 1681, the appearance of three Spanish ships made them quit the island in great haste, and they left behind a Mosquito Indian, named William, who was in the woods hunting for goats. Several of the buccaneers who were then with Watling were now with Cook, and, eager to discover if any traces could be found which would enable them to conjecture what was become of their former companion, but with small hope of finding him still here, as soon as they were near enough for a boat to be sent from the ship, they hastened to the shore. Dampier was in this first boat, as was also a Mosquito Indian named Robin; and, as they drew near the land, they had the satisfaction to see William at the sea-side waiting to receive them. Dampier has given the following affecting account of their meeting: "Robin, his countryman, was the first who leaped ashore from the boats, and, running to his brother Mosquito-man, threw himself flat on his face at his feet, who, helping him up and embracing him, fell flat with his face on the ground at Robin's feet, and was by him taken up also. We stood with pleasure to behold the surprise, tenderness, and solemnity of this interview, which was exceedingly affectionate on both sides ; and, when their ceremonies were over, we also, that stood gazing at them, drew near, each of us embracing him we had found here, who was overjoyed to see so many of his old friends come hither, as he thought, purposely to fetch him. He was named Will, as the other was Robin ; which names were given them by the English, for they have no names among themselves, and they take it as a favour to be named by us, and will complain if we do not appoint them some name when they are with us."

William had lived in solitude on Juan Fernandez above three years. The Spaniards knew of his being on the island, and Spanish ships had stopped there, the people belonging to which had made keen search after him ; but he kept himself concealed, and they could never discover his retreat. At the time Watling sailed from the island he had a musket, a knife, a small horn of powder and a few shot. "When his ammunition was expended, he contrived by notching his knife to saw the barrel of his gun into small pieces, wherewith he made harpoons, lances, hooks, and a long knife, heating the pieces of iron first in the fire, and then hammering them out as he pleased with stones. This may seem strange to those not acquainted with the sagacity of the Indians ; but it is no more than what the Mosquito men were accustomed to in their own country." He had worn out the clothes with which he landed, and was no otherwise clad than with a skin about his waist. He made fishing lines of the skins of seals cut into thongs. " He had built himself a hut, half-a-mile from the sea-shore, which he lined with goats' skins, and slept on his couch or *barbecu* of sticks, raised about two feet from the ground and spread with goats' skins." He saw the two ships commanded by Cook and Eaton the day before they anchored, and, from their manœuvring believing them to be English, he killed three goats, which he dressed with vegetables, thus preparing a treat for his friends on their landing ; and there has seldom been a more fair and joyful occasion for festivity.

Dampier reckoned two bays in Juan Fernandez proper for ships to anchor in ; " both at the east end, and in each there is a rivulet of good fresh water ". He mentions (it may be supposed on the authority of Spanish information) that this island was stocked with goats by Juan Fernandez, its discoverer, who, in a second voyage to it, landed three or four of these animals, and they quickly multiplied. Also, that Juan Fernandez had formed a plan of settling here, if he could have obtained a patent or royal grant of the island, which was refused him.*

The buccaneers found here a good supply of provisions in goats, wild vegetables, seals, sea-lions and fish. Dampier says: "The seals at Juan Fernandez are as big as calves, and have a fine thick short fur, the like I have not taken notice of anywhere but in these seas. The teeth of the sea-lion are the bigness

---

* The writer of *Commodore Anson's Voyage* informs us that Juan Fernandez resided some time on the island, and afterwards abandoned it.

of a man's thumb : in Captain Sharp's time some of
the buccaneers made dice of them.   Both the sea-lion
and the seal eat fish, which I believe is their common
food."

April the 8th, the "Batchelor's Delight" and
"Nicholas" sailed from Juan Fernandez for the
American coast, which they made in latitude 24° south,
and sailed northward, keeping sight of the land, but
at a good distance.   On the 3rd May, in latitude
9° 40' south, they took a Spanish ship laden with
timber.

Dampier remarks that "from the latitude of 24°
south, to 17°, and from 14° to 10° south, the land within
the coast is of a prodigious height.   It lies generally
in ridges parallel to the shore, one within another,
each surpassing the other in height, those inland being
the highest.   They always appear blue when seen
from sea, and are seldom obscured by clouds or fogs.
These mountains far surpass the Peak of Teneriffe,
or the land of Santa Martha."

On the 9th they anchored at the islands Lobos de
la Mar. "This Lobos consists of two little islands, each
about a mile round, of indifferent height, with a channel
between fit only for boats.   Several rocks lie on the
north side of the islands.   There is a small cove, or
sandy bay, sheltered from the winds, at the west end
of the easternmost island, where ships may careen.
There is good riding between the easternmost island
and the rocks, in ten, twelve or fourteen fathoms ; for
the wind is commonly at south, or south-south-east,
and the easternmost island lying east and west
shelters that road.   Both the islands are barren, with-

out fresh water, tree, shrub or herb ; but sea-fowls, seals and sea-lions were here in multitudes." *

On a review of their strength, they mustered in the two ships 108 men fit for service, besides their sick. They remained at the Lobos de la Mar Isles till the 17th, when, three vessels coming in sight, they took up their anchors and gave chase. They captured all the three, which were laden with provisions, principally flour, and bound for Panama. They learnt from the prisoners that the English ship "Cygnet" had been at Baldivia, and that the viceroy, on information of strange ships having entered the South Sea, had ordered treasure which had been shipped for Panama to be relanded. The buccaneers, finding they were expected on the coast, determined to go with their prizes first to the Galapagos Islands, and afterwards to the coast of New Spain.

They arrived in sight of the Galapagos on the 31st, but were not enough to the southward to fetch the southern islands, the wind being from south by east, which Dampier remarks is the common trade-wind in this part of the Pacific. Many instances occur in South Sea navigations which show the disadvantage of not keeping well to the south in going to the Galapagos.

The two ships anchored near the north-east part of one of the easternmost islands, in sixteen fathoms, the bottom white hard sand, a mile distant from the shore.

It was during this visit of the buccaneers to the Galapagos that the chart of these islands which was

* Dampier's *Voyages*, vol. i. chap. 5.

published with Cowley's voyage was made. Considering the small opportunity for surveying which
was afforded by their track, it may be reckoned a
good chart, and has the merit both of being the
earliest survey known of these islands, and of having
continued in use to this day, the latest charts we
have of the Galapagos being founded upon this
original, and (setting aside the additions) varying
little from it in the general outlines.

Where Cook and Eaton first anchored appears to
be the Duke of Norfolk's Island of Cowley's chart.
They found there sea turtle and land turtle, but could
stop only one night, on account of two of their prizes,
which, being deeply laden, had fallen too far to leeward
to fetch the same anchorage.

The day following they sailed on to the next
island westward (marked King James's Island in
the chart) and anchored at its north end, a quarter
of a mile distant from the shore, in fifteen fathoms.
Dampier observed the latitude of the north part of
this second island, 0° 28′ north, which is considerably
more north than it is placed in Cowley's chart. The
riding here was very uncertain, "the bottom being so
steep that if an anchor starts it never holds again".

An error has been committed in the printed narrative of Dampier, which it may be useful to notice. It
is there said : "The island at which we first anchored
hath water on the north end, falling down in a stream
from high steep rocks upon the sandy bay, where it
may be taken up". Concerning so essential an article
to mariners as fresh water, no information can be too
minute to deserve attention. In the manuscript journal,

Dampier says of the first island at which they anchored :
" We found there the largest land turtle I ever saw ;
but the island is rocky and barren, without wood or
water ". At the next island at which they anchored,
both Dampier and Cowley mention fresh water being
found. Cowley says: "This bay I called Albany Bay,
and another place York Road. Here is excellent
sweet water." Dampier also in the margin of his
written journal, where the second anchorage is mentioned, has inserted the note following : " At the north
end of the island we saw water running down from the
rocks ". The editor or corrector of the press has mistakenly applied this to the first anchorage.

Cowley, after assigning names to the different
islands, adds : " We could find no good water on any
of these places, save on the Duke of York's [i.e., King·
James's] Island. But at the north end of Albemarle
Island there were green leaves of a thick substance,
which we chewed to quench our thirst ; and there were
abundance of fowls on this island which could not live
without water, though we could not find it." *

* The latter part of the above extract is from Cowley's manuscript. Captain Colnet when at the Galapagos made a similar remark. He says: "I was perplexed to form a conjecture how the
small birds, which appeared to remain in one spot, supported themselves without water ; but some of our men informed me that as
they were reposing beneath a prickly pear-tree they observed an old
bird in the act of supplying three young ones with drink by squeezing
the berry of a tree into their mouths. It was about the size of a pea,
and contained a watery juice of an acid and not unpleasant taste.
The bark of the tree yields moisture, and, being eaten, allays the
thirst. The land tortoise gnaw and suck it. The leaf of this tree is
like that of the bay-tree ; the fruit grows like cherries ; the juice of
the bark dyes the flesh of a deep purple." Colnet's *Voyage to the
South Sea*, p. 53.

Animal food was furnished by the Galapagos Islands in profusion, and of the most delicate kind ; of vegetables nothing of use was found except the mammee, the leaves just noticed, and berries. The name "Galapagos" which has been assigned to these islands signifies "turtle" in the Spanish language, and was given to them on account of the great numbers of those animals, both of the sea and land kind, found there. Guanas, an amphibious animal well known in the West Indies, fish, flamingoes, and turtle-doves so tame that they would alight upon the men's heads, were all in great abundance ; and, convenient for preserving meat, salt was plentiful at the Galapagos. Some green snakes were the only other animals seen there.

The full-grown land turtle were from 150 to 200 lbs. in weight. Dampier says : " So sweet that no pullet can eat more pleasantly. They are very fat ; the oil saved from them was kept in jars and used instead of butter to eat with dough-boys or dumplings. . . . We lay here feeding sometimes on land turtle sometimes on sea turtle, there being plenty of either sort ; but the land turtle, as they exceed in sweetness, so do they in numbers : it is incredible to report how numerous they are."

The sea turtle at the Galapagos are of the larger kind of those called the green turtle. Dampier thought their flesh not so good as the green turtle of the West Indies.

Dampier describes the Galapagos Isles to be generally of good height : " Four or five of the easternmost islands are rocky, hilly and barren, producing neither

tree, herb, nor grass; but only a green prickly shrub
that grows ten or twelve feet high, as big as a man's
leg, and is full of sharp prickles in thick rows from top
to bottom, without leaf or fruit. In some places by
the sea-side grow bushes of Burton wood (a sort of
wood which grows in the West Indies), which is good
firing. Some of the westernmost of these islands are
nine or ten leagues long, have fertile land, with mould
deep and black; and these produce trees of various
kinds, some of great and tall bodies, especially the
mammee. The heat is not so violent here as in many
other places under the equator. The time of year for
the rains is in November, December and January."

At Albany Bay, and at other of the islands, the
buccaneers built storehouses, in which they lodged
five thousand packs of their prize flour, and a quantity
of sweetmeats, to remain as a reserved store to which
they might have recourse on any future occasion.
Part of this provision was landed at the islands northward of King James's Island, to which they went in
search of fresh water, but did not find any. They endeavoured to sail back to the Duke of York's Island,
Cowley says, "there to have watered," but a current,
setting northward, prevented them.

On the 12th June they sailed from the Galapagos
Islands for the island Cocos, where they proposed to
water. The wind at this time was south; but they
expected they should find, as they went northward,
the general trade-wind blowing from the east; and in
that persuasion they steered more easterly than the
line of direction in which Cocos lay from them, ima-
gining that when they came to the latitude of the

island, they would have to bear down upon it before the wind. Contrary, however, to this expectation, as they advanced northward they found the wind more westerly, till it settled at south-west by south, and they got so far eastward that they crossed the parallel of Cocos without being able to come in sight of it.

Missing Cocos, they sailed on northward for the coast of New Spain. In the beginning of July they made the west cape of the Gulf of Nicoya. " This cape is about the height of Beachy Head, and was named Blanco, on account of two white rocks lying about half-a-mile from it, which, to those who are far off at sea, appear as part of the mainland ; but on coming nearer, they appear like two ships under sail."*

The day on which they made this land the buc-caneer commander, John Cook, who had been some time ill, died. Edward Davis, the quarter-master, was unanimously elected by the company to succeed in the command.

* Dampier, vol. i. p. 112.

CHAPTER XIV.

Edward Davis commander. On the coast of New Spain and Peru. Algatrane, a bituminous earth. Davis is joined by other buccaneers. Eaton sails to the East Indies. Guayaquil attempted. Rivers of St. Jago and Tomaco. In the Bay of Panama. Arrivals of numerous parties of buccaneers across the isthmus from the West Indies.

DAMPIER describes the coast of New Spain immediately westward of the Cape Blanco last mentioned, as falling in to the north-east about four leagues, making a small bay, which is by the Spaniards called Caldera.* Within the entrance of this bay, a league from Cape Blanco, was a small brook of very good water running into the sea. The land here is low, making a saddle between two small hills. The ships anchored near the brook, in good depth, on a bottom of clean, hard sand; and at this place their deceased commander was taken on shore and buried.

The country appeared thin of inhabitants, and the few seen were shy of coming near strangers. Two Indians, however, were caught. Some cattle were seen grazing near the shore, at a beef *estançian* or farm,

---

* Dampier, vol. i. chap. 5. This description does not agree with the Spanish charts, but no complete regular survey appears yet to have been made of the coast of New Spain.

three miles distant from where the ships lay. Two
boats were sent thither to bring cattle, having with
them one of the Indians for a guide. They arrived at
the farm towards evening, and some of the buccaneers
proposed that they should remain quiet till daylight
next morning, when they might surround the cattle
and drive a number of them into a pen or inclosure;
others of the party disliked this plan, and one of the
boats returned to the ships. Twelve men, with the
other boat, remained, who hauled their boat dry up on
the beach, and went and took their lodgings for the
night by the farm. When the morning arrived, they
found the people of the country had collected, and saw
about forty armed men preparing to attack them.
The buccaneers hastened as speedily as they could
to the sea-side where they had left their boat, and
found her in flames. "The Spaniards now thought
they had them secure, and some called to them to ask
if they would be pleased to walk to their plantations;
to which never a word was answered." Fortunately
for the buccaneers, a rock appeared just above water
at some distance from the shore, and the way to it
being fordable, they waded thither. This served as a
place of protection against the enemy, "who only now
and then whistled a shot among them". It was at
about half ebb tide when they took to the rock for
refuge; on the return of the flood the rock became
gradually covered. They had been in this situation
seven hours when a boat arrived, sent from the ships
in search of them. The rise and fall of the tide here
was eight feet perpendicular, and the tide was still
rising at the time the boat came to their relief; so that

their peril from the sea when on the rock was not less than it had been from the Spaniards when they were on shore.

From Caldera Bay they sailed for Ria Lexa. The coast near Ria Lexa is rendered remarkable by a high peaked mountain, called Volcan Viejo (the Old Volcano). "When the mountain bears north-east, ships may steer directly in for it, which course will bring them to the harbour. Those that go thither must take the sea wind, which is from the south-south-west, for there is no going in with the land wind. The harbour is made by a low flat island, about a mile long and a quarter of a mile broad, which lies about a mile and a half from the mainland. There is a channel at each end of the island ; the west channel is the widest and safest, yet at the north-west point of the island there is a shoal of which ships must take heed, and when past the shoal must keep close to the island, on account of a sandy point which strikes over from the mainland. This harbour is capable of receiving 200 sail of ships. The best riding is near the mainland, where the depth is seven or eight fathoms, clean hard sand. Two creeks lead up to the town of Ria Lexa, which is two leagues distant from the harbour." *

The Spaniards had erected breastworks and made other preparation in expectation of such a visit as the present. The buccaneers, therefore, changed their intention, which had been to attack the town, and sailed on for the Gulf of Amapalla.

"The Bay or Gulf of Amapalla runs eight or ten

* Dampier, vol. i. chap. 5.

leagues into the country   On the south side of its
entrance is Point Casivina, in latitude 12° 40′ north ;
and on the north-west side is Mount San Miguel.
There are many islands in this gulf, all low except two,
named Amapalla and Mangera, which are both high
land.   These are two miles asunder, and between
them is the best channel into the gulf." *

The ships sailed into the gulf through the channel
between Point Casivina and the island Mangera.
Davis went with two canoes before the ships, and
landed at a village on the island Mangera.   The
inhabitants kept at a distance, but a Spanish friar
and some Indians were taken, from whom the buccaneers learnt that there were two Indian towns or
villages on the island Amapalla ; upon which information they hastened to their canoes, and made for that
island.   On coming near, some among the inhabitants
called out to demand who they were and what they
came for.   Davis answered by an interpreter that he
and his men were Biscayners sent by the king of
Spain to clear the sea of pirates, and that their
business in Amapalla Bay was to careen.   No other
Spaniard than the *padre* dwelt among these Indians,
and only one among the Indians could speak the
Spanish language, who served as a kind of secretary
to the *padre*.   The account the buccaneers gave of
themselves satisfied the natives, and the secretary
said they were welcome.   The principal town or
village of the island Amapalla stood on the top of
a hill, and Davis and his men, with the friar at their
head, marched thither.

* Dampier, vol. i. chap. 5.

At each of the towns on Amapalla, and also on Mangera, was a handsomely built church. The Spanish *padre* officiated at all three, and gave religious instruction to the natives in their own language. The islands were within the jurisdiction of the governor of the town of San Miguel, which was at the foot of the mount. "I observed," says Dampier, "in all the Indian towns under the Spanish Government that the images of the Virgin Mary, and of other saints, with which all their churches are filled, are painted of an Indian complexion, and partly in an Indian dress; but in the towns which arc inhabited chiefly by Spaniards the saints conform to the Spanish garb and complexion."

The ships anchored near the east side of the island Amapalla, which is the largest of the islands, in ten fathoms' depth, clean hard sand. On other islands in the bay were plantations of maize, with cattle, fowls, plantains, and abundance of a plum-tree common in Jamaica, the fruit of which Dampier calls the large hog plum. This fruit is oval, with a large stone and little substance about it, pleasant enough in taste; but he says he never saw one of these plums ripe that had not a maggot or two in it.

The buccaneers helped themselves to cattle from an island in the bay which was largely stocked, and which, they were informed, belonged to a nunnery. The natives willingly assisted them to take the cattle, and were content on receiving small presents for their labour. The buccaneers had no other service to desire of these natives, and, therefore, it must have been from levity and an ambition to give a specimen of their vocation, more than for any advantage expected, that they planned to take the opportunity, when the inhabitants should be assembled in their church, to shut the church doors upon them—the buccaneers themselves say, "to let the Indians know who we were, and to make a bargain with them". In executing this project, one of the buccaneers, being impatient at the leisurely movements of the inhabitants, pushed one of them rather rudely to hasten him into the church; but the contrary effect was produced, for the native, being frightened, ran away, and all the rest taking alarm "sprang out of the church like deer". As they fled, some of Davis's men fired at them as at an enemy, and, among other injury committed, the Indian secretary was killed.

Cowley relates their exploits here very briefly, but in the style of an accomplished gazette writer. He says: "We set sail from Realejo to the Gulf of St. Miguel, where we took two islands: one was inhabited by Indians, and the other was well stored with cattle".

Davis and Eaton here broke off consortship. The cause of their separating was an unreasonable claim of Davis's crew, who, having the stouter and better ship, would not agree that Eaton's men should share equally with themselves in the prizes taken. Cowley at this time quitted Davis's ship and entered with Eaton, who sailed from the Bay of Amapalla for the Peruvian coast. Davis also sailed the same way on the day following (September the 3rd), first releasing the priest of Amapalla; and, with a feeling of remorse something foreign to his profession, by way of atonement to the inhabitants for the annoyance and mischief they had sustained from the buccaneers, he left them one of the prize vessels with half a cargo of flour.

Davis sailed out of the gulf by the passage between the islands Amapalla and Mangera. In the navigation towards the coast of Peru they had the wind from the north-north-west and west, except during tornadoes, of which they had one or more every day, and whilst they lasted the wind generally blew from the south-east; but as soon as they were over the wind settled again in the north-west. Tornadoes are common near the Bay of Panama from June to November, and at this time were accompanied with much thunder, lightning and rain.

When they came to Cape San Francisco they found settled, fair weather, and the wind at south. On the 20th they anchored at the east side of the island Plata. The 21st, Eaton's ship anchored near them. Eaton had been at the island Cocos, and had lodged on shore there 200 packages of flour.

According to Eaton's description, Cocos Island is encompassed with rocks, "which make it almost inaccessible except at the north-east end, where there is a small but secure harbour, and a fine brook of fresh water runs there into the sea. The middle of the island is pretty high and destitute of trees, but looks green and pleasant with a herb by the Spaniards called *gramadiel*. All round the island by the sea the land is low, and there cocoa-nut trees grow in great groves."

At La Plata they found only one small run of fresh water, which was on the east side of the island, and trickled slowly down from the rocks. The Spaniards

had recently destroyed the goats here that they might
not serve as provision for the pirates.   Small sea turtle,
however, were plentiful, as were men-of-war birds and
boobies.   The tide was remarked to run strong at this
part of the coast, the flood to the south.

Eaton and his crew would willingly have joined
company again with Davis, but Davis's men persisted
in their unsociable claim to larger shares ; the two
ships, therefore, though designing alike to cruise on
the coast of Peru, sailed singly and separately,
Eaton on the 22nd, and Davis on the day
following.

Davis went to Point Santa Elena.   On its west
side is deep water and no anchorage.   In the bay on
the north side of the point is good anchorage, and
about a mile within the point was a small Indian
village, the inhabitants of which carried on a trade
with pitch and salt made there.   The point Santa
Elena is tolerably high, and overgrown with thistles,
but the land near it is sandy, low, and in parts over-
flowed, without tree or grass, and without fresh water,
but water-melons grew there large and very sweet.
When the inhabitants of the village wanted fresh water
they were obliged to fetch it from a river called the
Colanche, which is at the innermost part of the bay,
four leagues distant from their habitations.   The
buccaneers landed and took some natives prisoners.   A
small barque was lying in the bay at anchor, the crew of
which set fire to and abandoned her, but the buccaneers
boarded her in time to extinguish the fire.   A general
order had been given by the viceroy of Peru to all
ship-masters, that if they should be in danger of being

taken by pirates, they should set fire to their vessels and betake themselves to their boats.

The pitch, which was the principal commodity produced at Santa Elena, was supplied from a hot spring, of which Dampier gives the following account. " Not far from the Indian village, and about five paces within high-water mark, a bituminous matter boils out of a little hole in the earth. It is like thin tar ; the Spaniards call it *algatrane.* By much boiling it becomes hard like pitch, and is used by the Spaniards instead of pitch. It boils up most at high water, and the inhabitants save it in jars."*

A report was current here among the Spaniards "that many years before a rich Spanish ship was driven ashore at Point Santa Elena for want of wind to work her, that immediately after she struck she heeled off to seaward and sank in seven or eight fathoms of water, and that no one ever attempted to fish for her because there falls in here a great high sea ". †

Davis landed at a village named Manta, on the mainland about three leagues eastward of Cape San Lorenzo, and due north of a high conical mountain, called Monte Christo. The village was on a small ascent, and between it and the sea was a spring of good water. "About a mile and a half from the shore, right opposite the village, is a rock which is

---

* Dampier, vol. i. chap. 6.

† Dampier, vol. i. chap. 6. To search for this wreck with a view to recover the treasure in her was one of the objects of an ex pedition from England to the South Sea which was made a few years subsequent to this buccaneer expedition.

very dangerous, because it never appears above water, neither does the sea break upon it.   A mile within the rock is good anchorage in six, eight, or ten fathoms, hard sand and clear ground.   A mile from the road on the west side is a shoal which runs out a mile into the sea."*

The only booty made by landing at Manta was the taking two old women prisoners.   From them, however, the buccaneers obtained intelligence that many of their fraternity had lately crossed the isthmus from the West Indies, and were at this time on the South Sea, without ships, cruising about in canoes ; and that it was on this account the viceroy had given orders for the destruction of the goats at the island Plata.

Whilst Davis and his men, in the " Batchelor's Delight," were lying at the island Plata, unsettled in their plans by the news they had received, they were on the 2nd October joined by the "Cygnet," Captain Swan, and by a small barque manned with a crew of buccaneers, both of which anchored in the road.

The "Cygnet," as before noticed, was fitted out from London for the purpose of trade.   She had put in at Baldivia, where Swan, seeing the Spaniards suspicious of the visits of strangers, gave out that he was bound to the East Indies, and that he had endeavoured to go by the Cape of Good Hope, but that, meeting there with storms and unfavourable winds, and not being able to beat round that cape, he had changed his course and run for the Strait of Ma-

* Dampier, vol. i. chap. 6.

galhanes, to sail by the Pacific Ocean to India. This story was too improbable to gain credit. Instead of finding a market at Baldivia, the Spaniards there treated him and his people as enemies, by which he lost two men and had several wounded. He afterwards tried the disposition of the Spaniards to trade with him at other places, both in Chili and Peru, but nowhere met encouragement. He proceeded northward for New Spain still with the same view, but near the Gulf of Nicoya he fell in with some buccaneers who had come over the isthmus and were in canoes, and his men, Dampier says, forced him to receive them into his ship, and he was afterwards prevailed on to join in their pursuits. Swan had to plead as his excuse the hostility of the Spaniards towards him at Baldivia. These buccaneers with whom Swan associated had for their commander Peter Harris, a nephew of the Peter Harris who was killed in a battle with the Spaniards in the Bay of Panama, in 1680, when the buccaneers were commanded by Sawkins and Coxon. Swan stipulated with them that ten shares of every prize should be set apart for the benefit of his owners, and articles to that purport were drawn up and signed. Swan retained the command of the " Cygnet," with a crew increased by a number of the newcomers, for whose accommodation a large quantity of bulky goods belonging to the merchants was thrown into the sea. Harris with others of the buccaneers established themselves in a small barque they had taken.

On their meeting with Davis there was much joy and congratulation on all sides. They immediately agreed to keep together, and the separation of Eaton's

ship was now much regretted. They were still incommoded in Swan's ship for want of room; therefore,
the supercargoes giving consent, whatever part of the
cargo any of the crews desired to purchase, it was sold
to them upon trust, and more bulky goods were thrown
overboard. Iron, of which there was a large quantity,
was kept for ballast, and the finer goods, as silks,
muslins, stockings, &c., were saved. Whilst they continued at La Plata, Davis kept a small barque out
cruising, which brought in a ship from Guayaquil,
laden with timber, the master of which reported that
great preparations were making at Callao to attack the
pirates. This information made a reunion with Eaton
more earnestly desired, and a small barque manned
with twenty men was despatched to search along the
coast southward as far as to the Lobos Isles, with an
invitation to him to join them again. The ships in
the meantime followed leisurely in the same direction.

On the 30th they were off Cape Blanco, which
is between Payta and the Bay of Guayaquil. Southerly
winds prevail along the coast of Peru and Chili much
the greater part of the year, and Dampier remarks of
this Cape Blanco, that it was reckoned the most difficult to weather of any headland along the coast, the
wind generally blowing strong from south-south-west
or south by west, without being altered, as at other
parts of the coast, by the land winds. Yet it was held
necessary here to beat up close in with the shore, because (according to the accounts of Spanish seamen)
" on standing out to sea, a current is found setting
north-west, which will carry a ship farther off shore
in two hours than she can run in again in five ".

November the 3rd the buccaneers landed at Payta without opposition, the town being abandoned to them. They found nothing of value, " not so much as a meal of victuals being left them ".   The governor would not pay ransom for the town, though he fed the buccaneers with hopes till the sixth day, when they set it on fire.

At most of the towns on the coast of Peru the houses are built with bricks made of earth and straw kneaded together and dried in the sun ; many houses have no roof other than mats laid upon rafters, for it never rains, and they endeavour to fence only from the sun.   From the want of moisture, great part of the country near the coast will not produce timber, and most of the stone they have " is so brittle that anyone may rub it into sand with their finger ".

Payta had neither wood nor water, except what was carried thither.   The water was procured from a river about two leagues north-north-east of the town, where was a small Indian village called Colan. Dampier says : " This dry country commences northward about Cape Blanco, in about 4° south latitude, whence it reaches to latitude 30° south, in which extent they have no rain that I could ever observe or hear of ".   In the southern part of this tract, however (according to Wafer), they have great dews in the night, by which the valleys are rendered fertile, and are well furnished with vegetables.

Eaton had been at Payta, where he burnt a large ship in the road, but did not land.   He put on shore there all his prisoners, from which circumstance it was conjectured that he purposed to sail immediately for the East Indies; and such proved to be the fact.

The vessel commanded by Harris sailed badly, and was therefore quitted and burnt. On the 14th the other buccaneer vessels under Davis anchored near the north-east end of Lobos de Tierra, in four fathoms' depth. They took here penguins, boobies and seals. On the 19th they were at Lobos de la Mar, where they found a letter left by the barque sent in search of Eaton, which gave information that he had entirely departed from the American coast. The barque had sailed for the island Plata, expecting to re-join the ships there.

Eaton in his route to the East Indies stopped at Guahan, one of the Ladrone Islands, where himself and his crew acted towards the native islanders with the utmost barbarity, which Cowley relates as a subject of merriment.

On their first arrival at Guahan, Eaton sent a boat on shore to procure refreshments; but the natives kept at a distance, believing his ship to be one of the Manilla galleons, and his people Spaniards. Eaton's men served themselves with cocoa-nuts, but, finding difficulty in climbing, they cut the trees down to get at the fruit. The next time their boat went to the shore, the islanders attacked her, but were easily repulsed, and a number of them killed. By this time the Spanish governor was arrived at the part of the island near which the ship had anchored, and sent a letter addressed to her commander, written in four different languages—to wit, in Spanish, French, Dutch, and Latin—to demand of what country she was, and whence she came. Cowley says: "Our captain, thinking the French would be welcomer than the English, returned answer we were French, fitted out by private merchants to make fuller discovery of the world. The governor on this invited the captain to the shore, and at their first conference the captain told him that the Indians had fallen upon his men, and that we had killed some of them. He wished we had killed them all, and told us of their rebellion, that they had killed eight fathers of sixteen which were in a convent. He gave us leave to kill and take whatever we could find on one-half of the island where the rebels lived. We then made wars with these infidels, and went on shore every day, fetching provisions, and firing upon them wherever we saw them, so that the greatest part of them left the island. The Indians sent two of their captains to us to treat of peace, but we would not treat with them. The whole land is a garden. The governor was the same man who detained Sir John Narbrough's lieutenant at Baldivia. Our captain supplied him with four barrels of gunpowder and arms." *

Josef de Quiroga was at this time governor at Guahan, who afterwards conquered and unpeopled all the northern islands of the Ladrones. Eaton's crew took some of the islanders prisoners, three of whom jumped overboard to endeavour to escape. It was easy to retake them, as they had been bound with their hands behind them, but Eaton's men pursued them with the determined purpose to kill them, which

---

* Manuscript journal in the Sloane Collection.

they did in mere wantonness of sport.* At another
time, when they had so far come to an accommodation
with the islanders as to admit of their approach, the
ship's boat being on shore fishing with the seine, some
natives in canoes near her were suspected of intending
mischief. Cowley relates : " Our people that were in
the boat let go, in amongst the thickest of them, and
killed a great many of their number ". It is possible
that thus much might have been necessary for safety ;
but Cowley proceeds : " The others, seeing their mates
fall, ran away. Our other men which were on shore,
meeting them, saluted them also by making holes in
their hides."

From the Ladrones Eaton sailed to the north of
Luconia, and passed through among the islands
which were afterwards named by Dampier the Bashee
Islands. The account given by Cowley is as follows:
" There being half-a-point east variation, till we came
to latitude 20° 30′ north, where we fell in with a parcel
of islands lying to the northward of Luconia. On
the 23rd day of April we sailed through between the
second and third of the northernmost of them. We
met with a very strong current, like the race of Portland. At the third of the northernmost islands we
sent our boat on shore, where they found abundance
of nutmegs growing, but no people. They observed
abundance of rocks and foul ground near the shore,
and saw many goats upon the island."

Cowley concludes the narrative of his voyage with

* See Cowley's *Voyages*, p. 34.   Also, vol. iii. of *South Sea
Discoveries*, p. 305.

saying that he arrived home safe in England through
the infinite mercy of God.

To return to Edward Davis: at Lobos de la Mar
the Mosquito Indians struck as much turtle as served
all the crews. Shortly after, Davis made an attempt
to surprise Guayaquil, which miscarried through the
cowardice of one of his men and the coldness of Swan
to the enterprise. In the Bay of Guayaquil they
captured four vessels, one of them laden with woollen
cloth of Quito manufacture; the other three were ships
coming out of the river of Guayaquil with cargoes of
negroes.

The number of negroes in these vessels was a
thousand, from among which Davis and Swan chose
each about fifteen, and let the vessels go. Dampier
entertained on this occasion different views from his
companions. "Never," says he, "was put into the
hands of men a greater opportunity to enrich themselves. We had 1000 negroes, all lusty young men
and women, and we had 200 tons of flour stored up at
the Galapagos Islands. With these negroes we
might have gone and settled at Santa Maria on the
Isthmus of Darien, and have employed them in getting
gold out of the mines there. All the Indians living
in that neighbourhood were mortal enemies to the
Spaniards, were flushed by successes against them,
and for several years had been the fast friends of the
privateers. Add to which, we should have had the
North Sea open to us, and in a short time should have
received assistance from all parts of the West Indies.
Many thousands of buccaneers from Jamaica and the
French islands would have flocked to us; and we

should have been an overmatch for all the force the Spaniards could have brought out of Peru against us."

The proposal to employ slaves in the mines leaves no cause to regret that Dampier's plan was not adopted ; but that was probably not an objection with his companions. They naturally shrank from an attempt which in the execution would have required a regularity and order to which they were unaccustomed, and not at all affected.

The harbour of Guayaquil is the best formed port in Peru. In the river, three or four miles short of the town, stands a low island about a mile long, on either side of which is a fair channel to pass up or down. The western channel is the widest : the other is as deep. " From the upper part of the island to the town is about a league, and it is near as much from one side of the river to the other. In that spacious place ships of the greatest burthen may ride afloat ; but the best place for ships is near that part of the land on which the town stands. The country here is subject to great rains and thick fogs, which render it very unwholesome and sickly, in the valleys especially. Guayaquil, however, is not so unhealthy as Quito and other towns inland, but the northern part of Peru pays for the dry weather which they have about Lima and to the southward.

" Ships bound into the river of Guayaquil pass on the south side of the island Santa Clara to avoid shoals which are on the north side, whereon formerly ships have been wrecked. A rich wreck lay on the north side of Santa Clara not far from the island, and some plate which was in her was taken up : more might have been saved but for the cat-fish which swarm hereabouts.

"The cat-fish is much like a whiting ; but the head is flatter and bigger. It has a wide mouth, and certain small strings pointing out on each side of it like cats' whiskers. It hath three fins : one on the back, and one on either side. Each of these fins hath a sharp bone, which is very venomous if it strikes into a man's flesh. Some of the Indians that adventured to search this wreck lost their lives, and others the use of their limbs, by these fins. Some of the cat-fish weigh seven or eight pounds, and in some places there are cat-fish which are none of them bigger than a man's thumb ; but their fins are all alike venomous. They are most generally at the mouths of rivers (in the hot latitudes), or where there is much mud and ooze. The bones in their bodies are not venomous, and we never perceived any bad effect in eating the fish, which is very sweet and wholesome meat." *

The 13th, Davis and Swan, with their prizes, sailed from the Bay of Guayaquil to the island Plata, and found there the barque which had been in quest of Eaton's ship.

From Plata they sailed northward towards the Bay of Panama, landing at the villages along the coast to seek provisions. They were ill provided with boats, which exposed them to danger in making descents, by their not being able to land or bring off many men at one time ; and they judged that the best places for getting their wants in this respect sup-

* Dampier, vol. i. chap. 6.

plied would be in rivers of the continent, in which the Spaniards had no settlement, where, from the native inhabitants, they might obtain canoes by traffic or purchase, if not otherwise. Dampier remarks that there were many such unfrequented rivers in the continent to the northward of the Isle de la Plata, and that from the Equinoctial to the Gulf de San Miguel, in the Bay of Panama, which is above eight degrees of latitude, the coast was not inhabited by the Spaniards, nor were the Indians who lived there in any manner under their subjection, except at one part near the island Gallo, "where, on the banks of a gold river or two, some Spaniards had settled to find gold".

The land by the sea-coast to the north of Cape San Francisco is low and extremely woody, the trees are of extraordinary height and bigness, and in this part of the coast are large and navigable rivers. The white cotton-tree, which bears a very fine sort of cotton, called silk cotton, is the largest tree in these woods, and the cabbage-tree is the tallest. Dampier has given full descriptions of both. He measured a cabbage-tree 120 feet in length, and some were longer. "It has no limbs nor boughs except at the head, where there are branches something bigger than a man's arm. The cabbage-fruit shoots out in the midst of these branches, invested or folded in leaves, and is as big as the small of a man's leg, and a foot long. It is white as milk, and sweet as a nut if eaten raw, and is very sweet and wholesome if boiled."

The buccaneers entered a river with their boats, in or near latitude 2° north, which Dampier, from some Spanish pilot-book, calls the river of St. Jago. It was navigable some leagues within the entrance, and seems to be the river marked with the name "Patia" in the late Spanish charts, a name which has allusion to spreading branches.

Davis's men went six leagues up the river without seeing habitation or people. They then came in sight of two small huts, the inhabitants of which hurried into canoes with their household stuff, and paddled upwards against the stream faster than they could be pursued. More houses were seen higher up ; but the stream ran here so swift that the buccaneers would not be at the labour of proceeding. They found in the two deserted huts a hog, some fowls and plantains, which they dressed on the spot, and, after their meal, returned to the ships, which were at the island Gallo.

" The island Gallo is clothed with timber, and here was a spring of good water at the north-east end, with good landing in a small sandy bay, and secure riding in six or seven fathoms' depth." *

They entered with their boats another large river, called the Tomaco, the entrance of which is but three leagues from the island Gallo. This river was shoal at the mouth, and navigable for small vessels only. A little within was a village called Tomaco, some of the inhabitants of which they took prisoners, and carried off a dozen jars of good wine.

On the 1st of January they took a packet-boat bound for Lima, which the president of Panama had

* Dampier.

despatched to hasten the sailing of the Plate fleet
from Callao ; the treasure sent from Peru and Chili
to Old Spain being usually first collected at Panama,
and thence transported on mules to Porto Bello.   The
buccaneers judged that the Pearl Islands, in the Bay
of Panama, would be the best station they could
occupy for intercepting ships from Lima.

On the 7th they left Gallo, and pursued their
course northward.   An example occurs here of buccaneer order and discipline.   " We weighed," says
Dampier, " before day, and all got out of the road
except Captain Swan's tender, which never budged ;
for the men were all asleep when we went out, and,
the tide of flood coming on before they awoke, we
were forced to stay for them till the following tide."

On the 8th they took a vessel laden with flour.
The next day they anchored on the west side of the
island Gorgona, in thirty-eight fathoms' depth clear
ground, a quarter of a mile from the shore.   Gorgona
was uninhabited, and, like Gallo, covered with trees.
It is pretty high, and made remarkable by two saddles,
or risings and fallings on the top.   It is about two
leagues long, one broad, and is four leagues distant
from the mainland.   It was well watered at this time
with small brooks issuing from the high land.   At its
west end is another small island.   The tide rises and
falls seven or eight feet, and at low water shell-fish,
as periwinkles, mussels and oysters, may be taken.
At Gorgona were small black monkeys.   " When the
tide was out, the monkeys would come down to the
sea-shore for shell-fish.   Their way was to take up an
oyster and lay it upon a stone, and with another stone

to keep beating of it till they broke the shell." * The
pearl oyster was here in great plenty : they are flatter
than other oysters, are slimy, and taste copperish if
eaten raw, but were thought good when boiled. The
Indians and Spaniards hang the meat of them on strings
to dry. " The pearl is found at the head of the oyster,
between the meat and the shell. Some have twenty
or thirty small seed-pearl, some none at all, and some
one or two pretty large pearls. The inside of the
shell is more glorious than the pearl itself." †

They put some of their prisoners on shore at
Gorgona, and sailed thence on the 13th, being six
sail in company—that is to say, Davis's ship, Swan's
ship, three tenders, and their last prize. The 21st,
they arrived in the Bay of Panama, and anchored at
a small, low, and barren island named Galera.

On the 25th they went from Galera to one of the
southern Pearl Islands, where they lay the ships
aground to clean, the rise and fall of the sea at the
spring tides being ten feet perpendicular. The small
barques were kept out cruising, and on the 31st they
brought in a vessel bound for Panama from Lavelia, a
town on the west side of the bay, laden with Indian
corn, salt beef and fowls.

Notwithstanding it had been long reported that a
fleet was fitting out in Peru to clear the South Sea of
pirates, the small force under Davis, Swan and Harris,
amounting to little more than 250 men, remained
several weeks in uninterrupted possession of the Bay
of Panama, blocking up access to the city by sea,

* Wafer's *Voyages*, p. 196.
† Dampier, vol. i. chap. 7.

supplying themselves with provisions from the islands, and plundering whatsoever came in their way.

The Pearl Islands are woody, and the soil rich. They are cultivated with plantations of rice, plantains, and bananas, for the support of the city of Panama. Dampier says : " Why they are called the Pearl Islands I cannot imagine, for I did never see one pearl oyster about them, but of other oysters many. It is very pleasant sailing here, having the mainland on one side, which appears in divers forms, beautified with small hills, clothed with woods always green and flourishing ; and on the other side, the Pearl Islands, which also make a lovely prospect as you sail by them."

The buccaneers went daily in their canoes among the different islands, to fish, fowl, or hunt for guanas. One man so employed, and straggling from his party, was surprised by the Spaniards, and carried to Panama.

In the middle of February, Davis, who appears to have always directed their movements as the chief in command, went with his ships and anchored near the city of Panama. He negotiated with the governor an exchange of prisoners, and was glad by the release of forty Spaniards to obtain the deliverance of two buccaneers, one of them the straggler just mentioned, the other, one of Harris's men.

A short time after this exchange, as the buccaneer ships were at anchor near the island Taboga, which is about four leagues to the south of Panama, they were visited by a Spaniard in a canoe, who pretended he was a merchant and wanted to traffic with them privately. He proposed to come off to the ships in the night with a small vessel laden with such goods as the buccaneers desired to purchase. This was agreed to, and he came with his vessel when it was dark; but instead of a cargo of goods, she was fitted up as a fire-ship with combustibles. The buccaneers had suspected his intention and were on their guard; but, to ward off the mischief, were obliged to cut from their anchors and set sail.

In the morning they returned to their anchorage, which they had scarcely regained when a fresh cause of alarm occurred. Dampier relates : " We were striving to recover the anchors we had parted from, but the buoy-ropes being rotten broke, and, whilst we were puzzling about our anchors, we saw a great many canoes full of men pass between the island Taboga and another island, which at first put us into a new consternation. We lay still some time, till we saw they made directly towards us ; upon which we weighed and stood towards them. When we came within hail, we found that they were English and French privateers just come from the North Sea over the Isthmus of Darien. We presently came to an anchor again, and all the canoes came on board."

This new arrival of buccaneers to the South Sea consisted of 200 Frenchmen and 80 Englishmen, commanded by two Frenchmen named Grogniet and L'Escuyer. Grogniet had a commission to war on the Spaniards from a French West India governor. The Englishmen of this party upon joining Davis were received into the ships of their countrymen, and the largest of the prize vessels, which was a ship named the " San Rosario," was given to the Frenchmen.

From these new confederates it was learnt that another party consisting of 180 buccaneers, commanded by an Englishman named Townley, had crossed the isthmus, and were building canoes in the Gulf de San Miguel ; on which intelligence it was determined to sail to that gulf, that the whole buccaneer force in this sea might be joined. Grogniet, in return for the ship given to the French buccaneers, offered to Davis and Swan new commissions from the governor of Petit Goave, by whom he had been furnished with spare commissions with blanks, to be filled up and disposed of at his own discretion. Davis accepted Grogniet's present, "having before only an old commission which had belonged to Captain Tristian, and which, being found in Tristian's ship when she was carried off by Cook, had devolved as an inheritance to Davis". The commissions which, by whatever means, the buccaneers procured, were not much protection in the event of their falling into the hands of the Spaniards, unless the nation of which the buccaneer was a native happened to be then at war with Spain. Instances were not uncommon in the West Indies of the Spaniards hanging up their buccaneer prisoners with their commissions about their necks. But the commissions were allowed to be valid in the ports of other powers. Swan, however, refused the one offered him, and rested his justification on the orders he had received from the Duke of York ; in which he was directed neither to give offence to the Spaniards, nor to submit to receive affront from them ; they had done him injury in killing his men at Baldivia, and he held his orders to be a lawful commission to do himself right.

On the 3rd of March, as they approached the Gulf de San Miguel to meet the buccaneers under Townley, they were again surprised by seeing two ships standing towards them. These proved to be Townley and his men in two prizes they had already taken, one laden with flour, the other with wine, brandy and sugar; both designed for Panama. The wine came from Pisco, "which place is famous for wine, and was contained in jars of seven or eight gallons each. Ships which lade at Pisco stow the jars one tier on the top of another, so artificially that we could hardly do the like without breaking them; yet they often carry in this manner 1500 or 2000 or more in a ship, and seldom break one."

On this junction of the buccaneers, they went altogether to the Pearl Islands to make arrangements and to fit their prize vessels, as well as circumstances would admit, for their new occupation. Among the preparations necessary to their equipment it was not the last which occurred, that the jars from Pisco were wanted to contain their sea stock of fresh water; for which service they were in a short time rendered competent.

The 10th, they took a small barque in ballast from Guayaquil. On the 12th some Indians in a canoe came out of the river Santa Maria, purposely to inform them that a large body of English and French buccaneers were then on their march over the isthmus from the North Sea. This was not all; for on the 15th one of the small barques which were kept out

cruising fell in with a vessel in which were six Englishmen, who were part of a crew of buccaneers that had
been six months in the South Sea under the command
of a William Knight.   These six men had been sent
in a canoe in chase of a vessel, which they came up
with and took ; but they had chased out of sight of
their own ship, and could not afterwards find her.
Davis gave the command of this vessel to Harris, who
took possession of her with a crew of his own followers,
and he was sent to the river Santa Maria to look for
the buccaneers, of whose coming the Indians had
given information.

This was the latter part of the dry season in the
Bay of Panama.   Hitherto fresh water had been found
in plenty at the Pearl Islands, but the springs and
rivulets were now dried up.   The buccaneers examined within Point Garachina, but found no fresh
water.   They searched along the coast southward,
and on the 25th, at a narrow opening in the mainland
with two small rocky islands before it, about seven
leagues distant from Point Garachina, which Dampier
supposed to be Port de Pinas, they found a stream of
good water which ran into the sea ; but the harbour
was open to the south-west, and a swell set in, which
rendered watering there difficult and hazardous : the
fleet (for they were nine sail in company) therefore
stood for the island Taboga, " where," says Dampier,
" we were sure to find a supply ".

Their boats, being sent before the ships, came unexpectedly upon some of the inhabitants of Panama
who were loading a canoe with plantains, and took
them prisoners.   One among these, a mulatto, had the

imprudence to say he was in the fire-ship which had been sent in the night to burn the buccaneer ships ; upon which the buccaneers immediately hanged him.

They had chocolate, but no sugar ; and all the kettles they possessed, constantly kept boiling, were not sufficient to dress victuals for so many men. Whilst the ships lay at Taboga a detachment was sent to a sugar-work on the mainland, from which they returned with sugar and three coppers.

On the 11th of April they went from Taboga to the Pearl Islands, and were there joined by the flibustiers and buccaneers of whose coming they had been last apprised, consisting of 264 men, commanded by Frenchmen named Rose, Le Picard, and Des-marais. Le Picard was a veteran who had served under L'Olonois and Morgan. In this party came Raveneau de Lussan, whose journal is said to be the only one kept by any of the French who were in this expedition.

Lussan's narrative is written with much misplaced gaiety, which comes early into notice, and shows him to have been, even whilst young and unpractised in the occupation of a buccaneer, of a disposition delighting in cruelty. In the account of his journey overland from the West Indies, he relates instances which he witnessed of the great dexterity of the monkeys which inhabited the forests, and among others the following : " Je ne puis me souvenir sans rire de l'action que je vis faire a un de ces animaux, auquel apres avoir tiré plusieurs coups de fusil qui lui emportoient une partie du ventre, en sorte que toutes ses tripes sortoient, je le vis se tenir d'une de ses pates, ou mains si l'on veut, a une branche d'arbre, tandis que de l'autre il ramassoit ses intestins, qu'il se refouroit dans ce qui lui restoit de ventre ".*

Ambrose Cowley and Raveneau de Lussan are well matched for comparison, alike not only in their dis-positions, but in their conceptions, which made them imagine the recital of such actions would be read witb delight.

The buccaneers in the Bay of Panama were now nearly a thousand strong, and they held a consultation whether or not they should attack the city. They had just before learnt from an intercepted packet that the Lima fleet was at sea, richly charged with treasure; and that it was composed of all the naval force the Spaniards in Peru had been able to collect: it was, therefore, agreed not to attempt the city at the present, but to wait patiently the arrival of the Spanish fleet, and give it battle. The only enterprise they under-took on the mainland in the meantime was against the town of Chepo, where they found neither opposi-tion nor plunder.

The small island Chepillo, near the mouth of the river which leads to Chepo, Dampier reckoned the most pleasant of all the islands in the Bay of Panama. "It is low on the north side, and rises by a small ascent towards the south side. The soil is yellow, a kind of clay. The low land is planted with all sorts of delicate fruits." The islands in the bay being occupied by the buccaneers caused great scarcity of provision and distress at Panama, much of the con-sumption in that city having usually been supplied from

* *Journal du Voyage au Mer du Sud*, par Rav. de Lussan, p. 25.

the islands, which on that account and for their pleasantness were called the Gardens of Panama.

In this situation things remained till near the end of May, the buccaneers in daily expectation of seeing the fleet from Lima, of which it is now time to speak.

CHAPTER XV.

Edward Davis commander. Meeting of the Spanish and buccaneer fleets in the Bay of Panama. They separate without fighting. The buccaneers sail to the island Quibo. The English and French separate. Expedition against the city of Leon. That city and Ria Lexa burnt. Farther dispersion of the buccaneers.

THE Viceroy of Peru judged the fleet he had collected to be strong enough to encounter the buccaneers, and did not fear to trust the treasure to its protection; but he gave directions to the commander of the fleet to endeavour to avoid a meeting with them until after the treasure should be safely landed. In pursuance of this plan the Spanish admiral, as he drew near the Bay of Panama, kept more westward than the usual course, and fell in with the coast of Veragua to the west of the Punta Mala. Afterwards he entered the bay with his fleet, keeping close to the west shore; and, to place the treasure out of danger as soon as possible, he landed it at Lavelia, thinking it most probable his fleet would be descried by the enemy before he could reach Panama, which must have happened if the weather had not been thick, or if the buccaneers had kept a sharper look-out, by stationing tenders across the entrance of the bay. In consequence of this being neglected, the Spanish fleet arrived and anchored before the city of Panama without having been perceived by them, and immediately on their arrival the crews of the ships were reinforced with a number of European seamen who had purposely been sent overland from Porto Bello. Thus strengthened, and the treasure being placed out of danger, the Spanish admiral took up his anchors and stood from the road before Panama towards the middle of the bay, in quest of the buccaneers.

May the 28th, the morning was rainy ; the buccaneer fleet was lying at anchor near the island Pacheca, the northernmost of the Pearl Islands. At eleven o'clock in the forenoon the weather cleared up, when the Spanish fleet appeared in sight about three leagues distant from them to the west-north-west. The wind was light from the southward, and they were standing sharp trimmed towards the buccaneers.

Lussan dates this their meeting with the Spanish fleet to be on the 7th June. Ten days' alteration of the style had taken place in France three years before, and no alteration of style had yet been adopted in England.

The buccaneer fleet was composed of ten sail of vessels of different sizes, manned with 960 men, almost all Europeans; but, excepting the "Batchelor's Delight" and the "Cygnet," none of their vessels had cannon. Edward Davis was regarded as the admiral. His ship mounted thirty-six guns, and had a crew of 156 men, most of them English ; but, as he was furnished with a French commission, and France was still at war with Spain, he carried aloft a white flag, on which was painted a hand and sword. Swan's ship had sixteen guns, with a crew of 140 men, all English, and carried a St. George's flag at her main-topmast head. The rest of their fleet was well provided with small-arms, and the crews were dexterous in the use of them. Grogniet's ship was the most powerful, except in cannon, her crew consisting of 308 men.

The Spanish fleet numbered fourteen sail, six of which were provided with cannon; six others with musketry only, and two were fitted up as fire-ships. The buccaneer accounts say the Spanish admiral had forty-eight guns mounted, and 450 men; the vice-admiral forty guns, and men in proportion; the rear-admiral thirty-six guns, one of the other ships twenty-four, one eighteen, and one eight guns; and that the number of men in their fleet was above 2500, but more than one half of them Indians or slaves.

When the two fleets first had sight of each other, Grogniet's ship lay at anchor a mile to leeward of his confederates, on which account he weighed anchor and stood close upon a wind to the eastward, intending to turn up to the other ships; but in endeavouring to tack he missed stays twice, which kept him at a distance all the forepart of the day. From the superiority of the Spaniards in cannon, and of the buccaneer crews in musketry, it was evident that distant fighting was most to the advantage of the Spaniards, and that the buccaneers had to rest their hopes of success on close fighting and boarding. Davis was fully of this opinion, and at three o'clock in the afternoon, the enemy's fleet being directly to leeward and not far dis-

tant, he got his vessels under sail, and bore right down
upon them, making a signal at the same time to Grogniet to board the Spanish vice-admiral, who was some
distance separate from the other ships of his fleet.

Here may be contemplated the buccaneers at the
highest pitch of elevation to which they at any time
attained. If they obtained the victory it would give
them the sole dominion of the South Sea—and Davis,
the buccaneer commander, aimed at no less ; but he
was ill seconded, and was not possessed of authority
to enforce obedience on his commands.

The order given to Grogniet was not put in execution, and when Davis had arrived with his ship within cannon-shot of the Spaniards, Swan shortened sail
and lowered his ensign, to signify he was of opinion
that it would be best to postpone fighting till the
next day. Davis, wanting the support of two of
the most able ships of his fleet, was obliged to forego
his intention, and no act of hostility passed during the
afternoon and evening except the exchange of some
shot between his own ship and that of the Spanish
vice-admiral.

When it was dark the Spanish fleet anchored, and,
at the same time, the Spanish admiral took in his
light and ordered a light to be shown from one of his
small vessels, which he sent to leeward. The buccaneers were deceived by this artifice, believing the
light they saw to be that of the Spanish admiral, and
they continued under sail, thinking themselves secure
of the weathergage. At daylight the next morning
the Spaniards were seen well collected, whilst the buccaneer vessels were much dispersed. Grogniet and

Townley were to windward of the Spaniards; but all the rest, contrary to what they had expected, were to leeward. At sunrise the Spanish fleet got under sail and bore down towards the leeward buccaneer ships. The buccaneers thought it not prudent to fight under such disadvantages, and did not wait to receive them. They were near the small island Pacheca, on the south side of which are some islands yet smaller. Among these islands, Dampier says, is a narrow channel in one part not forty feet wide. Townley, being pressed by the Spaniards and in danger of being intercepted, pushed for this passage without any previous examination of the depth of water, and got safe through. Davis and Swan, whose ships were the fastest sailing in either fleet, had the credit of affording protection to their flying companions, by waiting to repulse the most advanced of the Spaniards. Dampier, who was in Davis's ship, says she was pressed upon by the whole Spanish force. "The Spanish admiral and the rest of his squadron began to play at us and we at them as fast as we could: yet they kept at distant cannonading. They might have laid us aboard if they would, but they came not within small-arms' shot, intending to maul us in pieces with their great guns." After a circuitous chase and running fight, which lasted till the evening, the buccaneers, Harris's ship excepted, which had been forced to make off in a different direction, anchored by the island Pacheca, nearly in the same spot whence they had set out in the morning.

On the 30th, at daylight, the Spanish fleet was seen at anchor three leagues to leeward. The breeze was

faint, and both fleets lay quiet till about ten o'clock
in the forenoon. The wind then freshened a little
from the south, and the Spaniards took up their
anchors; but instead of making towards the buccaneers, they sailed away in a disgraceful manner for
Panama. Whether they sustained any loss in this
skirmishing does not appear.   The buccaneers had
only one man killed outright.   In Davis's ship six
men were wounded, and half of her rudder was
shot away.

It might seem to those little acquainted with the
management of ships that it could make no material
difference whether the Spaniards bore down to engage
the buccaneers, or the buccaneers bore down to
engage the Spaniards, for that in either case when
the fleets were closed the buccaneers might have
tried the event of boarding.   But the difference here
was, that if the buccaneers had the weathergage it
enabled them to close with the enemy in the most
speedy manner, which was of much consequence where
the disparity in the number of cannon was so great.
When the Spaniards had the weathergage, they
would press the approach only near enough to give
effect to their cannon, and not near enough for
musketry to do them mischief. With this view, they
could choose their distance when to stop and bring
their broadsides to bear, and leave to the buccaneers
the trouble of making nearer approach against the
wind and a heavy cannonade.   Dampier, who has related the transactions of the 28th and 29th very briefly,
speaks of the weathergage here as a decisive advantage. He says: "In the morning (of the 29th),

therefore, when we found the enemy had got the weathergage of us, and were coming upon us with full sail, we ran for it ".

On this occasion there is no room for commendation on the valour of either party. The buccaneers, however, knew by the Spanish fleet coming to them from Panama that the treasure must have been landed, and therefore they could have had little motive for enterprise. The meeting was faintly sought by both sides, and no battle was fought except a little cannonading during the retreat of the buccaneers, which on their side was almost wholly confined to the ship of their commander. Both Dampier and Lussan acknowledge that Edward Davis brought the whole of the buccaneer fleet off safe from the Spaniards by his courage and good management.

On the 1st June the buccaneers sailed out of the Bay of Panama for the island Quibo. They had to beat up against south-west winds, and had much wet weather. In the middle of June they anchored on the east side of Quibo, where they were joined by Harris.

Quibo and the smaller islands near it Dampier calls collectively the Keys of Quibo. They are all woody. Good fresh water was found on the great island, which would naturally be the case with the wet weather ; and here were deer, guanas, and large black monkeys, whose flesh was esteemed by the buccaneers to be sweet and wholesome food.

A shoal which runs out from the south-east point of Quibo half-a-mile into the sea has been already noticed. A league to the north of this shoal, and a mile distant from the shore, is a rock which appears above water only at the last quarter ebb. Except the shoal and this rock, there is no other danger, and ships may anchor within a quarter-of-a-mile of the shore, in from six to twelve fathoms' clear sand and ooze.*

They stopped at Quibo to make themselves canoes, the trees there being well suited for the purpose, and some so large that a single trunk hollowed and wrought into shape would carry forty or fifty men. Whilst this work was performing, a strong party was sent to the mainland against Pueblo Nuevo, which town was now entered without opposition, but no plunder was obtained.

Lussan relates that two of the buccaneers were killed by serpents at Quibo. He says: "Here are serpents whose bite is so venomous that speedy death inevitably ensues, unless the patient can have immediate recourse to a certain fruit, which must be chewed and applied to the part bitten. The tree which bears this fruit grows here and in other parts of America. It resembles the almond-tree in France in height and in its leaves. The fruit is like the sea-chestnut *(Chataines de Mer)* but is of a grey colour, rather bitter in taste, and contains in its middle a whitish almond. The whole is to be chewed together before it is applied. It is called *(Graine à Serpent)* the 'serpent berry'."

The dissatisfaction caused by their being foiled in the Bay of Panama broke out in reproaches, and produced great disagreements among the buccaneers.

* Dampier, vol. i. chap. **8.**

Many blamed Grogniet for not coming into battle the first day. On the other hand, Lussan blames the behaviour of the English, "who," he says, "being the greater number, lorded it over the French," and says that Townley, liking Grogniet's ship better than his own, would have insisted on a change, if the French had not shown a determination to resist such an imposition. Another cause of complaint against the English was the indecent and irreverent manner in which they showed their hatred to the Roman Catholic religion. Lussan says : "When they entered the Spanish churches, it was their diversion to hack and mutilate everything with their cutlasses, and to fire their muskets and pistols at the images of saints". In consequence of these disagreements, 330 of the French joined together under Grogniet and separated from the English.

Before either of the parties had left Quibo, William Knight, a buccaneer already mentioned, arrived there in a ship manned with forty Englishmen and eleven Frenchmen. This small crew of buccaneers had crossed the isthmus about nine months before ; they had been cruising both on the coast of New Spain and on the coast of Peru, and the sum of their successes amounted to their being provided with a good vessel and a good stock of provisions. They had latterly been to the southward, where they learnt that the Lima fleet had sailed against the buccaneers before Panama, which was the first notice they received of other buccaneers than themselves being in the South Sea. On the intelligence they immediately sailed for the Bay of Panama, that they might be present and share in the capture of the Spaniards, which they believed would inevitably be the result of a meeting. On arriving in the Bay of Panama they learned what really had happened : nevertheless they proceeded to Quibo in search of their friends. The Frenchmen in Knight's ship left her to join their countrymen : Knight and the rest of the crew put themselves under the command of Davis.

The ship commanded by Harris was found to be in a decayed state and untenantable. Another vessel was given to him and his crew, but the whole company were so much crowded for want of ship room that a number remained constantly in canoes. One of the canoes which they built at Quibo measured thirty-six feet in length, and between five and six feet in width.

Davis and the English party, having determined to attack the city of Leon in the province of Nicaragua, sent an invitation to the French buccaneers to rejoin them. The French had only one ship, which was far from sufficient to contain their whole number, and they demanded, as a condition of their uniting again with the English, that another vessel should be given to themselves. The English could ill spare a ship, and would not agree to the proposition ; the separation, therefore, was final. Jean Rose, a Frenchman, with fourteen of his countrymen, in a new canoe they had built for themselves, left Grogniet to try their fortunes under Davis.

In this, and in other separations which subsequently took place among the buccaneers, it has been thought the most clear and convenient arrangement of narrative to follow the fortunes of the buccaneer commander Edward Davis and his adherents, without interruption, to the conclusion of their adventures in the South Sea; and afterwards to resume the proceedings of the other adventurers.

On the 20th of July, Davis, with eight vessels and 640 men, departed from the island Quibo for Ria Lexa, sailing through the channel between Quibo and the mainland, and along the coast of the latter, which was low and overgrown with thick woods, and appeared thin of inhabitants. August the 9th, at eight in the morning, the ships being then so far out in the offing that they could not be descried from the shore, Davis with 520 men went away in thirty-one canoes for the harbour of Ria Lexa. They set out with fair weather; but at two in the afternoon a tornado came from the land, with thunder, lightning, and rain, and with such violent gusts of wind that the canoes were all obliged to put right before it, to avoid being overwhelmed by the billows. Dampier remarks generally of the hot latitudes, as Lussan does of the Pacific Ocean, that the sea there is soon raised by the wind, and when the wind abates is soon down again. "Up wind up sea, down wind down sea," is proverbial between the tropics among seamen. The fierceness of the tornado continued about half-an-hour, after which the wind gradually abated, and the canoes again made towards the land. At seven in the evening it was calm, and the sea quite smooth. During the night the buccaneers, having the direction of a Spanish pilot, entered a narrow creek which led towards Leon; but the pilot could not undertake to proceed up till daylight lest he should mistake, there being several creeks communicating with each other.

The city of Leon bordered on the Lake of Nicaragua, and was reckoned twenty miles within the sea coast. They went only a part of this distance by the river, when Davis, leaving sixty men to guard the canoes, landed with the rest and marched towards the city, two miles short of which they passed through an Indian town. Leon had a cathedral and three other churches. It was not fortified, and the Spaniards, though they drew up their force in the great square or parade, did not think themselves strong enough to defend the place. About three in the afternoon the buccaneers entered, and the Spaniards retired.

All the buccaneers who landed did not arrive at Leon that same day. According to their ability for the march, Davis had disposed his men into divisions. The foremost was composed of all the most active, who marched without delay for the town, the other divisions following as speedily as they were able. The rear division being of course composed of the worst travellers, some of them could not keep pace even with their own division. They all came in afterwards except two, one of whom was killed, and the other taken prisoner. The man killed was a stout grey-headed old man of the name of Swan, aged about eighty-four years, who had served under Cromwell, and had ever since made privateering or buccaneering his occupation. This veteran would not be dissuaded from going on the enterprise against Leon; but his strength failed in the march, and after being left on the road he was found by the Spaniards, who endeavoured to make him their prisoner ; but he refused to surrender, and fired his musket amongst them, having in reserve a pistol still charged ; on which he was shot dead.

The houses in Leon were large, built of stone, but not high, with gardens about them. "Some have recommended Leon as the most pleasant place in all America ; and for health and pleasure it does surpass most places. The country round is of a sandy soil, which soon drinks up the rains to which these parts are much subject." *

The buccaneers being masters of the city, the governor sent a flag of truce to treat for its ransom. They demanded 300,000 dollars, and as much provision as would subsist 1000 men four months : also that the buccaneer taken prisoner should be exchanged. These demands it is probable the Spaniards never intended to comply with; however, they prolonged the negotiation till the buccaneers suspected it was for the purpose of collecting force. Therefore on the 14th they set fire to the city and returned to the coast. The town of Ria Lexa underwent a similar fate, contrary to the intention of the buccaneer commander.

Ria Lexa is unwholesomely situated in a plain among creeks and swamps, "and is never free from a noisome smell ". The soil is a strong yellow clay ; in the neighbourhood of the town were many sugar-works and beef-farms ; pitch, tar and cordage were made here —with all which commodities the inhabitants carried on

* Dampier.

a good trade. The buccaneers supplied themselves
with as much as they wanted of these articles, besides
which they received at Ria Lexa 150 head of cattle
from a Spanish gentleman, who had been released
upon his parole and promise oï making such payment
for his ransom. Their own man who had been made
prisoner was redeemed in exchange for a Spanish
lady, and they found in the town 500 packs of flour ;
which circumstances might have put the buccaneers
in good temper and have induced them to spare the
town ; " But," says Dampier, " some of our destructive crew, I know not by whose order, set fire to the
houses, and we marched away and left them burning".

After the Leon expedition no object of enterprise
occurred to them of sufficient magnitude to induce or to
enable them to keep together in such large force. Dispersed in small bodies, they expected a better chance of
procuring both subsistence and plunder. By general
consent, therefore, the confederacy which had been
preserved of the English buccaneers was relinquished,
and they formed into new parties according to their
several inclinations. Swan proposed to cruise along
the coast of New Spain, and north-westward as far as
to the entrance of the Gulf of California, and thence to
take his departure for the East Indies. Townley and
his followers agreed to try their fortunes with Swan as
long as he remained on the coast of New Spain ; after
which they proposed to return to the isthmus. In the
course of settling these arrangements William Dampier,
being desirous of going to the East Indies, took leave
of his commander, Edward Davis, and embarked with
Swan. Of these an account will be given hereafter.

CHAPTER XVI.

*Buccaneers under Edward Davis. At Amapalla Bay;
Cocos Island; the Galapagos Islands; coast of
Peru. Peruvian wine. Knight quits the South
Sea. Bezoar stones. Marine productions on
mountains. Vermejo. Davis joins the French
buccaneers at Guayaquil. Long sea engagement.*

WITH Davis there remained the vessels of Knight
and Harris, with a tender, making in all four
sail. August the 27th, they sailed from the harbour
of Ria Lexa, and as they departed Swan saluted them
with fifteen guns, to which Davis returned eleven.

A sickness had broken out among Davis's people,
which was attributed to the unwholesomeness of the
air, or the bad water, at Ria Lexa. After leaving the
place the disorder increased, on which account Davis
sailed to the Bay of Amapalla, where, on his arrival,
he built huts on one of the islands in the bay for the
accommodation of his sick men, and landed them.
Above 130 of the buccaneers were ill of a spotted
fever, and several died.

Lionel Wafer was surgeon with Davis, and has
given a brief account of his proceedings. Wafer with
some others went on shore to the mainland on the
south side of Amapalla Bay to seek for provisions.

They walked to a beef-farm which was about three miles from their landing. On the way they crossed a hot river in an open savannah, or plain, which they forded with some difficulty on account of its heat. This river issued from under a hill which was not a volcano, though along the coast there were several. "I had the curiosity," says Wafer, "to wade up the stream as far as I had daylight to guide me. The water was clear and shallow, but the steams were like those of a boiling pot, and my hair was wet with them. The river reeked without the hill a great way. Some of our men who had the itch bathed themselves here, and, growing well soon after, their cure was imputed to the sulphureousness or other virtue of this water." Here were many wolves, who approached so near and so boldly to some who had straggled from the rest of their party as to give them great alarm, and they did not dare to fire lest the noise of their guns should bring more wolves about them.

Davis remained some weeks at Amapalla Bay, and departed thence for the Peruvian coast, with the crews of his ships recovered. In their way southward they made Cocos Island, and anchored in the harbour at the north-east part, where they supplied themselves with excellent fresh water and cocoanuts. Wafer has given the following description : "The middle of Cocos Island is a steep hill, surrounded with a plain declining to the sea. This plain is thick set with cocoa-nut trees: but what contributes greatly to the pleasure of the place is, that a great many springs of clear and sweet water, rising to the top of the hill, are there gathered as in a deep large basin or pond, and the water having no channel, it overflows the verge of its basin in several places, and runs trickling down in pleasant streams. In some places of its overflowing, the rocky side of the hill being more than perpendicular and hanging over the plain beneath, the water pours down in a cataract, so as to leave a dry space under the spout, and form a kind of arch of water. The freshness which the falling water gives the air in this hot climate makes this a delightful place. We did not spare the cocoa-nuts. One day, some of our men being minded to make themselves merry went ashore and cut down a great many cocoa-nut trees, from which they gathered the fruit, and drew about twenty gallons of the milk. They then sat down and drank healths to the king and queen, and drank an excessive quantity; yet it did not end in drunkenness: but this liquor so chilled and benumbed their nerves that they could neither go nor stand. Nor could they return on board without the help of those who had not been partakers of the frolic, nor did they recover under four or five days' time." *

Here Peter Harris broke off consortship, and departed for the East Indies. The tender sailed at the same time, probably following the same route.

Davis and Knight continued to associate, and sailed together from Cocos Island to the Galapagos. At one of these islands they found fresh water; the buccaneer journals do not specify which island, nor anything that can be depended upon as certain of

* *Voyage and Description*, &c., by Lionel Wafer, p. 191, *et seq.*, London, 1699.

its situation. Wafer only says: "From Cocos we came to one of the Galapagos Islands. At this island there was but one watering place, and there we careened our ship." Dampier was not with them at this time, but in describing the Galapagos Isles he makes the following mention of Davis's careening place: "Part of what I say of these islands I had from Captain Davis, who was there afterwards, and careened his ship at neither of the islands that we were at in 1684, but went to other islands more to the westward, which he found to be good, habitable islands, having a deep fat soil capable of producing anything that grows in those climates: they are well watered, and have plenty of good timber. Captain Harris came hither likewise, and found some islands that had plenty of mammee trees, and pretty large rivers. They have good anchoring in many places, so that take the *Galapagos Islands by and large*, they are extraordinary good places for ships in distress to seek relief at." *

Wafer has not given the date of this visit, which was the second made by Davis to the Galapagos; but as he stopped several weeks in the Gulf of Amapalla for the recovery of his sick, and afterwards made some stay at Cocos Island, it must have been late in the year, if not after the end, when he arrived at the Galapagos, and it is probable, during, or immediately after, a rainy season.

The account published by Wafer, excepting what relates to the Isthmus of Darien, consists of short

---

* Dampier's manuscript journal.

notices set down from recollection, and occupying in
the whole not above fifty duodecimo pages. He
mentions a tree at the island of the Galapagos where
they careened, like a pear-tree, "low and not shrubby,
very sweet in smell, and full of very sweet gum".

Davis and Knight took on board their ships 500
packs or sacks of flour from the stores which had
formerly been deposited at the Galapagos. The birds
had devoured some in consequence of the bags having
been left exposed.

From the Galapagos they sailed to the coast of Peru,
and cruised in company till near the end of 1686.

They captured many vessels, which they released
after plundering, and attacked several towns along
the coast. They had sharp engagements with the
Spaniards at Guasco and at Pisco, the particulars of
which are not related; but they plundered both the
towns. They landed also at La Nasca, a small port on
the coast of Peru in latitude about 15° south, at which
place they furnished themselves with a stock of wine.
Wafer says : " This is a rich strong wine, in taste much
like madeira. It is brought down out of the country
to be shipped for Lima and Panama. Sometimes it
is kept here many years stopped up in jars of about
eight gallons each; the jars were under no shelter, but
exposed to the scorching sun, being placed along the
bay and between the rocks, every merchant having his
own wine marked." It could not well have been
placed more conveniently for the buccaneers.

They landed at Coquimbo, which Wafer describes
as "a large town with nine churches". What they did
there is not said. Wafer mentions a small river that

emptied itself in a bay, three miles from the town, in which, up the country, the Spaniards get gold. "The sands of the river by the sea, and round the whole bay, are all bespangled with particles of gold, insomuch that in travelling along the sandy bays our people were covered with a fine gold-dust, but too fine for any profit, for it would be an endless work to pick it up."

Statistical accounts of the vice-royalty of Peru, which during a succession of years were printed annually at the end of the *Lima Almanac*, notice the towns of Santa Maria de la Perilla, Guasca, Santiago de Miraflores, Cañete, Pisco, Huara, and Guayaquil, being sacked and in part destroyed by pirates in the years 1685, 1686 and 1687.

Davis and Knight having made much booty (Lussan says so much that the share of each man amounted to 5000 pieces of eight), they went to the island Juan Fernandez to refit, intending to sail thence for the West Indies ; but before they had recruited and prepared the ships for the voyage round the south of America, fortune made a new distribution of their plunder. Many lost all their money at play, and they could not endure, after so much peril, to quit the South Sea empty-handed, but resolved to revisit the coast of Peru. The more fortunate party embarked with Knight for the West Indies.

The luckless residue, consisting of sixty Englishmen and twenty Frenchmen, with Edward Davis at their head, remained with the "Batchelor's Delight" to begin their work afresh. They sailed from Juan Fernandez for the American coast, which they

made as far south as the island Mocha. By traffic
with the inhabitants they procured among other
provisions a number of the llama or Peruvian sheep.
Wafer relates that out of the stomach of one of these
sheep he took thirteen bezoar stones of several forms,
"some resembling coral, some round, and all green
when first taken out; but by long keeping they turned
of an ash colour".

In latitude 26° south, wanting fresh water, they
made search for the river Copiapo. They landed and
ascended the hills in hopes of discovering it. According
to Wafer's computation, they went eight miles within
the coast, ascending mountain beyond mountain till
they were a full mile in perpendicular height above
the level of the sea. They found the ground there
covered with sand and sea-shells, "which," says Wafer,
"I the more wondered at because there were no shell-
fish, nor could I ever find any shells on any part of
the sea-coast hereabouts, though I have looked for
them in many places". They did not discover the
river they were in search of, but shortly afterwards
they landed at Arica, which they plundered, and a
the river Ylo, where they took in fresh water. At
Arica was a house full of Jesuits' bark. Wafer relates :
"We also put ashore at Vermejo, in 10° south latitude.
I was one of those who landed to search for water. We
marched about four miles up a sandy bay, which we
found covered with the bodies of men, women and
children. These bodies to appearance seemed as if
they had not been above a week dead, but if touched
they proved dry and light as a sponge or piece of cork.
We were told by an old Spanish Indian whom we met that

in his father's time the soil there, which now yielded nothing, was well cultivated and fruitful : that the city of Wormia had been so numerously inhabited with Indians that they could have handed a fish from hand to hand until it had come to the Inca's hand. But that when the Spaniards came and laid siege to their city the Indians, rather than yield to their mercy, dug holes in the sand and buried themselves alive. The men as they now lie have by them their broken bows, and the women their spinning-wheels and distaffs with cotton yarn upon them. Of these dead bodies I brought on board a boy of about ten years of age with an intent to bring him to England, but was frustrated of my purpose by the sailors, who had a foolish conceit that the compass would not traverse right whilst there was a dead body on board, so they threw him overboard, to my great vexation."*

Near this part of the coast of Peru, in April, 1687, Davis had a severe action with a Spanish frigate named the "Katalina," in which the drunkenness of his crew gave opportunity to the Spanish commander, who had made a stout defence, to run his ship ashore upon the coast. They fell in with many other Spanish vessels, which, after plundering, they dismissed.

Shortly after the engagement with the Spanish frigate " Katalina," Davis made a descent at Payta to seek refreshments for his wounded men, and surprised there a courier with despatches from the Spanish commander at Guayaquil to the viceroy at Lima, by which he learnt that a large body of English and French

* Wafer's *Voyages*, p. 208.

buccaneers had attacked, and were then in possession of, the town of Guayaquil. The governor had been taken prisoner by the buccaneers, and the deputy, or next in authority, made pressing instances for speedy succour in his letter to the viceroy, which, according to Lussan, contained the following passage : " The time has expired some days which was appointed for the ransom of our prisoners. I amuse the enemy with the hopes of some thousands of pieces of eight, and they have sent me the heads of four of our prisoners ; but if they send me fifty I should esteem it less prejudicial than our suffering these ruffians to live. If your excellency will hasten the armament to our assistance, here will be a fair opportunity to rid ourselves of them."

Upon this news, and the farther intelligence that Spanish ships of war had been despatched from Callao to the relief of Guayaquil, Davis sailed for that place, and on the 14th May arrived in the Bay of Guayaquil, where he found many of his old confederates ; for these were the French buccaneers who had separated from him under Grogniet, and the English who had gone with Townley. Those two leaders had been overtaken by the perils of their vocation, and were no more. But whilst in their mortal career, and after their separation from Davis, though they had at one time been adverse almost to hostility against each other, they had met, been reconciled, and had associated together. Townley died first, of a wound he received in battle, and was succeeded in the command of the English by a buccaneer named George Hout or Hutt. At the attack of Guayaquil Grogniet was mortally wounded, and Le Picard was chosen by the

French to succeed him in the command. Guayaquil
was taken on the 20th of April; the plunder and a
number of prisoners had been conveyed by the buccaneers to their ships, which were at anchor by the
island Puna, when their unwearied good fortune
brought Davis to join them.

The taking of Guayaquil by the buccaneers under
Grogniet and Hutt will be more circumstantially
noticed in the sequel, with other proceedings of the
same crews. When Davis joined them, they were
waiting with hopes, nearly worn out, of obtaining a
large ransom which had been promised them for the
town of Guayaquil and for their prisoners.

The information Davis had received made him
deem it prudent, instead of going to anchor at Puna,
to remain with his ship on the look-out in the offing;
he, therefore, sent a prize vessel into the road to
acquaint the buccaneers there of his being near at
hand, and that the Spaniards were to be expected
shortly.

The captors of Guayaquil continued many days after
this to wait for ransom. They had some hundreds of
prisoners, for whose sakes the Spaniards sent daily to
the buccaneers large supplies of provisions, of which
the prisoners could expect to receive only the surplus
after the buccaneers should be satisfied. At length
the Spaniards sent 42,000 pieces of eight, the most
part in gold, and eighty packages of flour. The sum
was far short of the first agreement, and the buccaneers at Puna, to make suitable return, released only
a part of the prisoners, reserving for a subsequent
settlement those of the most consideration.

On the 26th they quitted the road of Puna and joined Davis. In the evening of the same day two large Spanish ships came in sight. Davis's ship mounted thirty-six guns ; and her crew, which had been much diminished by different engagements, was immediately reinforced with eighty men from Le Picard's party. Besides Davis's ship, the buccaneers had only a small ship and a *barca-longa* fit to come into action. Their prize vessels, which could do no service, were sent for security into shallow water.

On the morning of the 27th the buccaneers and Spaniards were both without the island Santa Clara. The Spaniards were the farthest out at sea, and had the sea-breeze first, with which they bore down till about noon, when, being just within the reach of cannon-shot, they hauled upon a wind and began a distant cannonade, which was continued till evening ; the two parties then drew off to about a league asunder and anchored for the night. On the morning of the 28th they took up their anchors, and the day was spent in distant firing and in endeavours to gain or to keep the wind of each other. The same kind of manœuvring and distant firing was put in practice on each succeeding day till the evening of the 2nd of June, which completed the seventh day of this obstinate engagement. The Spanish commander, being then satisfied that he had fought long enough, and hopeless of prevailing on the enemy to yield, withdrew in the night. On the morning of the 3rd the buccaneers were surprised, and not displeased, at finding no enemy in sight.

During all this fighting the buccaneers indulged

their vanity by keeping the governor of Guayaquil and other prisoners of distinction upon deck to witness the superiority of their management over that of the Spaniards. It was not, indeed, a post of much danger, for in the whole seven days' battle not one buccaneer was killed, and only two or three were wounded.

It may be some apology for the Spanish commander that, in consequence of Davis's junction with the captors of Guayaquil, he found a much greater force to contend with than he had been taught to expect. Fortune had been peculiarly unfavourable to the Spaniards on this occasion. Three ships of force had been equipped and sent in company against the buccaneers at Guayaquil. One of them, the "Katalina," by accident was separated from the others, and fell in with Davis, by whom she was driven on the coast, where she stranded. The Spanish armament, thus weakened one third, on arriving in the Bay of Guaya quil, found the buccaneer force there increased, by this same Davis, in a proportion greater than their own had been diminished. Davis and Le Picard left the choice of distance to the Spaniards in this meeting, not considering it their business to come to serious battle unless forced. They had reason to be satisfied with having defended themselves and their plunder; and after the enemy disappeared, finding the coast clear, they sailed to the island De la Plata, where they stopped to repair damages and to hold council.

They all now inclined homewards. The booty they had made, if it fell short of the expectations of some, was sufficient to make them eager to be where

they could use or expend it ; but they were not alike
provided with the means of returning to the North
Sea. Davis had a stout ship, and he proposed to go
the southern passage by the Strait of Magalhanes
or round Cape Horn. No other of the vessels in the
possession of the buccaneers was strong enough for
such a voyage. All the French, therefore, and many
of the English buccaneers bent their thoughts on returning overland, an undertaking that would inevitably
be attended with much difficulty, encumbered as they
were with their plunder, and the Darien Indians having
become hostile to them.

Almost all the Frenchmen in Davis's ship left her
to join their countrymen, and many of the English from
their party embarked with Davis. All thoughts of
farther negotiation with the Spaniards for the ransom
of prisoners was relinquished. Le Picard had given
notice, on quitting the Bay of Guayaquil, that payment
would be expected for the release of the remaining
prisoners, and that the buccaneers would wait for it
at Cape Santa Elena ; but they had passed that cape,
and it was apprehended that if they returned thither,
instead of receiving ransom, they might find the
Spanish ships of war, come to renew the attack on
them under other commanders. On the 10th they
landed their prisoners on the continent.

The next day they shared the plunder taken at
Guayaquil. The jewels and ornaments could not well
be divided, nor could their value be estimated to
general satisfaction : neither could they agree upon a
standard proportion between the value of gold and
silver. Every man was desirous to receive for his

share such parts of the spoil as were most portable,
and this was more especially of importance to those
who intended to march overland. The value of gold
was so much enhanced that an ounce of gold was
received in lieu of eighty dollars, and a Spanish pistole
went for fifteen dollars ; but these instances probably
took place in settling their gaming accounts. In the
division of the plunder these difficulties were obviated
by a very ingenious and unobjectionable mode of distribution. The silver was first divided : the other
articles were then put up to auction and bid for in
pieces of eight, and, when all were so disposed of, a
second division was made of the silver produced by
the sale.

Davis and his company were not present at the
taking of Guayaquil, but the services they had rendered
had saved both the plunder and the plunderers, and
gave them a fair claim to share. Neither Wafer nor
Lussan speak to this point, from which it may be
inferred that everything relating to the division was
settled among them amicably, and that Davis and his
men had no reason to be dissatisfied. Lussan gives a
loose statement of the sum total and of the single
shares. " Notwithstanding that these things were sold
so dearly, we shared for the taking of Guayaquil only
four hundred pieces of eight to each man, which would
make in the whole about fifteen hundred thousand
livres." The number of buccaneers with Grogniet
and Hutt immediately previous to the attack of
Guayaquil was 304. Davis's crew, at the time he
separated from Knight, consisted of eighty men. He
had afterwards lost men in several encounters, and it

is probable the whole number present at the sharing
of the plunder of Guayaquil was short of 350.   Allowing the extra shares to officers to have been 150,
making the whole number of shares 500, the amount
of plunder will fall short of Lussan's estimate.

On the 12th the two parties finally took leave of
each other and separated, bound by different routes
for the Atlantic.

CHAPTER XVII.

Edward Davis; his third visit to the Galapagos. One of those islands, named Santa Maria de l'Aguada by the Spaniards, a careening place of the buccaneers. Sailing thence southward, they discover land. Question, whether Edward Davis's discovery is the land which was afterwards named Easter Island? Davis and his crew arrive in the West Indies.

DAVIS again sailed to the Galapagos Islands to victual and refit his ship. Lionel Wafer was still with him, and appears to have been one of those to whom fortune had been most unpropitious. Wafer does not mention either the joining company with the French buccaneers, or the plunder of Guayaquil, and particularises few of his adventures. He says: "I shall not pursue all my coasting along the shore of Peru with Captain Davis. We continued rambling about to little purpose, sometimes at sea, sometimes ashore, till, having spent much time and visited many places, we were got again to the Galapagos, from whence we were determined to make the best of our way out of these seas."

At the Galapagos they again careened; and there they victualled the ship, taking on board a large supply of flour, curing fish, salting flesh of the land turtle for sea store; and they saved as much of the oil of the land turtle as filled sixty jars (of eight gallons each), which proved excellent and was thought not inferior to fresh butter.

Captain Colnet was at the Galapagos Isles in the years 1793 and 1794, and found traces still fresh which marked the haunts of the buccaneers. He says: "At every place where we landed on the western side of King James's Isle, we might have walked for miles through long grass and beneath groves of trees. It only wanted a stream to compose a very charming landscape. This isle appears to have been a favourite resort of the buccaneers, as we found seats made by them of earth and stone, and a considerable number of broken jars scattered about, and some whole, in which the Peruvian wine and liquors of the country are preserved. We also found daggers, nails, and other implements. The watering-place of the buccaneers was at this time (the latter part of April or beginning of May) entirely dried up, and there was only found a small rivulet between two hills, running into the sea, the northernmost of which hills forms the south point of Fresh Water Bay. There is plenty of wood, but that near the shore is not large enough for other use than firewood. In the mountains the trees may be larger, as they grow to the summits. I do not think the watering-place we saw is the only one on the island, and I have no doubt, if wells were dug anywhere beneath the hills and not near the lagoon behind the sandy beach, that fresh water would be found in great plenty." *

* Colnet's *Voyage to the Pacific*, pp. 156-7.

Since Captain Colnet's voyage Captain David Porter of the American United States' frigate "Essex" has seen and given descriptions of the Galapagos Islands. He relates an anecdote which accords with Captain Colnet's opinion of there being fresh water at King James's Island. He landed, on its west side, four goats (one male and three female) and some sheep, to graze. As they were tame, and of their own accord kept near the landing-place, they were left every night without a keeper, and water was carried to them in the morning. " But one morning, after they had been on the island several days and nights, the person who attended them went on shore as usual to give them water, but no goats were to be found : they had all as with one accord disappeared. Several persons were sent to search after them for two or three days, but without success." Captain Porter concluded that they had found fresh water in the interior of the island and chose to remain near it. "One fact," he says, "was noticed by myself and many others the day preceding their departure, which must lead us to believe that something more than chance directed their movements, which is, that they all drank an unusual quantity of water on that day, as though they had determined to provide themselves with a supply to enable them to reach the mountains." *

Davis and his men had leisure for search and to make every kind of experiment ; but no one of his party has given any description or account of what was trans-

---

* *Journal of a Cruise to the Pacific Ocean*, by Captain David Porter, in the years 1812-13 and 1814.

acted at the Galapagos in this his third visit.   Light, however, has been derived from late voyages.

It has been generally believed, but not till lately ascertained, that Davis passed most of the time he was amongst the Galapagos, at an island which the Spaniards have designated by the name of Santa Maria de l'Aguada, concerning the situation of which the Spaniards as well as geographers of other countries have disagreed.   A Spanish pilot reported to Captain Woodes Rogers that Santa Maria de l'Aguada lay by itself (*i.e.*, was not one of a group of islands) in latitude 1° 20′ or 1° 30′ south, was a pleasant island, well stocked with wood, and with plenty of fresh water.*   Moll, De Vaugondy, and others, combining the accounts given by Dampier and Woodes Rogers, have placed a Santa Maria de l'Aguada several degrees to the westward of the whole of Cowley's group.   Don Antonio de Ulloa, on the contrary, has laid it down as one of the Galapagos Isles, but among the most south-eastern of the whole group.   More consonant with recent information, Pascoe Thomas, who sailed round the world with Commodore Anson, has given from a Spanish manuscript the situations of different islands of the Galapagos, and among them that of Santa Maria de l'Aguada.   The most western in the Spanish list published by Thomas is named Santa Margarita, and is the same with the Albemarle Island in Cowley's chart. The Santa Maria de l'Aguada is set down in the same Spanish list in latitude 1° 10′ south, and 19′ in

* *Cruising Voyage round the World*, by Captain Woodes Rogers in the years 1708 to 1711, pp. 211 and 265, 2nd edition.   London, 1718.

longitude more east than the longitude given of Santa Margarita, which situation is due south of Cowley's King James's Island.

Captain Colnet saw land due south of King James's Island, which he did not anchor at or examine, and appears to have mistaken for the King Charles's Island of Cowley's chart. On comparing Captain Colnet's chart with Cowley's, it is evident that Captain Colnet has given the name of Lord Chatham's Isle to Cowley's King Charles's Island, the bearings and distance from the south end of Albemarle Island being the same in both, *i.e.*, due east about 20 leagues. It follows that the Charles Island of Colnet's chart was not seen by Cowley, and that it is the Santa Maria de l'Aguada of the Spaniards. It has lately been frequented by English and American vessels employed in the South Sea whale fishery, who have found a good harbour on its north side, with wood and fresh water ; and marks are yet discoverable that it was formerly a careening place of the buccaneers. Mr. Arrowsmith has added this harbour to Captain Colnet's chart, on the authority of information communicated by the master of a South Sea whaler.

From Captain David Porter's journal, it appears that the watering-place at Santa Maria de l'Aguada is three miles distant from any part of the sea-shore, and that the supply it yields is not constant. On arriving a second time at the Galapagos, in the latter part of August, Captain Porter sent a boat on shore to this island. Captain Porter relates: "I gave directions that our former watering-places there should be examined, but was informed that they were entirely dried up ".

Cowley's chart, being originally a buccaneer performance, and not wholly out of use, is annexed to this
account ; with the insertion, in unshaded outline, of
the Santa Maria de l'Aguada, according to its situation
with respect to Albemarle Island, as laid down in the
last edition of Captain Colnet's chart, published by
Mr. Arrowsmith. This unavoidably makes a difference in the latitude, equal to the difference between
Cowley's and Captain Colnet's latitude of the south
end of Albemarle Island. In Captain Colnet's chart
the north end of Santa Maria de l'Aguada is laid
down in 1° 15′ south.

The voyage of the "Essex" gives reasonable
expectation of an improved chart of the Galapagos
Isles, the Rev. Mr. Adams, who sailed as chaplain
in that expedition, having employed himself actively
in surveying them.

When the season approached for making the
passage round Cape Horn, Davis and his company
quitted their retreat. The date of their sailing is not
given. Wafer relates : " From the Galapagos Islands
we went again for the southward, intending to touch
nowhere till we came to the Island Juan Fernandez.
In our way thither, being in the latitude of 12° 30′ south,
and about 150 leagues from the main of America,
about four o'clock in the morning our ship felt a
terrible shock, so sudden and violent that we took it
for granted she had struck upon a rock. When the
amazement was a little over we cast the lead and
sounded, but found no ground, so we concluded it
must certainly be some earthquake. The sea, which
ordinarily looks green, seemed then of a whitish

colour ; and the water which we took up in the buckets for the ship's use we found to be a little mixed with sand. Some time after we heard that at that very time there was an earthquake at Callao, which did mischief both there and at Lima.

" Having recovered from our fright, we kept on to the southward. We steered south by east half-easterly, until we came to the latitude of 27° 20' south, when about two hours before day we fell in with a small, low, sandy island, and heard a great roaring noise, like that of the sea beating upon the shore, right ahead of the ship. Whereupon, fearing to fall foul upon the shore before day, the ship was put about. So we plied off till day, and then stood in again with the land, which proved to be a small flat island, without the guard of any rocks. We stood in within a quarter-of-a-mile of the shore, and could see it plainly, for it was a clear morning. To the westward, about twelve leagues by judgment, we saw a range of high land which we took to be islands, for there were several partitions in the prospect. This land seemed to reach about fourteen or sixteen leagues in a range, and there came thence great flocks of fowls. I and many of our men would have made this land, and have gone ashore at it, but the captain would not permit us. The small island bears from Copiapo almost due east [west was intended] 500 leagues, and from the Galapagos, under the line, is distant 600 leagues." *

Dampier was not present at this discovery ; but he met his old commander afterwards, and relates in-

---

* Wafer's *Voyages*, p. 214 *et seq.*

formation he received concerning it in the following words : "Captain Davis told me lately that after his departing from us at Ria Lexa he went, after several traverses, to the Galapagos, and that, standing thence southward for wind to bring him about the Tierra del Fuego, in the latitude of 27° south, about 500 leagues from Copiapo, on the coast of Chili, he saw a small sandy island just by him ; and that they saw to the westward of it a long tract of pretty high land, tending away toward the north-west, out of sight ".*

The two preceding paragraphs contain the whole which is said either in Wafer or Dampier concerning this land. The apprehension of being late in the season for the passage round Cape Horn seems to have deterred Davis from making examination of his discovery. The latitude and specified distance from Copiapo were particulars sufficient to direct future search ; and twenty-five years afterwards Jacob Roggewein, a Dutch navigator, guided by those marks, found land ; but, it being more distant from the American continent than stated by Davis or Wafer, Roggewein claimed it as a new discovery. A more convenient place for discussing this point, which has been a lasting subject of dispute among geographers, would be in an account of Roggewein's voyage ; but a few remarks here may be satisfactory.

Wafer kept neither journal nor reckoning, his profession not being that of a mariner ; and from circumstances which occur in Davis's navigation to the Atlantic, it may reasonably be doubted whether a

* Dampier, vol. i. chap. xiii. p. 352.

regular reckoning or journal was kept by any person on board, and whether the 500 leagues' distance of the small island from the American coast, mentioned by Davis and Wafer, was other than a conjectured distance. They had no superior by whom a journal of their proceedings would be required or expected. If a regular journal had really been kept, it would most probably have found its way to the press.

Jacob Roggewein, the Dutch admiral, was, more than any other navigator, willing to give himself the credit of making new discoveries, as the following extracts from the journal of his expedition will evince : " We looked for Hawkins's Maiden Land, but could not find it ; but we discovered an island 200 leagues in circuit, in latitude 52° south, about 200 leagues distant to the east of the coast of South America, which we named Belgia Austral ". That is as much as to say, Admiral Roggewein could not find Hawkins's Maiden Land ; but he discovered land on the same spot, which he named Belgia Austral. Afterwards, proceeding in the same disposition, the journal relates : " We directed our course from Juan Fernandez towards Davis's Land, but to the great astonishment of the admiral (Roggewein) it was not seen. I think we either missed it or that there is no such land. We went on towards the west, and on the anniversary of the resurrection of our Saviour we came in sight of an island. We named it Paaschen or Oster Eylandt (*i.e.*, Easter Island)."

Paaschen or Easter Island, according to modern charts and observations, is nearly 690 leagues distant from Copiapo, which is in the same parallel on the

continent of America. The statement of Davis and
Wafer makes the distance only 512 leagues, which is a
difference of 178 leagues. It is not probable that
Davis could have had good information of the longi-
tudes of the Galapagos Islands and Copiapo ; but with
every allowance, so large an error as 178 leagues in a
run of 600 leagues might be thought incredible, if its
possibility had not been demonstrated by a much
greater being made by the same persons in this same
homeward passage, as will be related. In the latitude
and appearance of the land the descriptions of Davis
and Wafer are correct, Easter Island being a mountainous land, which will make partitions in the distant prospect, and appear like a number of islands.

Roggewein's claim to Paaschen or Easter Island
as a new discovery has had countenance and
support from geographers, some of the first eminence,
but has been made a subject of jealous contest and
not of impartial investigation. If Roggewein discovered an island farther to the west of the American
coast than Davis's Land, it must follow that Davis's
Land lies between his discovery and the continent ;
but that part of the South Sea has been so much ex-
plored that if any high land had existed between
Easter Island and the American coast it could not have
escaped being known. There is not the least impro-
bability that ships, in making a passage from the
Galapagos Isles through the south-east trade-wind,
should come into the neighbourhood of Easter Island.

Edward Davis has generally been thought a native
of England, but, according to Lussan—and nothing
appears to the contrary—he was a native of Holland.

The majority of the buccaneers in the ship, however, were British. How far to that source may be traced the disposition to refuse the buccaneers the credit of the discovery, and how much national partialities have contributed to the dispute, may be judged from this circumstance, that Easter Island being Davis's Land has never been doubted by British geographers, and has been questioned only by those of other nations.

The merit of the discovery is nothing, for the buccaneers were not in search of land, but came without design in sight of it, and would not look at what they had accidentally found. And whether the discovery is to be attributed to Edward Davis or to his crew ought to be esteemed of little concern to the nations of which they were natives, seeing the discoverers were men outlawed, and whose acts were disowned by the governments of their countries.

Passing from considerations of claims to consideration of the fact, there is not the smallest plea for questioning, nor has anyone questioned the truth of the buccaneers having discovered a high island west of the American coast, in or near the latitude of 27° south. If different from Easter Island, it must be supposed to be situated between that and the continent. But however much it has been insisted or argued that Easter Island is not Davis's Land, no chart has yet pretended to show two separate islands, one for Edward Davis's discovery, and one for Roggewein's. The one island known has been in constant requisition for double duty, and must continue so until another island of the same description shall be found.

Davis arrived at Juan Fernandez "at the latter

end of the year," and careened there. Since the buccaneers were last at the island the Spaniards had put
dogs on shore for the purpose of killing the goats.
Many, however, found places among precipices,
where the dogs could not get at them, and the buccaneers shot as many as served for their daily con-
sumption. Here, again, five men of Davis's crew, who
had gamed away their money and "were unwilling to
return out of these seas as poor as they came in,"
determined on staying at Juan Fernandez, to take the
chance of some other buccaneer ship, or privateer,
touching at the island. A canoe, arms, ammunition,
and various implements were given to them, with a
stock of maize for planting, and some for their immediate subsistence, and each of these gentlemen had
a negro attendant landed with him.

From Juan Fernandez Davis sailed to the islands
Mocha and Santa Maria, near the continent, where
he expected to have procured provisions ; but he found
both those islands deserted and laid waste, the
Spaniards having obliged the inhabitants to remove,
that the buccaneers might not obtain supplies there.
The season was advanced ; therefore, without expend-
ing more time in search for provisions, they bent their
course southward. They passed round Cape Horn
without seeing land, but fell in with many islands of
ice, and ran so far eastward before they ventured to
steer a northerly course that afterwards, when in the
parallel of the river De la Plata they steered westward
to make the American coast—which they believed to be
only one hundred leagues distant—they sailed " four
hundred and fifty leagues to the west in the same lati-

tude," before they came in sight of land ; whence many began to apprehend they were still in the South Sea,* and this belief would have gained ground, if a flight of locusts had not alighted on the ship, which a strong flurry of wind had blown off from the American coast.

They arrived in the West Indies in the spring of the year 1688, at a time when a proclamation had recently been issued offering the king's pardon to all buccaneers who would quit that way of life and claim the benefit of the proclamation.

It was not the least of fortune's favours to this crew of buccaneers that they should find it in their power, without any care or forethought of their own, to terminate a long course of piratical adventures in quietness and security. Edward Davis was afterwards in England, as appears by the notice given of his discovery by William Dampier, who mentions him always with peculiar respect. Though a buccaneer, he was a man of much sterling worth, being an excellent commander, courageous, never rash, and endued in a superior degree with prudence, moderation, and steadiness, qualities in which the buccaneers generally have been most deficient. His character is not stained with acts of cruelty ; on the contrary, wherever he commanded, he restrained the ferocity of his companions. It is no small testimony to his abilities that the whole of the buccaneers in the South Sea during his time, in every enterprise wherein he bore part, voluntarily placed themselves under his guidance, and paid him obedience as their leader ; and no symptom occurs of

* Wafer's *Voyages*, p. 220.

their having at any time wavered in this respect or
shown inclination to set up a rival authority.   It may
also be said that the only matter in which they were
not capricious was their confidence in his management;
and in it they found their advantage, if not their preservation.

CHAPTER XVIII.

Adventures of Swan and Townley on the coast of New Spain, until their separation.

THE South Sea adventures of the buccaneer chief Davis being brought to a conclusion, the next related will be those of Swan and his crew in the "Cygnet," they being the first of the buccaneers who after the battle in the Bay of Panama left the South Sea. William Dampier, who was in Swan's ship, kept a journal of their proceedings, which is published, and the manuscript also has been preserved.

Swan and Townley, the reader may recollect, were left by Edward Davis in the harbour of Ria Lexa in the latter part of August, 1685, and had agreed to keep company together, westward, towards the entrance of the Gulf of California.

They remained at Ria Lexa some days longer to take in fresh water, "such as it was," and they experienced from it the same bad effects which it had on Davis's men; for, joined to the unwholesomeness of the place, it produced a malignant fever, by which several were carried off.

On September the 3rd they put to sea, four sail in company, *i.e.*, the "Cygnet," Townley's ship, and two tenders; the total of the crews being 340 men.

The sea was not favourable for getting westward
along this coast.   Westerly winds were prevalent, and
scarcely a day passed without one or two violent tornadoes, which were accompanied with frightful flashes
of lightning and claps of thunder ; " the like," says
Dampier, " I did never meet with before nor since ".

These tornadoes generally came out of the north-
east, very fierce, and did not last long.   When the
tornado was past the wind again settled westward.
On account of these storms, Swan and Townley kept
a large offing ; but towards the end of the month the
weather became settled.   On the 24th, Townley, and
106 men in nine canoes, went on westward, whilst the
ships lay by two days with furled sails, to give them
time to get well forward, by which they would come
the more unexpectedly upon any place along the
coast.

Townley proceeded, without finding harbour or
inlet, to the Bay of Tecuantepeque, where, putting
ashore at a sandy beach, the canoes were all overset by
the surf, one man drowned, and some muskets lost.
Townley, however, drew the canoes up dry, and
marched into the country ; but, notwithstanding that
they had not discovered any inlet on the coast, they
found the country intersected with great creeks not
fordable, and were forced to return to their canoes.
A body of Spaniards and Indians came to reconnoitre
them from the town of Tecuantepeque, to seek which
place was the chief purpose of the buccaneers when
they landed.   " The Spanish books," says Dampier,
" mention a large river there, but whether it was run
away at this time, or rather that Captain Townley and

his men were shortsighted, I know not; but they did
not find it."

October the 2nd, the canoes returned to the ships.
The wind was fresh and fair from the east-north-east,
and they sailed westward, keeping within short distance
of the shore, but found neither harbour nor opening.
They had soundings all the way, the depth being
twenty-one fathoms, a coarse sandy bottom, at eight
miles' distance from the land. Having run about
twenty leagues along the coast, they came to a small
high island called Tangola, on which they found wood
and water, and near it good anchorage. "This island
is about a league distant from the main, which is pretty
high, and savannah land by the sea; but within land
it is higher and woody." "We coasted a league
farther, and came to Guatulco, in latitude 15° 30',
which is one of the best ports in this kingdom of
Mexico. Nearly a mile from the mouth of the harbour,
on the east side, is a little island close by the mainland. On the west side of the mouth of the harbour
is a great hollow rock, which, by the continual working of the sea in and out, makes a great noise, and
may be heard a great way; every surge that comes in
forces the water out at a little hole at the top, as out
of a pipe, from whence it flies out just like the blowing of a whale, to which the Spaniards liken it and call
it El Buffadore. Even at the calmest seasons the
beating of the sea makes the water spout out at the
hole, so that this is always a good mark to find the harbour of Guatulco by. The harbour runs in north-
west, is about three miles deep and one mile broad.
The west side of the harbour is the best for small

ships to ride in ; anywhere else you are open to south-west winds which often blow here. There is clean ground anywhere, and good gradual soundings from sixteen to six fathoms ; it is bounded by a smooth sandy shore, good for landing ; and at the bottom of the harbour is a fine brook of fresh water running into the sea. The country is extraordinarily pleasant and delightful to behold at a distance." *

There appeared to be so few inhabitants at this part of the coast that the buccaneers were not afraid to land their sick. A party of men went eastward to seek for houses and inhabitants, and at a league dis-tance from Guatulco they found a river, named by the Spaniards El Capalita, which had a swift current, and was deep at the entrance. They took a few In-dians prisoners, but learnt nothing of the country from them. On the 6th, Townley, with 140 men, marched fourteen miles inland, and in all that way found only one small Indian village, the inhabitants of which cultivated and cured a plant called "vinello," which grows on a vine and is used to perfume chocolate and sometimes tobacco.

The 10th, the canoes were sent westward ; and on the 12th the ships followed, the crews being well re-covered of the Ria Lexa fever. "The coast (from Guatulco) lies along west and a little southerly for twenty or thirty leagues." † On account of a current which set eastward they anchored near a small green island named Sacrificio, about a league to the west of Guatulco, and half-a-mile from the main. In the

---

* Dampier, vol. i. chap. 8.   † *Ib.* vol. i. chap. 9.

channel between was five or six fathoms' depth, and
the tide ran there very swift.

They advanced westward, but slowly. The canoes
were again overset in attempting to land near Port de
Angeles, at a place where cattle were seen feeding,
and another man was drowned. Dampier says : "We
were at this time abreast of Port de Angeles, but those
who had gone in the canoes did not know it, because
the Spaniards describe it to be as good a harbour as
Guatulco. It is a broad open bay, with two or three
rocks at the west side. There is good anchorage all
over the bay, in depth from thirty to twelve fathoms,
but you are open to all winds till you come into twelve
fathoms, and then you are sheltered from the west-
south-west, which is here the common trade-wind.
Here always is a great swell, and landing is bad. The
place of landing is close by the west side, behind a few
rocks. Latitude 15° north. The tide rises about five
feet. The land round Port de Angeles is pretty high,
the earth sandy and yellow, in some places red." The
buccaneers landed at Port de Angeles, and supplied
themselves with cattle, hogs, poultry, maize and salt,
and a large party of them remained feasting three days
at a farm-house. The 27th, they sailed on westward.

Some of their canoes in seeking Port de Angeles
had been as far westward as Acapulco. On their way
back they found a river, into which they went, and
filled fresh water. Afterwards they entered a lagune
or lake of salt water, where fishermen had cured and
stored up fish, of which the buccaneers took away a
quantity.

On the evening of the 27th Swan and Townley

anchored in sixteen fathoms' depth, near a small rocky island six leagues westward of Port de Angeles, and about half-a-mile distant from the mainland. The next day they sailed on, and in the night of the 28th, being abreast the lagune above-mentioned, a canoe manned with twelve men was sent to bring off more of the fish. The entrance into the lagune was not more than a pistol-shot wide, and on each side were rocks high enough and convenient to screen or conceal men. The Spaniards having more expectation of this second visit than they had of the first, a party of them provided with muskets took station behind these rocks. They waited patiently till the canoe of the buccaneers was fairly within the lagune, and then fired their volley and wounded five men. The buc-caneer crew were not a little surprised, yet returned the fire ; but, not daring to repass the narrow entrance, they rowed to the middle of the lagune, where they lay out of the reach of shot. There was no other pas-sage out but the one by which they had entered, which, besides being so narrow, was a quarter of a mile in length, and it was too desperate an undertaking to attempt to repass it. Not knowing what else to do, they lay still two whole days and three nights in hopes of relief from the ships.

It was not an uncommon circumstance among the buccaneers for parties sent away on any particular design to undertake some new adventure ; the long absence of the canoe, therefore, created little surprise in the ships which lay off at sea waiting without solici-tude for her return, till Townley's ship, happening to stand nearer to the shore than the rest, heard muskets

fired in the lagune. He then sent a strong party in
his canoes, which obliged the Spaniards to retreat from
the rocks and leave the passage free for the hitherto
penned-up buccaneers. Dampier gives the latitude of
this lagune, "about 16° 40′ north".

They coasted on westward, with fair weather and
a current setting to the west. On the 2nd November,
they passed a rock called by the Spaniards the Alcatraz
(pelican). "Five or six miles to the west of the rock
are seven or eight white cliffs, which are remarkable
because there are none other so white and so thick
together on all the coast. A dangerous shoal lies
south by west from those cliffs, four or five miles off at
sea. Two leagues to the west of these cliffs is a pretty
large river, which forms a small island at its mouth.
The channel on the east side is shoal and sandy;
the west channel is deep enough for canoes to enter."
The Spaniards had raised a breastwork on the banks
of this channel, and they made a show of resisting the
buccaneers; but, seeing they were determined on
landing, they quitted the place, on which Dampier
honestly remarks: "One chief reason why the
Spaniards are so frequently routed by us, though much
our superiors in number, is their want of firearms, for
they have but few unless near their large garrisons".

A large quantity of salt intended for salting the
fish caught in the lagune was taken here. Dampier
says: "The fish in these lagunes were of a kind called
snooks, which are neither sea-fish nor fresh-water fish;
it is about a foot long, round, and as thick as the small
of a man's leg, has a pretty long head, whitish scales,
and is good meat".

A mulatto whom they took prisoner told them that a ship of twenty guns had lately arrived at Acapulco from Lima. Townley and his crew had long been dissatisfied with their ship, and, in hopes of getting a better, they stood towards the harbour of Acapulco. On the 7th they made the high land over Acapulco, "which is remarkable by a round hill standing between two other hills, both higher, the westernmost of which is the biggest and the highest, and has two hillocks like two paps at the top". Dampier gives the latitude of Acapulco 17° north.*

This was not near the usual time either of the departure or of the arrival of the Manilla ships, and except at those times Acapulco is almost deserted on account of the situation being unhealthy. Acapulco is described as hot, unwholesome, pestered with gnats, and having nothing good but the harbour. Merchants depart from it as soon as they have transacted their business. Townley accordingly expected to bring off the Lima ship quietly and with little trouble. In the evening of the 7th, the ships being then so far from land that they could not be descried, Townley with 140 men departed in twelve canoes for the harbour of Acapulco. They did not reach Port Marques till the second night, and on the third night they rowed softly and unperceived by the Spaniards into Acapulco harbour. They found the Lima ship moored close to the castle, and after reconnoitring thought it would not be in their power to bring her off; so they paddled

---

* Late observations place Acapulco in latitude 16° 51′ 41″ north, and longitude 100° west of Greenwich.

back quietly out of the harbour, and returned to their ships, tired and disappointed.

Westward from the port of Acapulco they passed a sandy bay, or beach, above twenty leagues in length, the sea all the way beating with such force on the shore that a boat could not approach with safety. "There was clean anchoring ground at a mile or two from the shore. At the west end of this bay, in 17° 30' north, is the hill of Petaplan, which is a round point stretching out into the sea, and at a distance seems an island." * This was reckoned twenty-five leagues from Acapulco. A little to the west of the hill are several round white rocks. They sailed within the rocks, having eleven fathoms' depth, and anchored on the north-west side of the hill. Their mosquito men took here some small turtle and small jew-fish.

They landed, and at an Indian village took a mulatto woman and her children, whom they carried on board. They learnt from her that a caravan drawn by mules was going with flour and other goods to Acapulco, but that the carrier had stopped on the road from apprehension of the buccaneers.

The ships weighed their anchors and ran about two leagues farther westward, to a place called Chequetan, which Dampier thus describes: "A mile and a half from the shore is a small key (or island), and within it is a very good harbour, where ships may careen; here is also a small river of fresh water, and wood enough".

On the 14th, in the morning, about one hundred

* Dampier.

buccaneers set off in search of the carrier, taking the woman prisoner for a guide. They landed a league to the west of Chequetan, at a place called Estapa, and their conductress led them through a wood by the side of a river, about a league, which brought them to a savannah full of cattle; and here at a farm-house the carrier and his mules were lodged. He had forty packs of flour, some chocolate, small cheeses, and earthenware. The eatables, with the addition of eighteen beeves which they killed, the buccaneers laid on the backs of above fifty mules which were at hand, and drove them to their boats. A present of clothes was made to the woman, and she with two of her children was set at liberty; but the other child, a boy seven or eight years old, Swan kept, against the earnest intreaties of the mother. Dampier says: "Captain Swan promised her to make much of him, and was as good as his word. He proved afterwards a fine boy for wit, courage, and dexterity."

They proceeded westward along the coast, which was high land full of ragged hills, but with pleasant and fruitful valleys between. The 25th, they were abreast a hill, "which towered above his fellows, and was divided in the top, making two small parts. It is in latitude 18° 8′ north. The Spaniards mention a town called Thelupan near this hill."

The 26th, the captains (Swan and Townley) went in the canoes with 200 men to seek the city of Colima, which was reported to be a rich place; but their search was fruitless. They rowed twenty leagues along shore and found no good place for landing, neither did they see house or inhabitant, although they passed

by a fine valley called the Valley of Maguella, except
that towards the end of their expedition they saw a
horseman, who they supposed had been stationed as a
sentinel, for he rode off immediately on their appearance. They landed with difficulty, and followed the
track of the horse on the sand, but lost it in the woods.

On the 28th they saw the volcano of Colima,
which is in about 18° 36′ north latitude, five or six
leagues from the sea, and appears with two sharp
points, from each of which issued flames or smoke.
The valley of Colima is ten or twelve leagues wide
by the sea; it abounds in cacao-gardens, fields of corn,
and plantain walks. The coast is a sandy shore, on
which the waves beat with violence. Eastward of the
valley the land is woody. A river ran here into the
sea, with a shoal or bar at its entrance, which boats
could not pass. On the west side of the river was
savannah land.

December the 1st they were near the port of
Salagua, which Dampier reckoned in latitude 18°
52′ north. He says : " It is only a pretty deep bay
divided in the middle with a rocky point, which makes,
as it were, two harbours.* Ships may ride secure in
either, but the west harbour is the best ; the depth of
water is ten or twelve fathoms, and a brook of fresh
water runs into the sea there."

Two hundred buccaneers landed at Salagua, and,
finding a broad road which led inland, followed it for
about four leagues, over a dry stony country, much
overgrown with short wood, without seeing habitation

* See chart in Spilbergen's *Voyage*.

or inhabitant ; but in their return they met and took
prisoners two mulattoes, who informed them that the
road they had been travelling led to a great city called
Oarrah, which was distant as far as a horse will travel
in four days, and that there was no place of consequence nearer.   The same prisoner said the Manilla
ship was daily expected to stop at this part of the
coast to land passengers, for that the arrival of the
ships at Acapulco from the Philippines commonly
happened about Christmas, and scarcely ever more
than eight or ten days before or after.

Swan and Townley sailed on for Cape Corrientes.
Many among the crews were at this time taken ill with
a fever and ague which left the patients dropsical.
Dampier says the dropsy is a disease very common
on this coast.   He was one of the sufferers, and continued ill a long time, and several died.

The coast southward of Cape Corrientes is of
moderate height and full of white cliffs.   The inland
country is high and barren, with sharp peaked hills.
Northward of this rugged land, is a chain of mountains
which terminates eastward with a high steep mountain,
which has three sharp peaks and resembles a crown,
and is therefore called by the Spaniards Coronada.
On the 11th they came in sight of Cape Corrientes.
When the cape bore north by west, the Coronada
mountain bore east-north-east.*

On arriving off Cape Corrientes the buccaneer
vessels spread for the advantage of enlarging their
look-out, the " Cygnet " taking the outer station at

* Dampier's manuscript journal.

about ten leagues' distance from the cape. Provisions, however, soon became scarce, on which account Townley's tender and some of the canoes were sent to the land to seek a supply. The canoes rowed up along shore against a northerly wind to the Bay de Vanderas; but the barque could not get round Cape Corrientes. On the 18th Townley complained he wanted fresh water, whereupon the ships quitted their station near the cape and sailed to some small islands called the Keys of Chametly, which are situated to the south-east of Cape Corrientes, to take in fresh water.

The descriptions of the coast of New Spain given by Dampier, in his account of his voyage with the buccaneers, contain many particulars of importance which are not to be found in any other publication. Dampier's manuscript and the printed narrative frequently differ, and it is sometimes apparent that the difference is not the effect of inadvertence or mistake in the press, but that it was intended as a correction from a reconsideration of the subject. The printed narrative says at this part : " These Keys or Islands of Chametly are about sixteen or eighteen leagues to the eastward of Cape Corrientes. They are small, low, woody, and environed with rocks. There are five of them lying in the form of a half moon, not a mile from the shore of the main, and between them and the mainland is very good riding secure from any wind." In the manuscript it is said : " The Islands Chametly make a secure port. They lie eight or nine leagues from Port Navidad."

* Dampier, vol. i. p. 257.

It is necessary to explain that Dampier, in describing his navigation along the coast of New Spain, uses the terms eastward and westward not according to the precise meaning of the words, but to signify being more or less advanced along the coast from the Bay of Panama. By westward, he invariably means more advanced towards the Gulf of California; by eastward, the contrary.

The ships entered within the Chametly Islands by the channel at the south-east end, and anchored in five fathoms' depth, on a bottom of clean sand. They found there good fresh water and wood, and caught plenty of rock-fish with hook and line. No inhabitants were seen, but there were huts, made for the temporary convenience of fishermen who occasionally went there to fish for the inhabitants of the city of La Purificacion. These islands, forming a commodious port affording fresh water and other conveniences, from the smallness of their size are not made visible in the Spanish charts of the coast of New Spain in present use.* Whilst the ships watered at the Keys or Isles of Chametly, a party was sent to forage on the mainland, whence they carried off about forty bushels of maize.

On the 22nd they left the Keys of Chametly, and returned to their cruising station off Cape Corrientes, were they were rejoined by the canoes which had been sent to the Bay de Vanderas. Thirty-seven men had landed there from the canoes, who went three miles

* In some old manuscript Spanish charts, the Chametly Isles are laid down south-east half south about twelve leagues distant from Cape Corrientes.

into the country, where they encountered a body of Spaniards, consisting both of horse and foot. The buccaneers took advantage of a small wood for shelter against the attack of the horse, yet the Spaniards rode in among them ; but the Spanish captain and some of their foremost men being killed, the rest retreated. Four of the buccaneers were killed, and two desperately wounded. The Spanish infantry were more numerous than the horse, but they did not join in the attack, because they were armed only with lances and swords ; " nevertheless," says Dampier, " if they had come in, they would certainly have destroyed all our men ". The buccaneers conveyed their two wounded men to the water side on horses, one of which, when they arrived at their canoes, they killed and dressed, not daring to venture into the savannah for a bullock, though they saw many grazing.

Swan and Townley preserved their station off Cape Corrientes only till 1st January, 1686, when their crews became impatient for fresh meat, and they stood into the Bay de Vanderas to hunt for beef. The depth of water in this bay is very great, and the ships were obliged to anchor in sixty fathoms.

" The valley of Vanderas is about three leagues wide, with a sandy bay against the sea, and smooth landing. In the midst of this bay (or beach) is a fine river, into which boats may enter ; but it is brackish at the latter part of the dry season, which is in March and part of April. The valley is enriched with fruitful savannahs, mixed with groves of trees fit for any use, and fruit trees grow wild in such plenty as if nature designed this place only for a garden. The

savannahs are full of fat bulls and cows, and horses ;
but no house was in sight."

Here they remained hunting beeves till the 7th of
the month. Two hundred and forty men landed every
day, sixty of whom were stationed as a guard, whilst
the rest pursued the cattle, the Spaniards all the time
appearing in large companies on the nearest hills.
The buccaneers killed and salted meat sufficient to
serve them two months, which expended all their salt.
Whilst they were thus occupied in the pleasant valley
of Vanderas, the galleon from Manilla sailed past Cape
Corrientes, and pursued her course in safety to
Acapulco. This they learned afterwards from prisoners;
but it was by no means unexpected : on the contrary,
they were in general so fully persuaded it would be the
consequence of their going into the Bay de Vanderas,
that they gave up all intention of cruising for her
afterwards.

The main object for which Townley had gone thus
far north being disposed of, he and his crew resolved to return southward. Some Darien Indians
had remained to this time with Swan : they were now
committed to the care of Townley, and the two ships
broke off consortship and parted company.

CHAPTER XIX.

*The "Cygnet" and her crew on the coast of Nueva
Galicia, and at the Tres Marias Islands.*

SWAN and his crew determined, before they
quitted the American coast, to visit some Spanish
towns farther north, in the neighbourhood of rich
mines, where they hoped to find good plunder, and to
increase their stock of provisions for the passage across
the Pacific to India.

January the 7th, the "Cygnet" and her tender sailed
from the Valley of Vanderas, and before night passed
Point Ponteque, the northern point of the Vanderas
Bay. Point Ponteque is high, round, rocky, and barren : at a distance it looks like an island. Dampier
reckoned it ten leagues distant, in a direction north,
20° west, from Cape Corrientes, the variation of the
compass observed near the cape being 4° 28' easterly.*

A league west from Point Ponteque are two small
barren islands, round which lie scattered several high,
sharp, white rocks. The "Cygnet" passed on the east
side of the two islands, the channel between them and
Point Ponteque appearing clear of danger. "The sea-
coast beyond Point Ponteque runs in north-east, all

* According to Captain Vancouver, Point Ponteque and Cape
Corrientes are nearly north and south of each other. Dampier was
nearest inshore.

ragged land, and afterwards out again north-north-west, making many ragged points, with small sandy bays between. The land by the sea is low and woody ; but the inland country is full of high, sharp, rugged and barren hills."

Along this coast they had light sea and land breezes and fair weather. They anchored every evening, and got under sail in the morning with the land-wind. On the 14th they had sight of a small white rock, which had resemblance to a ship under sail. Dampier gives its latitude 21° 51' north, and its distance from Cape Corrientes thirty-four leagues. It is three leagues from the main, with depth in the channel near the island, twelve or fourteen fathoms.

The 15th, at noon, the latitude was 22° 11' north. The coast here lay in a north-north-west direction. The 16th, they steered " north-north-west as the land runs ". At noon the latitude was 22° 41' north. The coast was sandy and shelving, with soundings at six fathoms' depth a league distant. The sea set heavy on the shore. They caught here many cat-fish.

On the 20th they anchored a league to the east of a small group of isles, named the Chametlan Isles, after the name of the district or captainship (Alcaldia mayor) in the province of Culiacan, opposite to which they are situated. Dampier calls them the Isles of Chametly, " different from the Isles or Keys of Chametly at which we had before anchored. These are six small islands in latitude 23° 11' north, about three leagues distant from the mainland,* where a salt

* The manuscript says the farthest of the Chametlan Isles from the mainland is not more than four miles distant.

lake has its outlet into the sea. Their meridian distance from Cape Corrientes is twenty-three leagues
(west). The coast here, and for about ten leagues before coming abreast these islands, lies north-west and
south-east."

On the Chametlan Isles they found guanas and
seals, and a fruit of a sharp pleasant taste, by Dampier
called the Penguin fruit, "of a kind which grows so
abundantly in the bay of Campeachy that there is no
passing for their high prickly leaves".

In the mainland, six or seven leagues north-north-
west from the Isles of Chametlan, is a narrow opening
into a lagune, with depth of water sufficient for boats to
enter. This lagune extends along the back of the sea-
beach about twelve leagues, and makes many low man-
grove islands. The latitude given of the entrance
above-mentioned is 23° 30′ north, and it is called by
the Spaniards Rio de Sal.

Half a league northward of Rio de Sal was said to
be the river Culiacan, with a rich Spanish town of the
same name. Swan went with the canoes in search of
it, and followed the coast thirty leagues from abreast
the Chametlan Isles, without finding any river to the
north of the Rio de Sal. All the coast was low and
sandy, and the sea beat high on the shore. The ships
did not go further within the gulf than to 23° 45′
north, in which latitude, on the 30th, they anchored in
eight fathoms' depth, three miles distant from the mainland, the meridian distance from Cape Corrientes being
thirty-four leagues west, by Dampier's reckoning.

In their return southward Swan with the canoes
entered the Rio de Sal lagune, and at an estancian

on the western side they took the owner prisoner.
They found in his house a few bushels of maize, but
the cattle had been driven out of their reach.
Dampier relates : " The old Spanish gentleman who
was taken at the estancian near the Rio de Sal was a
very intelligent person.   He had been a great traveller
in the kingdom of Mexico, and spoke the Mexican
language very well.   He said it is a copious language,
and much esteemed by the Spanish gentry in those
parts, and of great use all over the kingdom ; and that
many Indian languages had some dependency on it."

The town of Mazatlan was within five leagues of
the north-east part of the lagune, and Swan with one
hundred and fifty men went thither.   The inhabitants
wounded some of the buccaneers with arrows, but
could make no effectual resistance.   There were rich
mines near Mazatlan, and the Spaniards of Compostella, which is the chief town in this district, kept slaves
at work in them.   The buccaneers, however, found no
gold here, but carried off some Indian corn.

February 2nd, the canoes went to an Indian town
called Rosario, situated on the banks of a river and
nine miles within its entrance.   " Rosario was a fine
little town of sixty or seventy houses, with a good
church."   The river produced gold, and mines were in
the neighbourhood ; but here, as at Mazatlan, they got
no other booty than Indian corn, of which they conveyed to their ships between eighty and ninety bushels.

On the 3rd, the ships anchored near the river
Rosario in seven fathoms, oozy ground, a league
from the shore, the latitude of the entrance of the
river 22° 51′ north.   A small distance within the coast,

and bearing north-east by north from the ship, was a round hill like a sugar-loaf; and north-westward of that hill was another "pretty long hill," called Caput Cavalli, or the Horse's Head.

On the 8th the canoes were sent to search for a river named the Oleta, which was understood to lie in latitude 22° 27' north, but, the weather proving foggy, they could not find it.

On the 11th they anchored abreast the south point of the entrance of a river called De Santiago, in seven fathoms, soft oózy bottom, about two miles from the shore; a high white rock called Maxentelbo, bore from their anchorage west-north-west, distant about three leagues, and a high hill in the country, with a saddle or bending, called the hill Xalisco, bore south-east. "The river St. Iago is in latitude 22° 15' north; the entrance lies east and west with the rock Maxentelbo. It is one of the principal rivers on this coast: there is ten foot water on the bar at low water, but how much the tide rises and falls was not observed. The mouth of the river is nearly half a mile broad, with very smooth entering. Within the entrance it widens, for three or four rivers meet there and issue all out together. The water is brackish a great way up; but fresh water is to be had by digging two or three feet deep in a sandy bay just at the mouth of the river. Northward of the entrance, and north-east by east from Maxentelbo, is a round white rock."

"Between the latitudes 22° 41' and 22° 10' north, which includes the river De Santiago, the coast lies north-north-west and south-south-east." *

* Dampier, vol. i. chap. 9.

No inhabitants were seen near the entrance of the river Santiago, but the country had a fruitful appearance, and Swan sent seventy men, in four canoes, up the river to seek for some town or village. After two days spent in examining different creeks and rivers, they came to a field of maize which was nearly ripe, and immediately began to gather ; but whilst they were loading the canoes they saw an Indian, whom they caught, and from him they learnt that at four leagues' distance from them was a town named Santa Pecaque. With this information they returned to the ship ; and the same evening Swan, with eight canoes and 140 men, set off for Santa Pecaque, taking the Indian for a guide. This was on the 15th of the month.

They rowed during the night about five leagues up the river, and at six o'clock in the morning landed at a place where it was about a pistol-shot wide, with pretty high banks on each side, the country plain and even. Twenty men were left with the canoes, and Swan with the rest marched towards the town, by a road which led partly through woodland and partly through savannahs well stocked with cattle. They arrived at the town by ten in the forenoon, and entered without opposition, the inhabitants having quitted it on their approach.

The town of Santa Pecaque was small, regularly built after the Spanish mode, with a parade in the middle, and balconies to the houses which fronted the parade. It had two churches. The inhabitants were mostly Spaniards, their principal occupation being husbandry. It is distant from Compostella about twenty-one leagues. Compostella itself was at that time reckoned not to contain more than seventy white families, which made about one-eighth part of its inhabitants.

There were large storehouses, with maize, salt-fish, salt, and sugar at Santa Pecaque, provisions being kept there for the subsistence of some hundreds of slaves who worked in silver mines not far distant. The chief purpose for which the "Cygnet" had come so far north on this coast was to get provisions, and here was more than sufficient to supply her wants. For transporting it to their canoes, Swan divided the men into two parties, which it was agreed should go alternately, one party constantly to remain to guard the stores in the town. The afternoon of the first day was passed in taking rest and refreshment, and in collecting horses. The next morning fifty-seven men, with a number of horses laden with maize, each man also carrying a small quantity, set out for the canoes, at which they arrived and safely deposited their burthens. The Spaniards had given some disturbance to the men who guarded the canoes, and had wounded one, on which account they were reinforced with seven men from the carrying party, and in the afternoon the fifty returned to Santa Pecaque. Only one trip was made in the course of the day.

On the morning of the 18th the party which had guarded the town the day before took their turn for carrying. They loaded twenty-four horses, and every man had his burthen. This day they took a prisoner who told them that nearly a thousand men, of all colours, Spaniards, Indians, negroes, and mulattoes, were assembled at the town of Santiago, which was only three leagues distant from Santa Pecaque. This information made Captain Swan of opinion that separating his men was attended with much danger; and he determined that the next morning he would quit the town with the whole party. In the meantime he employed his men to catch as many horses as they could, that when they departed they might carry off a good load.

On the 19th Swan called his men out early, and gave orders to prepare for marching; but the greater number refused to alter the mode they had first adopted, and said they would not abandon the town until all the provision in it was conveyed to the canoes. Swan was forced to acquiesce, and to allow one half of the company to go as before. They had fifty-four horses laden; Swan advised them to tie the horses one to another, and the men to keep in two bodies, twenty-five before and the same number behind. His directions, however, were not followed: "the men would go their own way, every man leading his horse". The Spaniards had before observed their careless manner of marching, and had prepared their plan of attack for this morning, making choice of the ground they thought most for their advantage, and placing men there in ambush. The buccaneer convoy had not been gone above a quarter of an hour when those who kept guard in the town heard the report of guns. Captain Swan called on them to march out to the assistance of their companions; but some even then opposed him, and spoke with contempt of the danger and their enemies, till two horses, saddled, with holsters, and without riders, came galloping into the town frightened, and one had at its side a carbine newly dis-

charged.   On this additional sign that some event had
taken place which it imported them to know, Swan
immediately marched out of the town, and all his men
followed him.   When they came to the place where
the engagement had happened, they beheld their companions that had gone forth from the town that morning, every man lying dead in the road, stripped, and so
mangled that scarcely any one could be known.   This
was the most severe defeat the buccaneers suffered in
all their South Sea enterprises.

The party living very little exceeded the number
of those who lay dead before them ; yet the Spaniards
made no endeavour to interrupt their retreat, either in
their march to the canoes, or in their falling down the
river, but kept at a distance.   " It is probable," says
Dampier, " the Spaniards did not cut off so many of
our men without loss of many of their own.   We lost
this day fifty-four Englishmen and nine blacks ; and
among the slain was my ingenious friend Mr. Ringrose,
who wrote that part of the *History of the Buccaneers*
which relates to Captain Sharp.   He had engaged in
this voyage as supercargo of Captain Swan's ship."
" Captain Swan had been forewarned by his astrologer
of the great danger they were in ; and several of the
men who went in the first party had opposed the
division of their force : some of them foreboded their
misfortune, and heard, as they lay down in the church
in the night, grievous groanings which kept them from
sleeping." *

Swan and his surviving crew were discouraged
from attempting anything more on the coast of New

* Manuscript journal.

Galicia, although they had laid up but a small stock of provisions. On the 21st they sailed from the river of Santiago for the south cape of California, where it was their intention to careen the ship; but the wind had settled in the north-west quarter, and after struggling against it a fortnight, on the 7th of March they anchored in a bay at the east end of the middle of the Tres Marias Islands, in eight fathoms, clean sand. The next day they took a berth within a quarter of a mile of the shore, the outer points of the bay bearing east-north-east and south-south-west.

None of the Tres Marias Islands were inhabited. Swan named the one at which he had anchored, Prince George's Island. Dampier describes them of moderate height, and the westernmost island to be the largest of the three. "The soil is stony and dry, producing much of a shrubby kind of wood, troublesome to pass; but in some parts grow plenty of straight large cedars. The sea-shore is sandy, and there a green, prickly plant grows, whose leaves are much like the penguin leaf; the root is like the root of the sempervivum, but larger, and when baked in an oven is reckoned good to eat. The Indians of California are said to have great part of their subsistence from these roots. We baked some, but none of us greatly cared for them. They taste exactly like the roots of our English burdock boiled."

At this island were guanas, raccoons, rabbits, pigeons, doves, fish, turtle, and seal. They careened here, and made a division of the store of provisions, two-thirds to the "Cygnet" and one-third to the tender, "there being one hundred eaters in the ship, and fifty on board the tender". The maize they had saved measured 120 bushels.

Dampier relates the following anecdote of himself at this place. " I had been a long time sick of a dropsy, a distemper whereof many of our men died; so here I was laid and covered all but my head in the hot sand. I endured it nearly half-an-hour, and then was taken out. I sweated exceedingly while I was in the sand; and I believe it did me much good, for I grew well soon after."

This was the dry season, and they could not find here a sufficient supply of fresh water, which made it necessary for them to return to the continent. Before sailing Swan landed a number of prisoners, Spaniards and Indians, which would have been necessary on many accounts besides that of the scantiness of provisions, if it had been his design to have proceeded forthwith westward for the East Indies; but as he was going again to the American coast, which was close at hand, the turning his prisoners ashore on a desolate island appears to have been in revenge for the disastrous defeat sustained at Santa Pecaque, and for the Spaniards having given no quarter on that occasion.

They sailed on the 26th, and two days after anchored in the Bay of Vanderas near the river at the bottom of the bay; but the water of this river was now brackish. Search was made along the south shore of the bay, and two or three leagues towards Cape Corrientes a small brook of good fresh water was found, and good anchorage near to a small round island which lies half-a-mile from the main, and about four leagues north-eastward of the cape. Just within this island they brought the ships to anchor in twenty-five fathoms' depth, the brook bearing from them east half north half-a-mile distant, and Point Ponteque north-west by north six leagues.

The Mosquito men struck here nine or ten jew-fish, the heads and finny pieces of which served for present consumption, and the rest was salted for sea-store. The maize and salted fish composed the whole of their stock of eatables for their passage across the Pacific, and at a very straitened allowance would scarcely be sufficient to hold out sixty days.

CHAPTER XX.

The "Cygnet". Her passage across the Pacific Ocean.
At the Ladrones. At Mindanao.

MARCH the 31st, they sailed from the American coast, steering at first south-west, and afterwards more westerly till they were in latitude 13° north, in which parallel they kept. "The kettle was boiled but once a day," says Dampier, "and there was no occasion to call the men to victuals. All hands came up to see the quarter-master share it, and he had need to be exact. We had two dogs and two cats on board, and they likewise had a small allowance given them, and they waited with as much eagerness to see it shared as we did." In this passage they saw neither fish nor fowl of any kind, except at one time, when by Dampier's reckoning they were 4975 miles west from Cape Corrientes, and then numbers of the sea-birds called boobies were flying near the ships, which were supposed to come from some rocks not far distant. Their longitude at this time may be estimated at about 180 degrees from the meridian of Greenwich.*

Fortunately they had a fresh trade-wind, and made great runs every day. "On 20th May, which," says

* Dampier's reckoning made the difference of longitude between Cape Corrientes and the island Guahan 125 degrees, which is 16 degrees more than it has been found by modern observations.

Dampier, "we begin to call the 21st, we were in latitude 12° 50′ north and steering west. At two p.m. the
barque tender, being two leagues ahead of the "Cygnet,"
came into shoal water, and those on board plainly saw
rocks under her, but no land was in sight. They
hauled on a wind to the southward and hove the lead,
and found but four fathoms' water. They saw breakers
to the westward. They then wore round, and got their
starboard tacks on board and stood northward. The
"Cygnet" in getting up to the barque ran over a shoal
bank, where the bottom was seen and fish among the
rocks ; but the ship ran past it before we could heave the
lead. Both vessels stood to the northward, keeping upon
a wind, and sailed directly north, having the wind at
east-north-east till five in the afternoon, having at that
time run eight miles and increased our latitude so
many minutes. We then saw the island Guam
(Guahan) bearing north-north-east, distant from us
about eight leagues, which gives the latitude of the
island (its south end) 13° 20′ north. We did not
observe the variation of the compass at Guam. At
Cape Corrientes we found it 4° 21′ easterly, and an
observation we made when we had gone about a third
of the passage showed it to be the same. I am inclined
to think it was less at Guam."

The shoal above mentioned is called by the Spaniards, the Banco de Santa Rosa, and the part over
which the "Cygnet" passed, according to the extract
from Dampier, is about south by west half west from the
south end of Guahan, distant ten or eleven leagues.

* Dampier, manuscript journal, and vol i. chap. 10 of his printed
Voyages.

An hour before midnight they anchored on the west side of Guahan, a mile from the shore. The Spaniards had here a small fort and a garrison of thirty soldiers, but the Spanish governor resided at another part of the island. As the ships anchored, a Spanish priest, in a canoe, went on board, believing them to be Spaniards from Acapulco. He was treated with civility, but detained as a kind of hostage to facilitate any negotiation necessary for obtaining provisions, and Swan sent a present to the Spanish governor by the Indians of the canoe.

No difficulty was experienced on this head. Both Spaniards and the few natives seen here were glad to dispose of their provisions to so good a market as the buccaneer ships. Dampier conjectured the number of the natives at this time on Guahan not to exceed a hundred. In the last insurrection, which was a short time before Eaton stopped at the Ladrones, the natives, finding they could not prevail against the Spaniards, destroyed their plantations and went to other islands. "Those of the natives who remained in Guahan," says Dampier, "if they were not actually concerned in that broil, their hearts were bent against the Spaniards; for they offered to carry us to the fort, and assist us to conquer the island."

Whilst Swan lay at Guahan the Spanish Acapulco ship came in sight of the island. The governor immediately sent off notice to her of the buccaneer ships' being in the road, on which she altered her course towards the south, and by so doing got among the shoals, where she struck off her rudder and did not get clear for three days. The natives at Guahan told

the buccaneers that the Acapulco ship was in sight of
the island, "which," says Dampier, "put our men in a
great heat to go out after her, but Captain Swan persuaded them out of that humour".

Dampier praises the ingenuity of the natives of the
Ladrone Islands, and particularly in the construction
of their sailing canoes, or, as they are sometimes called,
their flying proes, of which he has given the following
description : " Their proe or sailing canoe is sharp at
both ends ; the bottom is of one piece, of good substance, neatly hollowed, and is about twenty-eight feet
long ; the under or keel part is made round, but in-
clining to a wedge ; the upper part is almost flat,
having a very gentle hollow, and is about a foot
broad ; from hence both sides of the boat are carried
up to about five feet high with narrow plank, and each
end of the boat turns up round very prettily.   But
what is very singular, one side of the boat is made
perpendicular like a wall, while the other side is round-
ing as other vessels are, with a pretty full belly.
The dried husks of the cocoa-nuts serve for oakum.
At the middle of the vessel the breadth aloft is four or
five feet or more, according to the length of the boat.
The mast stands exactly in the middle, with a long
yard that peeps up and down like a ship's mizzen-yard ;
one end of it reaches down to the head of the boat,
where it is placed in a notch made purposely to keep
it fast: the other end hangs over the stern.   To this yard
the sail is fastened, and at the foot of the sail is another
small yard to keep the sail out square, or to roll the
sail upon when it blows hard ; for it serves instead of
a reef to take up the sail to what degree they please.

Along the belly side of the boat, parallel with it, at about seven feet distance, lies another boat or canoe, very small, being a log of very light wood almost as long as the great boat, but not above a foot and a half wide at the upper part, and sharp like a wedge at each end. The little boat is fixed firm to the other by two bamboos placed across the great boat, one near each end, and its use is to keep the great boat upright from oversetting. They keep the flat side of the great boat against the wind, and the belly side, consequently, with its little boat, is upon the lee. * The vessel has a head at each end, so as to be able to sail with either foremost; they need not tack as our vessels do, but when they ply to windward and are minded to make a board the other way, they only alter the setting of the sail by shifting the end of the yard, and they take the broad paddle, with which they steer instead of a rudder, to the other end of the vessel. I have been particular in describing these, their sailing canoes, because I believe they sail the best of any boats in the world. I tried the swiftness of one of them with our log : we had twelve knots on our reel, and she ran it all out before the half-minute glass was half out. I believe she would run twenty-four miles in an hour. It was very pleasant to see the little boat running so swift by the other's side. I was told that one of these proes, being sent express

---

* The Ladrone flying proe described in Commodore Anson's voyage sailed with the belly or rounded side and its small canoe to windward ; by which it appears that these proes were occasionally managed either way, probably according to the strength of the wind ; the little parallel boat or canoe preserving the large one upright by its weight when to windward, and by its buoyancy when to leeward.

from Guahan to Manilla (a distance above 480 leagues) performed the voyage in four days."

Dampier has described the bread-fruit, which is among the productions of the Ladrone Islands. He had never seen nor heard of it anywhere but at these islands. Provisions were obtained in such plenty at Guahan that in the two vessels they salted about fifty hogs for sea use. The friar was released, with presents in return for his good offices, and to compensate for his confinement.

June the 2nd, they sailed from Guahan for the island Mindanao. The weather was uncertain: "the westerly winds were not as yet in strength, and the easterly winds commonly over-mastered them and brought the ships on their way to Mindanao".

There is much difference between the manuscript journal of Dampier and the published narrative concerning the geography of the east side of Mindanao. The manuscript says : " We arrived off Mindanao the 21st day of June ; but being come in with the land, knew not what part of the island the city was in, therefore we ran down to the northward, between Mindanao and St. John, and came to an anchor in a bay which lieth in six degrees north latitude".

In the printed narrative it is said : " The 21st day of June we arrived at the island St. John, which is on the east side of Mindanao and distant from it three or four leagues. It is in latitude about 7° or 8° north. This island is in length about thirty-eight leagues, stretching north-north-west and south-south-east, and is in breadth about twenty-four leagues in the middle of the island. The northernmost end is broader, and the southern narrower. This island is of good height, and is full of small hills. The land at the south-east end (where I was ashore) is of a black fat mould ; and the whole island seems to partake of the same, by the vast number of large trees that it produceth, for it looks all over like one great grove. As we were passing by the south-east end we saw a canoe of the natives under the shore, and one of our boats went after to have spoken with her, but she ran to the shore, and the people leaving her fled to the woods. We saw no more people here, nor sign of inhabitant at this end. When we came aboard our ship again we steered away for the island Mindanao, which was fair in sight of us, it being about ten leagues distant from this part of St. John. The 22nd day we came within a league of the east side of Mindanao, and having the wind at south-east, we steered towards the north end, keeping on the east side till we came into the latitude of 7° 40′ north, and there we anchored in a small bay a mile from the shore in ten fathoms, rocky foul ground. Mindanao being guarded on the east side by St. John's Island, we might as reasonably have expected to find the harbour and city on this side as anywhere else ; but coming into the latitude in which we judged the city might be, we found no canoes or people that indicated a city or place of trade being near at hand, though we coasted within a league of the shore." *

This difference between the manuscript and printed journal cannot well be accounted for. The most remarkable particular of disagreement is in the

* Dampier, vol. i. chap. 11.

latitude of the bay wherein they anchored. At this
bay they had communication with the inhabitants,
and learnt that the Mindanao city was to the westward. They could not prevail on any Mindanao man
to pilot them; the next day, however, they weighed
anchor, and sailed back southward till they came to a
part they supposed to be the south-east end of Mindanao, and saw two small islands about three leagues
distant from it.

There is reason to believe that the two small islands
here noticed were Sarangan and Candigar; according
to which, Dampier's island, St. John, will be the land
named Cape San Augustin in the present charts. And
hence arises a doubt whether the land of Cape San
Augustin is not an island separate from Mindanao.
Dampier's navigation between them does not appear
to have been far enough to the northward to ascertain
whether he was in a strait or a gulf.

The wind blew constant and fresh from the westward, and it took them till the 4th of July to get into
a harbour or sound a few leagues to the north-west
from the two small islands. This harbour or sound
ran deep into the land; at the entrance it is only
two miles across, but within it is three leagues wide,
with seven fathoms' depth, and there is good depth for
shipping four or five leagues up, but with some rocky
foul ground. On the east side of this bay are small
rivers and brooks of fresh water. The country on the
west side was uncultivated land, woody, and well
stocked with wild deer, which had been used to live
there unmolested, no people inhabiting on that side of
the bay. Near the shore was a border of savannah or

meadow-land which abounded in long grass. Dampier
says : " The adjacent woods are a covert for the deer in
the heat of the day, but mornings and evenings they
feed in the open plains, as thick as in our parks in
England. I never saw anywhere such plenty of wild
deer. We found no hindrance to our killing as many
as we pleased, and the crews of both the ships were fed
with venison all the time we remained here."

They quitted this commodious port on the 12th ;
the weather had become moderate, and they proceeded
westward for the river and city of Mindanao. The
southern part of the island appeared better peopled
than the eastern part ; they passed many fishing boats,
"and now and then a small village".

On the 18th they anchored before the river
of Mindanao in fifteen fathoms' depth, the bottom
hard sand, about two miles distant from the shore, and
three or four miles from a small island which was
without them to the southward. The river is small,
and had not more than ten or eleven feet depth over
the bar at spring tides. Dampier gives the latitude of
the entrance 6° 22′ north.

The buccaneer ships on anchoring saluted with
seven guns, under English colours, and the salute
was returned with three guns from the shore. " The
city of Mindanao is about two miles from the sea. It
is a mile long, of no great breadth, winding with the
banks of the river on the right hand going up, yet it
has many houses on the opposite side of the river."
The houses were built upon posts, and at this time, as
also during a great part of the succeeding month, the
weather was rainy, and "the city seemed to stand as in

a pond, so that there was no passing from one house to another but in canoes ".

The island Mindanao was divided into a number of small states. The port at which the "Cygnet" and her tender now anchored, with a large district of country adjacent, was under the dominion of a sultan or prince who appears to have been one of the most powerful in the island. The Spaniards had not established their dominion over all the Philippine Islands, and the inhabitants of this place were more apprehensive of the Hollanders than of any other Europeans, and on that account expressed some discontent when they understood the "Cygnet" was not come for the purpose of making a settlement. On the afternoon of their arrival Swan sent an officer with a present to tl.e sultan, consisting of scarlet cloth, gold lace, a scimitar, and a pair of pistols, and likewise a present to another great man, who was called the general, of scarlet cloth and three yards of silver lace. The next day Captain Swan went on shore and was admitted to an audience in form. The sultan showed him two letters from English merchants, expressing their wish to establish a factory at Mindanao, to do which he said the English should be welcome. A few days after this audience the "Cygnet" and tender went into the river, the former being lightened first to get her over the bar. Here, similar to the custom in the ports of China, an officer belonging to the sultan went on board and measured the ships.

Voyagers or travellers who visit strange countries generally find or think it necessary to be wary and circumspect: mercantile voyagers are on the watch for occasions of profit, and the inquisitiveness of men of observation will be regarded with suspicion ; all which, however familiarity of manners may be assumed, keeps cordiality at a distance, and causes them to continue strangers. The present visitors were differently circumstanced and of different character : their pursuits at Mindanao were neither to profit by trade nor to make observation. Long confined with pockets full of money which they were impatient to exchange for enjoyment, with minds little troubled by considerations of economy, they at once entered into familiar intercourse with the natives, who were gained almost as much by the freedom of their manners as by their presents, and with whom they immediately became intimates and inmates. The same happened to Drake and his companions when, returning enriched with spoil from the South Sea, they stopped at the island Java; and we read no instance of Europeans arriving at such sociable and friendly intercourse with any of the natives of India, as they became with the people of Java during the short time they remained there, except in the similarly circumstanced instance of the crew of the "Cygnet" among the Mindanayans.

By the length of their stay in Mindanao Dampier was enabled to enter largely into descriptions of the natives and of the country, and he has related many entertaining particulars concerning them. Those only in which the buccaneers were interested will be noticed here.

The buccaneers were at first prodigal in their gifts. When any of them went on shore they were welcomed and invited to the houses, and were courted to form

particular attachments. Among many nations of the
East a custom has been found to prevail, according to
which a stranger is expected to choose some individual
native to be his friend or comrade ; and a connection
so formed, and confirmed with presents, is regarded, if
not as sacred, with such high respect, that it is held
most dishonourable to break it. The visitor is at all
times afterwards welcome to his comrade's house.
The tayoship, with the ceremony of exchanging names,
among the South Sea islanders is a bond of fellowship
of the same nature. The people of Mindanao enlarged
and refined upon this custom, and allowed to the
stranger a pagally or platonic friend of the other sex.
The wives of the richest men may be chosen, and she is
permitted to converse with her pagally in public. " In
a short time," say Dampier, " several of our men, such
as had good clothes and store of gold, had a comrade
or two, and as many pagallies." Some of the crew
hired, and some purchased houses, in which they lived
with their comrades and pagallies, and with a train of
servants, as long as their means held out. " Many of
our squires," continues Dampier, " were in no long
time eased of the trouble of counting their money. This
created a division of the crew into two parties, that is to
say, of those who had money and those who had none.
As the latter party increased, they became dissatisfied
and unruly for want of action, and continually urged the
captain to go to sea ; which not being speedily complied
with, they sold the ships' stores and the merchants'
goods to procure arrack." Those whose money held
out were not without their troubles. The Mindanayans were a people deadly in their resentments.

Whilst the "Cygnet" lay at Mindanao sixteen buccaneers were buried, most of whom, Dampier says, died by poison. "The people of Mindanao are expert at poisoning, and will do it upon small occasions. Nor did our men want for giving offence, either by rogueries or by familiarities with their women, even before their husbands' faces. They have poisons which are slow and lingering, for some who were poisoned at Mindanao did not die till many months after."

Towards the end of the year they began to make preparation for sailing. It was then discovered that the bottom of the tender was eaten through by worms in such a manner that she would scarcely swim longer in port, and could not possibly be made fit for sea. The "Cygnet" was protected by a sheathing which covered her bottom, the worms not being able to penetrate farther than to the hair which was between the sheathing and the main plank.

In the beginning of January (1687) the "Cygnet" was removed to without the bar of the river. Whilst she lay there, and when Captain Swan was on shore, his journal was accidentally left out, and thereby liable to the inspection of the crew, some of whom had the curiosity to look in it, and found there the misconduct of several individuals on board noted down in a manner that seemed to threaten an after-reckoning. This discovery increased the discontents against Swan to such a degree that when he heard of it he did not dare to trust himself on board, and the discontented party took advantage of his absence and got the ship under sail. Captain Swan sent on board Mr. Harthope, one of the supercargoes, to see if he could effect a reconciliation. The principal mutineers showed to Mr. Harthope the captain's journal, "and repeated to him all his ill actions, and they desired that he would take the command of the ship ; but he refused, and desired them to tarry a little longer whilst he went on shore and communed with the captain, and he did not question but all differences would be reconciled. They said they would wait till two o'clock ; but at four o'clock, Mr. Harthope not having returned, and no boat being seen coming from the shore, they made sail and put to sea with the ship, leaving their commander and thirty-six of the crew at Mindanao." Dampier was among those who went in the ship, but he disclaims having had any share in the mutiny.

CHAPTER XXI.

*The "Cygnet" departs from Mindanao. At the Ponghou
Isles. At the Five Islands. Dampier's account
of the Five Islands. They are named the Bashee
Islands.*

IT was on the 14th of January the "Cygnet"
sailed from before the river Mindanao. The
crew chose one John Reed, a Jamaica man, for
their captain. They steered westward along the
coast of the south side of the island, "which here
tends west by south, the land of a good height,
with high hills in the country". The 15th
they were abreast a town named Chambongo (in
the charts Samboangan), which Dampier reckoned
to be thirty leagues distant from the river of Mindanao. The Spaniards had formerly a fort there,
and it is said to be a good harbour. "At the
distance of two or three leagues from the coast
are many small low islands or keys, and two or three
leagues to the southward of these keys is a long
island stretching north-east and south-west about
twelve leagues." *

* Dampier, vol. i. chap. 14. The long island is named Basseelan
in the charts, but the shape there given it does not agree well with
Dampier's description.

When they were past the south-west part of Mindanao they sailed northward towards Manilla, plundering the country vessels that came in their way. What was seen here of the coasts is noticed slightly and with uncertainty. They met two Mindanao vessels laden with silks and calicoes; and near Manilla they took some Spanish vessels, one of which had a cargo of rice.

From the Philippine Islands they went to the island Pulo Condore, where two of the men who had been poisoned at Mindanao died. "They were opened by the surgeon, in compliance with their dying request, and their livers were found black, light, and dry, like pieces of cork."

From Pulo Condore they went cruising to the Gulf of Siam and to different parts of the China seas. What their success was Dampier did not think proper to tell, for it would not admit of being palliated under the term "buccaneering". Among their better projects and contrivances one, which could only have been undertaken by men confident in their own seamanship and dexterity, was to search at the Prata Island and shoal for treasure which had been wrecked there, the recovery of which no one had ever before ventured to attempt. In pursuit of this scheme they unluckily fell too far to leeward, and were unable to beat up against the wind.

In July they went to the Ponghou Islands, expecting to find there a port which would be a safe retreat. On the 20th of that month they anchored at one of the islands, where they found a large town and a tartar garrison. This was not a place where they could rest with ease and security. Having the wind at south-west, they again got under sail, and directed their course to look for some islands which in the charts were laid down between Formosa and Luconia without any name, but marked with the figure 5 to denote their number. These buccaneers, or rather pirates, had no other information concerning the five islands than seeing them on the charts, and hoped to find them without inhabitants.

Dampier's account of the five islands would lose in many respects if given in any other than his own words, which, therefore, are here transcribed :—

" August the 6th we made the islands ; the wind was at south, and we fetched in with the westernmost, which is the largest, on which we saw goats, but could not get anchor-ground, therefore we stood over to others about three leagues from this, and the next forenoon anchored in a small bay on the east side of the easternmost island in fifteen fathoms, a cable's length from the shore ; and before our sails were furled we had a hundred small boats aboard with three, four, and some with six men in them. There were three large towns on the shore within the distance of a league. Most of our people being aloft (for we had been forced to turn in close with all sail abroad, and when we anchored furled all at once) and our deck being soon full of Indian natives, we were at first alarmed and began to get our small-arms ready ; but they were very quiet, only they picked up such old iron as they found upon our deck. At last one of our men perceived one of them taking an iron pin out of a gun-carriage and laid hold of him, upon which he bawled out and the rest leaped into their boats or overboard, and they all made away for the shore. But when we perceived their fright we made much of him we had in hold, and gave him a small piece of iron, with which we let him go, and he immediately leaped overboard and swam to his consorts, who hovered near the ship to see the issue. Some of the boats came presently aboard again, and they were always afterward very honest and civil. We, presently after this, sent our canoe on shore, and they made the crew welcome with a drink they call 'bashee,' and they sold us some hogs. We bought a fat goat for an old iron hoop, a hog of seventy or eighty pounds' weight for two or three pounds of iron, and their 'bashee' drink and roots for old nails or bullets. Their hogs were very sweet, but many were measled. We filled fresh water here at a curious brook close by the ship.

"We lay here till the 12th, when we weighed to seek for a better anchoring place. We plied to windward, and passed between the south end of this island and the north end of another island south of this. These islands were both full of inhabitants, but there was no good riding. We stopped a tide under the southern island. The tide runs there very strong, the flood to the north, and it rises and falls eight feet. It was the 15th day of the month before we found a place we might anchor at and careen, which was at another island not so big as either of the former.

"We anchored near the north-east part of this smaller island, against a small sandy bay, in seven fathoms' clean hard sand, a quarter of a mile from the shore. We presently set up a tent on shore, and

every day some of us went to the towns of the natives,
and were kindly entertained by them.   Their boats
also came on board to traffic 'with us every day; so that,
besides provision for present use, we bought and
salted seventy or eighty good fat hogs, and laid up a
good stock of potatoes and yams.

" These islands lie in 20° 20' north.*   As they are
laid down in the charts marked only with a figure of
5, we gave them what names we pleased.   The
Dutchmen who were among us named the westernmost, which is the largest, the Prince of Orange's
Island.   It is seven or eight leagues long, about two
leagues wide, and lies almost north and south.
Orange Island was not inhabited.   It is high land, flat
and even at the top, with steep cliffs against the sea ;
for which reason we could not go ashore there, as we
did on all the rest.

" The island where we first anchored we called the
Duke of Grafton's Isle, having married my wife out of
his duchess's family and leaving her at Arlington
House at my going abroad.   Grafton Isle is about
four leagues long, stretching north and south, and one
and a half wide.

" The other great island our seamen called the Duke
of Monmouth's Island.   It is about three leagues long,
and a league wide.

" The two smaller islands, which lie between Monmouth and the south end of Orange Island : the
westernmost, which is the smaller, we called Goat

* M. de Surville in 1769, and much more lately Captain A.
Murray, of the English East India Company's service, found the
south end of Monmouth Island to be in 20° 17' north.

Island, from the number of goats we saw there. The easternmost, at which we careened, our men unanimously called Bashee Island, because of the plentiful quantity of that liquor which we drank there every day. This drink, called 'bashee,' the natives make with the juice of the sugar-cane, to which they put some small blackberries. It is well boiled and then put into great jars, in which it stands three or four days to ferment. Then it settles clear, and is presently fit to drink. This is an excellent liquor, strong, and I believe wholesome, and much like our English beer both in colour and taste. Our men drank briskly of it during several weeks, and were frequently drunk with it, and never sick in consequence. The natives sold it to us very cheap, and from the plentiful use of it our men called all these islands the Bashee Islands.

"To the northward of the five islands are two high rocks." [These rocks are not inserted in Dampier's manuscript chart, and only one of them in the published chart; whence is to be inferred that the other was beyond the limit of the chart.]

"These islanders are short, squat people, generally round-visaged, with thick eyebrows; their eyes of a hazel colour, small, yet bigger than those of the Chinese; they have short, low noses; their teeth white; their hair black, thick, and lank, which they wear short; their skins are of a dark copper-colour. They wear neither hat, cap, nor turban to keep off the sun. The men had a cloth about their waist, and the women wore short cotton petticoats which reached below the knee. These people had iron; but whence it came we knew not. The boats they build are much after the fashion of our Deal yawls, but smaller; and every man has a boat, which he builds himself. They have also large boats which will carry forty or fifty men each.

"They are neat and cleanly in their persons, and are withal the quietest and civilest people I ever met with. I could never perceive them to be angry one with another. I have admired to see twenty or thirty boats aboard our ship at a time, all quiet, and endeavouring to help each other on occasion; and if cross accidents happened, they caused no noise nor appearance of distaste. When any of us came to their houses they would entertain us with such things as their houses or plantations would afford; and if they had no 'bashee' at home would buy of their neighbours, and sit down and drink freely with us; yet neither then nor sober could I ever perceive them to be out of humour.

"I never observed them to worship anything; they had no idols, neither did I perceive that one man was of greater power than another: they seemed to be all equal, only every man ruling in his own house, and children respecting and honouring their parents. Yet it is probable they have some law or custom by which they are governed; for whilst we lay here we saw a young man buried alive in the earth, and it was for theft as far as we could understand from them. There was a great deep hole dug, and abundance of people came to the place to take their last farewell of him. One woman particularly made great lamentations, and took off the condemned person's ear-rings. We supposed her to be his mother. After he had taken leave of her and some others, he was put into the pit and covered over with earth. He did not struggle, but yielded very quietly to his punishment, and they crammed the earth close upon him and stifled him.

"Monmouth and Grafton Isles are very hilly, with steep precipices; and, whether from fear of pirates, of foreign enemies, or factions among their own clans, their towns and villages are built on the most steep and inaccessible of these precipices, and on the sides of rocky hills; so that in some of their towns three or four rows of houses stand one above another in places so steep that they go up to the first row with a ladder, and in the same manner ascend to every street upwards. Grafton and Monmouth Islands are very thick set with these hills and towns. The two small islands are flat and even, except that on Bashee Island there is one steep craggy hill. The reason why Orange Island has no inhabitants, though the largest and as fertile as any of these islands, I take to be because it is level and exposed to attack; and for the same reason Goat Island, being low and even, hath no inhabitants. We saw no houses built on any open plain ground. Their houses are but small and low, the roofs about eight feet high.

"The valleys are well watered with brooks of fresh water. The fruits of these islands are plantains, bananas, pine-apples, pumpkins, yams and other roots, and sugar-canes, which last they use mostly for their 'bashee' drink. Here are plenty of goats and hogs, and but a few fowls. They had no grain of any kind.

"On the 26th of September our ship was driven to sea by a strong gale at north by west, which made her drag her anchors. Six of the crew were on shore, who could not get on board. The weather continued stormy till the 29th. The 1st of October we recovered the anchorage from which we had been driven, and immediately the natives brought on board our six seamen, who related that after the ship was out of sight the natives were more kind to them than they had been before, and tried to persuade them to cut their hair short, as was the custom among themselves, offering to each of them if they would, a young woman to wife, a piece of land, and utensils fit for a planter. These offers were declined, but the natives were not the less kind ; on which account we made them a present of three whole bars of iron."

Two days after this reciprocation of kindness the buccaneers bade farewell to these friendly islanders.

CHAPTER XXII.

*The " Cygnet ".   At the Philippines, Celebes, and
Timor.   On the coast of New Holland.   End
of the " Cygnet ".*

FROM the Bashee Islands the " Cygnet " steered
at first south-south-west, with the wind at west,
and on that course passed "close to the eastward of
certain small islands that lie just by the north end of
the island Luconia ".

They went on southward by the east of the
Philippine Islands.   On the 14th they were near a
small, low, woody island, which Dampier reckoned to
lie east 20 leagues from the south-east end of Mindanao.   The 16th they anchored between the small
islands Candigar and Sarangan ; but afterwards found
at the north-west end of the eastern of the two islands
a good and convenient small cove, into which they
went and careened the ship.   They heard here that
Captain Swan and those of the crew left with him
were still at the city of Mindanao.

The " Cygnet " and her restless crew continued
wandering about the eastern seas, among the Philippine Islands, to Celebes, and to Timor.   December
the 27th, steering a southerly course, they passed by
the west side of Rotte, and by another small island

near the south-west end of Timor. Dampier says :
" Being now clear of all the islands, and having
the wind at west and west by north, we steered
away south-south-west,* intending to touch at New
Holland to see what that country would afford
us ".

The wind blew fresh, and kept them under low sail :
sometimes with only their courses set, and sometimes
with reefed topsails. The 31st at noon their latitude
was 13° 20' south. About ten o'clock at night they
tacked and stood to the northward for fear of a shoal,
which their charts laid down in the track they were
sailing, and in latitude 13° 50' south. At three in the
morning they tacked again and stood south by west
and south-south-west. As soon as it was light they
perceived a low island and shoal right ahead. This
shoal, by their reckoning, is in latitude 13° 50', and
lies south by west from the west end of Timor.† " It
is a small spit of sand appearing just above the water's
edge, with several rocks about it eight or ten feet
high above water. It lies in a triangular form, each
side in extent about a league and a half. We could
not weather it, so bore away round the east end and
stood again to the southward, passing close by it and
sounding, but found no ground. This shoal is laid
down in our drafts not above sixteen or twenty

* Manuscript journal.

† In the printed *Voyage* the shoal is mistakenly said to lie south
by west from the east end of Timor. The manuscript journal, and
the track of the ship as marked in the charts to the first volume of
Dampier's *Voyages*, agree in making the place of the shoal south by
west from the west end of Timor ; whence they had last taken their
departure, and from which their reckoning was kept.

leagues from New Holland; but we ran afterwards sixty leagues making a course due south before we fell in with the coast of New Holland, which we did on the 4th January in latitude 16° 50′ south." Dampier remarks here that, unless they were set westward by a current, the coast of New Holland must have been laid down too far westward in the charts; but he thought it not probable that they were deceived by currents, because the tides on that part of the coast were found very regular, the flood setting towards the north-east.

The coast here was low and level, with sand-banks. The "Cygnet" sailed along the shore north-east by east twelve leagues, when she came to a point of land with an island so near it that she could not pass between. A league before coming to this point, that is to say, westward of the point, was a shoal which ran out from the mainland a league. Beyond the point the coast ran east and east-southerly, making a deep bay with many islands in it. On the 5th they anchored in this bay, about two miles from the shore, in twenty-nine fathoms. The 6th they ran nearer in and anchored about four miles eastward of the point before-mentioned, and a mile distant from the nearest shore, in eighteen fathoms' depth, the bottom clean sand.

People were seen on the land, and a boat was sent to endeavour to make acquaintance with them, but the natives did not wait. Their habitations were sought for, but none were found. The soil here was dry and sandy, yet fresh water was found by digging for it. They warped the ship into a small sandy cove at a spring tide as far as she would float, and at low water she was high aground, the sand being dry beyond her for half a mile ; for the sea rose and fell here about five fathoms perpendicularly.   During the neap tides the ship lay wholly aground, the sea not approaching nearer than within a hundred yards of her. Turtle and manatee were struck here, as much every day as served the whole crew.

Boats went from the ship to different parts of the bay in search of provisions.   For a considerable time they met with no inhabitants ; but at length a party going to one of the islands saw there about forty natives—men, women, and children.   " The island was too small for them to conceal themselves.   The men at first made threatening motions with lances and wooden swords, but a musket was fired to scare them and they stood still.   The women snatched up their infants and ran away howling, their other children running after squeaking and bawling.   Some invalids who could not get away lay by the fire making a doleful noise, but after a short time they grew sensible that no mischief was intended them, and they became quiet."   Those who had fled soon returned, and some presents made, succeeded in rendering them familiar.   Dampier relates : " We filled some of our barrels with water at wells which had been dug by the natives, but it being troublesome to get to our boats, we thought to have made these men help us, to which end we put on them some old ragged clothes, thinking this finery would make them willing to be employed.   We then brought our new servants to the wells and put a barrel on the shoulders of each, but all the signs we could make were to no purpose, for they stood like statues staring at one another and grinning like so many monkeys. These poor creatures seem not accustomed to carry burthens, and I believe one of our ship-boys of ten years old would carry as much as one of their men. So we were forced to carry our water ourselves, and they very fairly put off the clothes again and laid them down. They had no great liking to them at first, neither did they seem to admire anything that we had."

"The inhabitants of this country are the most miserable people in the world. The Hottentots, compared with them, are gentlemen. They have no houses, animals, or poultry. Their persons are tall, straight-bodied, thin, with long limbs : they have great heads, round foreheads, and great brows. Their eyelids are always half closed to keep the flies out of their eyes, for they are so troublesome here that no fanning will keep them from one's face, so that from their infancy they never open their eyes as other people do ; and, therefore, they cannot see far, unless they hold up their heads as if they were looking at something over them. They have great bottle noses, full lips, wide mouths ; the two fore-teeth of their upper jaw are wanting in all of them ; neither have they any beards. Their hair is black, short, and curled, and their skins coal-black like that of the negroes in Guinea. Their only food is fish, and they constantly search for them at low water, and they make little weirs or dams with stones across little coves of the sea. At one time our boat, being among the islands seeking for game, espied a drove of these people swimming from one island to another, for they have neither boats, canoes, nor bark-logs. We always gave them victuals when we met any of them. But after the first time of our being among them they did not stir for our coming."

It deserves to be remarked to the credit of human nature that these poor people, in description the most wretched of mankind in all respects, that we read of, stood their ground for the defence of their women and children, against the shock and first surprise at hearing the report of firearms.

The "Cygnet" remained at this part of New Holland till the 12th of March, and then sailed westward for the west coast of Sumatra.

On the 28th they fell in with a small, woody, un-inhabited island in latitude 10° 20′ south, and, by Dampier's reckoning, 12° 6′ of longitude from the part of New Holland at which they had been. There was too great depth of water everywhere round the island for anchorage. A landing-place was found near the south-west point, and on the island a small brook of fresh water, but the surf would not admit of any to be taken off to the ship. Large craw-fish, boobies, and men-of-war birds were caught, as many as served for a meal for the whole crew.

April the 7th they made the coast of Sumatra. Shortly after, at the Nicobar Islands, Dampier and some others quitted the "Cygnet". Read, the captain, and those who yet remained with him continued their piratical cruising in the Indian Seas, till, after a variety of adventures and changes of commanders, they put into St. Augustine's Bay, in the island of

Madagascar, by which time the ship was in so crazy a condition that the crew abandoned her and she sunk at her anchors. Some of the men embarked on board European ships, and some engaged themselves in the service of the petty princes of that island.

Dampier returned to England in 1691.

CHAPTER XXIII.

French buccaneers under François Grogniet and Le Picard, to the death of Grogniet.

HAVING accompanied the "Cygnet" to her end, the history must again be taken back to the breaking up of the general confederacy of buccaneers, which took place at the island Quibo, to give a connected narrative of the proceedings of the French adventurers from that period to their quitting the South Sea.

Three hundred and forty-one French buccaneers (or, to give them their due, privateers, war then existing between France and Spain) separated from Edward Davis in July, 1685, choosing for their leader Captain François Grogniet.

They had a small ship, two small barques, and some large canoes, which were insufficient to prevent their being incommoded for want of room, and the ship was so ill-provided with sails as to be disqualified for cruising at sea. They were likewise scantily furnished with provisions, and necessity for a long time confined their enterprises to the places on the coast of New Spain in the neighbourhood of Quibo. The towns of Pueblo Nuevo, Ria Lexa, Nicoya, and others were plundered by them, some more than once, by which they obtained provisions, and little of other plunder except prisoners, from whom they extorted ransom either in provisions or money.

In November they attacked the town of Ria Lexa. Whilst in the port a Spanish officer delivered to them a letter from the vicar-general of the province of Costa Rica, written to inform them that a truce for twenty years had been concluded between France and Spain. The vicar-general, therefore, required of them to forbear committing farther hostility, and offered to give them safe conduct overland to the North Sea, and a passage to Europe in the galleons of his Catholic Majesty to as many as should desire it. This offer not according with the inclinations of the adventurers, they declined accepting it, and, without entering into enquiry, professed to disbelieve the intelligence.

November the 14th they were near the Point Burica. Lussan says : " We admired the pleasant appearance of the land, and, among other things, a walk or avenue, formed by five rows of cocoa-nut trees, which extended in continuation along the coast fifteen leagues with as much regularity as if they had been planted by line ".

In the beginning of January, 1686, two hundred and thirty of these buccaneers went in canoes from Quibo against Chiriquita, a small Spanish town on the continent, between Point Burica and the island Quibo. Chiriquita is situated up a navigable river, and at some distance from the sea-coast. " Before this river are eight or ten islands, and shoals on which the sea breaks at low water ; but there are channels between them through which ships may pass." *

* *A Voyage by Edward Cooke*, vol. i. p. 371. London, 1712.

The buccaneers arrived in the night at the entrance of the river, unperceived by the Spaniards; but, being without guides and in the dark, they mistook and landed on the wrong side of the river. They were two days occupied in discovering the right way, but were so well concealed by the woods that at daylight on the morning of the third day they came upon the town and surprised the whole of the inhabitants, who, says Lussan, had been occupied the last two days in disputing which of them should keep watch and go the rounds.

Lussan relates here that himself and five others were decoyed to pursue a few Spaniards to a distance from the town, where they were suddenly attacked by one hundred and twenty men. He and his companions however, he says, played their parts an hour and a half "en vrai Flibustiers," and laid thirty of the enemy on the ground, by which time they were relieved by the arrival of some of their friends. They set fire to the town, and got ransom for their prisoners: in what the ransom consisted Lussan has not said.

Their continuance in one station at length prevailed on the Spaniards to collect and send a force against them. They had taken some pains to instil into the Spaniards a belief that they intended to erect fortifications and establish themselves at Quibo. Their view in this it is not easy to conjecture, unless it was to discourage their prisoners from pleading poverty, for they obliged those from whom they could not get money to labour and to procure bricks and material for building to be sent for their ransom. On the 27th of January a small fleet of Spanish

vessels approached the island of Quibo. The buccaneer ship was without cannon, and lay near the
entrance of a river which had only depth sufficient
for their small vessels. The buccaneers, therefore,
took out of the ship all that could be of use, and ran
her aground, and with their small barques and canoes
took a station in the river. The Spaniards set fire to
the abandoned ship, and remained by her to collect
the iron-work; but they showed no disposition to
attack the French in the river, and on the 1st of
February they departed from the island.

The buccaneers, having lost their ship, set hard to
work to build themselves small vessels. In this month
of February fourteen of their number died by sickness
and accidents.

They had projected an attack upon Granada, but
want of present subsistence obliged them to seek
supply nearer, and a detachment was sent with that
view to the river of Pueblo Nuevo. Some vessels of
the Spanish flotilla which had lately been at Quibo
were lying at anchor in the river, which the flibustiers
mistook for a party of the English buccaneers. In
this belief they went within pistol-shot and hailed, and
were then undeceived by receiving for answer a volley
of musketry. They fired on the Spaniards in return,
but were obliged to retreat, and in this affair they lost
four men killed outright, and between thirty and forty
were wounded.

Preparatory to their intended expedition against
Granada, they agreed upon some regulations for preserving discipline and order, the principal articles of
which were that cowardice, theft, drunkenness, or

disobedience should be punished with forfeiture of all share of booty taken.

On the evening of the 22nd they were near the entrance of the Gulf of Nicoya, in a little fleet, consisting of two small barques, a row galley and nine large canoes. A tornado came on in the night which dispersed them a good deal. At daylight they were surprised at counting thirteen sail in company, and before they discovered which was the strange vessel five more sail came in sight. They soon joined each other, and the strangers proved to be a party of the buccaneers of whom Townley was the head.

Townley had parted company from Swan not quite two months before. His company consisted of 115 men, embarked in a ship and five large canoes. Townley had advanced with his canoes along the coast before his ship to seek provisions, he and his men being no better off in that respect than Grogniet and his followers. On their meeting, as above related, the French did not forget Townley's former overbearing conduct towards them : they, however, limited their vengeance to a short triumph. Lussan says : "We, now finding ourselves the strongest, called to mind the ill offices he had done us, and to show him our resentment we made him and his men in the canoes with him our prisoners. We then boarded his ship, of which we made ourselves masters, and pretended that we would keep her. We let them remain some time under this apprehension, after which we made them see that we were more honest and civilised people than they were, and that we would not profit by our advantage over them to revenge ourselves ;

for, after keeping possession about four or five hours,
we returned to them their ship and all that had
been taken from them." The English showed their
sense of this moderation by offering to join in the
attack on Granada, which offer was immediately
accepted.

The city of Granada is situated in a valley bordering on the lake of Nicaragua, and is about sixteen
leagues distant from Leon. The buccaneers were provided with guides, and to avoid giving the Spaniards
suspicion of their design Townley's ship and the two
barques were left at anchor near Cape Blanco, whilst the
force destined to be employed against Granada proceeded in the canoes to the place at which it was proposed to land, directions being left with the ship and
barques to follow in due time.

The 7th of April 345 buccaneers landed from the
canoes about twenty leagues north-westward of Cape
Blanco, and began their march conducted by the guides,
who led them through woods and unfrequented ways.
They travelled night and day till the 9th, in hopes to
reach the city before they were discovered by the inhabitants, or their having landed should be known by
the Spaniards.

The province of Nicaragua, in which Granada
stands, is reckoned one of the most fertile in New
Spain. The distance from where the buccaneers
landed, to the city, may be estimated about sixty
miles. Yet they expected to come upon it by surprise;
and, in fact, they did travel the greater part of the way
without being seen by any inhabitant. Such a mark
of the state of the population corresponds with all the

accounts given of the wretched tyranny exercised by the Spaniards over the nations they have conquered.

The buccaneers, however, were discovered in their second day's march by people who were fishing in a river, some of whom immediately posted off with the intelligence. The Spaniards had some time before been advertised by a deserter that the buccaneers designed to attack Granada, but they were known to entertain designs upon so many places, and to be so fluctuating in their plans, that the Spaniards could only judge from certain intelligence where most to guard against their attempts.

On the night of the 9th fatigue and hunger obliged the buccaneers to halt at a sugar plantation four leagues distant from the city. One man, unable to keep up with the rest, had been taken prisoner. The morning of the 10th they marched on, and from an eminence over which they passed had a view of the lake of Nicaragua, on which were seen two vessels sailing from the city. These vessels the buccaneers afterwards learnt were freighted with the richest movables that at short notice the inhabitants had been able to embark, to be conveyed for security to an island in the lake which was two leagues distant from the city.

Granada was large and spacious, with magnificent churches and well-built houses. The ground is destitute of water, and the town is supplied from the lake; nevertheless there were many large sugar plantations in the neighbourhood, some of which were like small towns, and had handsome churches. Granada was not regularly fortified, but had a place of arms surrounded with a wall, in the nature of a citadel, and furnished

with cannon. The great church was within this en-
closed part of the town. The buccaneers arrived about
two o'clock in the afternoon, and immediately assaulted
the place of arms, which they carried with the loss of
four men killed and eight wounded, most of them
mortally. The first act of the victors, according to
Lussan, was to sing *Te Deum* in the great church ;
and the next, to plunder. Provisions, military stores,
and a quantity of merchandise were found in the town,
the latter of which was of little or no value to the
captors. The next day they sent to enquire if the
Spaniards would ransom the town and the merchandise.
It had been rumoured that the buccaneers would be
unwilling to destroy Granada because they proposed
at some future period to make it their baiting place in
returning to the North Sea, and the Spaniards scarcely
condescended to make answer to the demand for ransom. The buccaneers in revenge set fire to the houses.
" If we could have found boats," says Lussan, " to have
gone on the lake, and could have taken the two vessels
laden with the riches of Granada, we should have
thought this a favourable opportunity for returning to
the West Indies."

On the 15th they left Granada to return to the
coast, which journey they performed in the most
leisurely manner. They took with them a large
cannon, with oxen to draw it, and some smaller guns,
which they laid upon mules. The weather was hot
and dry, and the road so clouded with dust as almost
to stifle both men and beasts. Sufficient provision of
water had not been made for the journey, and the oxen
all died. The cannon was of course left on the road.

Towards the latter part of the journey, water and refreshments were procured at some villages and houses, the inhabitants of which furnished supplies as a condition that their dwellings should be spared.

On the 26th they arrived at the sea and embarked in their vessels, taking on board with them a Spanish priest whom the Spaniards would not redeem by delivering up their buccaneer prisoner. Most of the men wounded in the Granada expedition died of cramps.

The 28th they came upon Ria Lexa unexpectedly, and made one hundred of the inhabitants prisoners. By such means little could be gained more than present subsistence, and that was rendered very precarious by the Spaniards removing their cattle from the coast. It was, therefore, determined to put an end to their unprofitable continuance in one place, but they could not agree where next to go. All the English, and one half of the French, were for sailing to the Bay of Panama. The other half of the French, 148 in number, with Grogniet at their head, declared for trying their fortunes north-westward. Division was made of the vessels and provisions. The whole money which the French had acquired by their depredations amounted to little more than 7000 dollars, and this sum they generously distributed among those of their countrymen who had been lamed or disabled.

May the 19th they parted company. Those bound for the Bay of Panama, of whom Townley appears to have been regarded as the head, had a ship, a barque, and some large canoes. Townley proposed an attack on the town of Lavelia or La Villia, at which place the treasure from the Lima ships had been

landed in the preceding year, and this proposal was
approved.

Tornadoes and heavy rains kept them among the
Keys of Quibo till the middle of June. On the 20th
of that month they arrived off the Punta Mala, and
during the day they lay at a distance from the land
with sails furled. At night the principal part of their
force made for the land in the canoes, but they had
been deceived in the distance. Finding that they
could not reach the river which leads to Lavelia before
day, they took down the sails and masts, and went to
three leagues' distance from the land, where they lay
all the day of the 21st. Lussan, who was of this party
of buccaneers, says that they were obliged to practise
the same manœuvre on the day following. In the
middle of the night of the 22nd 160 buccaneers landed
from the canoes at the entrance of the river. They
were some hours in marching to Lavelia, yet the town
was surprised and above three hundred of the inhabitants made prisoners. This was in admirable con-
formity with the rest of the management of the
Spaniards. The fleet from Lima, laden with treasure
intended for Panama, had more than a year before
landed the treasure and rich merchandise at Lavelia,
as a temporary measure of security against the buccaneers, suited to the occasion. The government at
Panama and the other proprietors would not be at the
trouble of getting it removed to Panama, except in such
portions as might be required by some present convenience, and allowed a great part to remain in Lavelia,
a place of no defence, although during the whole time
buccaneers had been on the coast of Veragua, or Nica-

ragua, to whom it now became an easy prey, through indolence and a total want of vigilance, as well in the proprietors as in those whom they employed to guard it.

Three Spanish barques were riding in the river, one of which the crews sank, and so dismantled the others that no use could be made of them; but the buccaneers found two boats in serviceable condition at a landing-place a quarter of a league below the town. The riches they now saw in their possession equalled their most sanguine expectations, and, if secured, they thought would compensate for all former disappointments. The merchandise in Lavelia was estimated in value at a million and a half of piastres. The gold and silver found there amounted only to 15,000 piastres.

The first day of being masters of Lavelia was occupied by the buccaneers in making assortments of the most valuable articles of the merchandise. The next morning they loaded eighty horses with bales, and a guard of eighty men went with them to the landing-place where the two boats above-mentioned were lying. In the way one man of this escort was taken by the Spaniards. The two prize boats were by no means large enough to carry all the goods which the buccaneers proposed to take from Lavelia, and on that account directions had been despatched to the people in the canoes at the entrance of the river to advance up towards the town. These directions they attempted to execute; but the land bordering the river was woody, which exposed the canoes to the fire of a concealed enemy, and after losing one man they desisted from advancing. For the same cause it was thought proper not to send off the two loaded boats without a strong guard, and they did not move during this day. The buccaneers sent a letter to the Spanish alcade to demand if he would ransom the town, the merchandise, and the prisoners, but the alcade refused to treat with them. In the afternoon, therefore, they set fire to the town and marched to the landing-place where the two boats lay, and there rested for the night.

The river of Lavelia is broad but shallow. Vessels of forty tons can go a league and a half within the entrance. The landing-place is yet a league and a half farther up, and the town is a quarter of a mile from the landing-place.*

On the morning of the 25th the two boats, laden as deep as was safe, began to fall down the river, having on board nine men to conduct them. The main body of the buccaneers at the same time marched along the bank on one side of the river, for their protection. A body of Spaniards, screened by the woods and unseen by the buccaneers, kept pace with them on the other side of the river at a small distance within the bank. The buccaneers had marched about a league, and the boats had descended as far, when they came to a point of land on which the trees and underwood grew so thick as not to be penetrated without some labour and expense of time, to which they did not choose to submit, but preferred making a circuit which took them about a quarter of a mile from the river. The Spaniards on the opposite side were on the watch, and not slow in taking advantage of their absence. They came to the bank, whence they fired upon the men in the laden

* *Raveneau de Lussan*, p. 117.

boats, four of whom they killed and wounded one ; the other four abandoned the boats and escaped into the thicket. The Spaniards took possession of the boats, and finding there the wounded buccaneer, they cut off his head and fixed it on a stake, which they set up by the side of the river at a place by which the rest of the buccaneers would necessarily have to pass.

The main body of the buccaneers regained the side of the river in ignorance of what had happened, and, not seeing the boats, were for a time in doubt whether they were gone forward or were still behind. The first notice they received of their loss was from the men who had escaped from the boats, who made their way through the thicket and joined them.

Thus did this crew of buccaneers within a short space of time win by circumspection and adroitness and lose by negligence the richest booty they had ever made. If quitting the bank of the river had been a matter of necessity and unavoidable, there was nothing but idleness to prevent their conveying their plunder the remainder of the distance to their boats by land.

In making their way through the woods they found the rudder, sails, and other furniture of the Spanish barques in the river; the barques themselves were near at hand and the buccaneers embarked in them, but the flood-tide making they came to an anchor and lay still for the night.

The next morning as they descended the river they saw the boats which they had so richly freighted now cleared of their lading and broken to pieces, and near to their wreck was the head which the Spaniards had stuck up. This spectacle, added to the mortifying loss of their booty, threw the buccaneers into a frenzy, and they forthwith cut off the heads of four prisoners and set them on poles in the same place. In the passage down the river four more of the buccaneers were killed by the firing of the Spaniards from the banks.

The day after their retreat from the river of Lavelia a Spaniard went off to them to treat for the release of the prisoners, and they came to an agreement that 10,000 pieces of eight should be paid for their ransom. Some among them who had wives were permitted to go on shore that they might assist in procuring the money ; but on the 29th the same messenger again went off and acquainted them that the alcade major would not only not suffer the relations of the prisoners to send money for their ransom, but that he had arrested some of those whom the buccaneers had allowed to land. On receiving this report these savages without hesitation cut off the heads of two of their prisoners and delivered them to the messenger, to be carried to the alcade with their assurance that if the ransom did not speedily arrive the rest of the prisoners would be treated in the same manner. The next day the ransom was settled for the remaining prisoners, and for one of the captured barques, the Spaniards paying partly with money, partly with provisions and necessaries, and with the release of the buccaneer they had taken. In the agreement for the barque, the Spaniards required a note specifying that if the buccaneers again met her they should make prize only of the cargo and not of the vessel.

After the destruction of Lavelia it might be sup-

posed that the prepetrators of so much mischief would
not be allowed with impunity to remain in the Bay of
Panama; but such was the weakness or negligence of
the Spaniards that this small body of freebooters
continued several months in this same neighbourhood,
and at times under the very walls of the city. On
another point, however, the Spaniards were more
active, and with success; for they concluded a treaty
of peace and alliance with the Indians of the isthmus,
in consequence of which the passage overland
through the Darien country was no longer open to
the buccaneers, and some small parties of them who
attempted to travel across were intercepted and cut
off by the Spaniards, with the assistance of the
natives.

The Spaniards had at Panama a military corps,
distinguished by the appellation of Greeks, which was
composed of Europeans of different nations, not
natives of Spain. Among the atrocities committed
by the crew under Townley, they put to death one of
these Greeks, who was also commander of a Spanish
vessel, because on examining him for intelligence
they thought he endeavoured to deceive them; and, in
aggravation of the deed, Lussan relates the circumstance in the usual manner of his pleasantries: "We
paid him for his treachery by sending him to the other
world".

On the 20th August, as they were at anchor within
sight of the city of Panama, they observed boats
passing and repassing between some vessels and the
shore, and a kind of bustle which had the appearance of
an equipment. The next day the buccaneers anchored

near the island Taboga ; and there, on the morning of
the 22nd, they were attacked by three armed vessels from
Panama.   The Spaniards were provided with cannon,
and the battle lasted half the day, when, owing to an
explosion of gunpowder in one of the Spanish vessels,
the victory was decided in favour of the buccaneers.
Two of the three Spanish vessels were taken, as was
also one other which, during the fight, arrived from
Panama as a reinforcement.   In the last-mentioned
prize cords were found prepared for binding their
prisoners in the event of their being victorious, and
this the buccaneers deemed provocation sufficient for
them to slaughter the whole crew.   This battle,
so fatal to the Spaniards, cost the buccaneers only
one man killed outright and twenty-two wounded.
Townley was among the wounded.

Two of the prizes were immediately manned from
the canoes, the largest under the command of Le
Picard, who was the chief among the French of this
party.

They had many prisoners; and one was sent
with a letter to the president of Panama to demand
ransom for them, also medicines and dressings for
the wounded, and the release of five buccaneers who
they learnt were prisoners of the Spaniards.   The
medicines were sent, but the president would not
treat either of ransom or the release of the buccaneer
prisoners.   The buccaneers despatched a second
message to the president, in which they threatened
that if the five buccaneers were not immediately
delivered to them the heads of all the Spaniards in
their possession should be sent to him.   The president

paid little attention to this message, not believing
that such a threat would be executed ; but the bishop
of Panama, regarding what had recently happened at
Lavelia as an earnest of what the buccaneers were
capable of, was seriously alarmed. He wrote a letter
to them, which he sent by a special messenger, in
which he exhorted them in the mildest terms not to
shed the blood of innocent men, and promised, if they
would have patience, to exert his influence to procure
the release of the buccaneer prisoners. His letter
concluded with the following remarkable paragraph,
which shows the great hopes entertained by the
Roman Catholics respecting Great Britain during
the reign of King James II. " I have information," says the bishop, "to give you, that the
English are all become Roman Catholics, and that
there is now a Catholic church at Jamaica."

The good prelate's letter was pronounced by the
buccaneers to be void of truth and sincerity and an
insult to their understanding. They had already
received the price of blood, shed not in battle nor in
their own defence ; and now, devoting themselves to
their thirst for gain, they would not be diverted from
their sanguinary purpose, but came to the resolution
of sending the heads of twenty Spaniards to the
president, and with them a message purporting that,
if they did not receive a satisfactory answer to all their
demands by the 28th of the month, the heads of the
remaining prisoners should answer for it. Lussan
says: " The president's refusal obliged us, though with
some reluctance, to take the resolution to send him
twenty heads of his people in a canoe. This method

was indeed a little violent, but it was the only way to bring the Spaniards to reason." *

What they had resolved they put into immediate execution. The president of Panama was entirely overcome by their inhuman proceedings, and in the first shock and surprise he yielded without stipulation to all they had demanded. On the 28th the buccaneer prisoners (four Englishmen and one Frenchman) were delivered to them, with a letter from the president, who said he left to their own consciences the disposal of the Spanish prisoners yet remaining in their hands.

To render the triumph of cruelty and ferocity more complete, the buccaneers, in an answer to the president, charged the whole blame of what they had done to his obstinacy; in exchange for the five buccaneers they sent only twelve of their Spanish prisoners, and they demanded 20,000 pieces of eight as ransom of the remainder, which demand, however, they afterwards mitigated to half that sum and a supply of refreshments. On the 4th of September the ransom was paid, and the prisoners were released.

September the 9th the buccaneer commander, Townley, died of the wound he received in the last battle. The English and French buccaneers were faithful associates, but did not mix well as comrades. In a short time after Townley's death the English desired that a division should be made of the prize vessels, artillery, and stores, and that those of their nation should keep together in the same vessels: and

---

* "Ce moyen êtoit a la verité un peu violent, mais c'etoit l'unique pour mettre les Espagnols à la raison."

this was done, without other separation taking place at the time.

In November they left the Bay of Panama and sailed westward to their old station near the Point de Burica, where, by surprising small towns, villages, and farms, a business at which they had become extremely expert, they procured provisions, and, by the ransom of prisoners, some money.

In January (1687) they intercepted a letter from the Spanish commandant at Sonsonnate addressed to the president of Panama, by which they learned that Grogniet had been in Amapalla Bay, and that three of his men had been taken prisoners. The commandant remarked in his letter that the peace made with the Darien Indians, having cut off the retreat of the buccaneers, would drive them to desperation, and render them like so many mad dogs; he advised, therefore, that some means should be adopted to facilitate their retreat, that the Spaniards in the South Sea might again enjoy repose. " They have landed," he said, "in these parts ten or twelve times without knowing what they were seeking, but wheresoever they come they spoil and lay waste everything."

A few days after intercepting this letter they took prisoner a Spanish horseman. Lussan says : "We interrogated him with the usual ceremonies, that is to say, we gave him the torture, to make him tell us what we wanted to know ".

Many such villainies were undoubtedly committed by these banditti, more than appear in their narratives or than they dared to make known. Lussan, who writes a history of his voyage, not before the end of

the second year of his adventures in the South Sea,
relates that they put a prisoner to the torture; and it
would have appeared as an individual instance if he
had not, probably through inadvertence, acknowledged
it to have been their established practice. Lussan,
on his return to his native land, pretended to reputation and character, and he found countenance and
favour from his superiors; it is, therefore, to be presumed that he would suppress every transaction in
which he was a participator which he thought of too
deep a nature to be received by his patrons with indulgence. A circumstance which tended to make this
set of buccaneers worse than any that had preceded
them, was, its being composed of men of two nations
between which there has existed a constant jealousy
and emulation. They were each ambitious to outdo
the other in acts of daringness, and were thereby
instigated to every kind of excess.

On the 20th, near Caldera Bay, they met
Grogniet with sixty French buccaneers in three canoes.
Grogniet had parted from Townley at the head of 148
men. They had made several descents on the coast.
At the Bay of Amapalla they marched fourteen
leagues within the coast to a gold-mine, where they
took many prisoners and a small quantity of gold
Grogniet wished to return overland to the West-
Indian Sea, but the majority of his companions
were differently inclined, and eighty-five quitted him
and went to try their fortunes towards California.
Grogniet nevertheless persevered in the design, with the
remainder of his crew, to seek some part of the coast
of New Spain, thin of inhabitants, where they might

land unknown to the Spaniards and march without obstruction through the country to the shore of the Atlantic without other guide than a compass. The party they now met with prevailed on them to defer the execution of this project to a season of the year more favourable, and in the meantime to unite with them.

In February they set fire to the town of Nicoya. Their gains by these descents were so small that they agreed to leave the coast of New Spain and to go against Guayaquil; but on coming to this determination the English and the French fell into high dispute for the priority of choice in the prize vessels which they expected to take, insomuch that upon this difference they broke off partnership. Grogniet, however, and about fifty of the French, remained with the English, which made the whole number of that party 142 men, and they all embarked in one ship, the canoes not being safe for an open sea navigation. The other party numbered 162 men, all French, and embarked in a small ship and a *Barca longa*. The most curious circumstance attending this separation was, that both parties persevered in the design upon Guayaquil, without any proposal being made by either to act in concert. They sailed from the coast of New Spain near the end of February, not in company, but each using all their exertions to arrive first at the place of destination. They crossed the Equinoctial line separately, but afterwards at sea accidentally fell in company with each other again, and at this meeting they accommodated their differences and renewed their partnership.

April the 13th they were near Point Santa Elena, on the coast of Peru, and met there a prize vessel belonging to their old commander, Edward Davis, and his company, but which had been separated from him. She was laden with corn and wine, and eight of Davis's men had the care of her. They had been directed, in case of separation, to rendezvous at the island Plata; but the uncertainty of meeting Davis there, and the danger they should incur if they missed him, made them glad to join in the expedition against Guayaquil, and the provisions with which the vessel was laden made them welcome associates to the buccaneers engaged in it.

Their approach to the city of Guayaquil was conducted with the most practised circumspection and vigilance. On first getting sight of Point Santa Elena, they took in their sails and lay with them furled as long as there was daylight. In the night they pursued their course, keeping at a good distance from the land, till they were to the southward of the island Santa Clara. Two hundred and sixty men then (the 15th April) departed from the ships in canoes. They landed at Santa Clara, which was uninhabited, and at a part of the island Puna, distant from any habitation, proceeding only during the night time and lying in concealment during the day.

In the night of the 17th they approached the river Guayaquil. At daylight they were perceived by a guard on watch near the entrance, who lighted a fire as a signal to other guards stationed farther on, by whom, however, the signal was not observed. The buccaneers put as speedily as they could to the nearest land, and a party of the most alert made a circuit through the woods and surprised the guard at the first signal station before the alarm had spread farther. They stopped near the entrance till night. All day of the 19th they rested at an island in the river, and at night advanced again. Their intention was to have passed the town in their canoes and to have landed above it, where they would be the least expected, but the flood tide with which they ascended the river did not serve long enough for their purpose, and on the 20th, two hours before day, they landed a short distance below the town, towards which they began to march, but the ground was marshy and overgrown with brushwood. Thus far they had proceeded undiscovered, when one of the buccaneers left to guard the canoes struck a light to smoke tobacco, which was perceived by a Spanish sentinel on the shore opposite, who immediately fired his piece and gave alarm to the fort and town. This discovery and the badness of the road caused the buccaneers to defer the attack till daylight. The town of Guayaquil is built round a mountain, on which were three forts which overlooked the town. The Spaniards made a tolerable defence, but by the middle of the day they were driven from all their forts, and the town was left to the buccaneers, detachments of whom were sent to endeavour to bring in prisoners, whilst a chosen party went to the great church to chant *Te Deum*.

Nine buccaneers were killed and twelve wounded in the attack. The booty found in the town was considerable—in jewels, merchandise and silver, particularly in church plate, besides 92,000 dollars in money—and they took seven hundred prisoners, amongst whom were the governor and his family. Fourteen vessels lay at anchor in the port, and two ships were on the stocks nearly fit for launching.

On the evening of the day that the city was taken, the governor (being a prisoner) entered into treaty with the buccaneers for the city, fort, shipping, himself and all the prisoners to be redeemed for a million pieces of eight, to be paid in gold, and 400 packages of flour; and to hasten the procurement of the money, which was to be brought from Quito, the vicar-general of the district, who was also a prisoner, was released.

The 21st, in the night, by the carelessness of a buccaneer one of the houses took fire, which communicated to other houses with such rapidity that one third of the city was destroyed before its progress was stopped. It had been specified in the treaty that the buccaneers should not set fire to the town. "Therefore," says Lussan, "lest in consequence of this accident the Spaniards should refuse to pay the ransom, we pretended to believe it was their doing."

Many bodies of the Spaniards killed in the assault of the town remained unburied where they had fallen, and the buccaneers were apprehensive that some infectious disorder would thereby be produced. They hastened, therefore, to embark on board the vessels in the port, their plunder and 500 of their prisoners, with which, on the 25th, they fell down the river to the island Puna, where they proposed to wait for the ransom.

On the 2nd of May Captain Grogniet died of a

wound he received at Guayaquil. Le Picard was afterwards the chief among the French buccaneers.

The 5th of May had been named for the payment of the ransom, from which time the money was daily and with increasing impatience expected by the buccaneers. It was known that Spanish ships of war were equipping at Callao purposely to attack them, and also that their former commander, Edward Davis, with a good ship, was near this part of the coast. They were anxious to have his company, and on the 4th despatched a galley to seek him at the island Plata, the place of rendezvous he had appointed for his prize.

The 5th passed without any appearance of ransom money, as did many following days. The Spaniards, however, regularly sent provisions to the ships at Puna every day, otherwise the prisoners would have starved, but in lieu of money they substituted nothing better than promises. The buccaneers would have felt it humiliation to appear less ferocious than on former occasions, and they recurred to their old mode of intimidation. They made the prisoners throw dice to determine which of them should die, and the heads of four on whom the lot fell, were delivered to a Spanish officer in answer to excuses for delay which he had brought from the lieutenant-governor of Guayaquil, with an intimation that at the end of four days more five hundred heads should follow if the ransom did not arrive.

On the 14th their galley which had been sent in search of Davis returned, not having found him at the island Plata; but she brought notice of two strange sail being near the cape Santa Elena. These proved to be Edward Davis's ship and a prize. Davis had received intelligence, as already mentioned, of the buccaneers having captured Guayaquil, and was now come purposely to join them. He sent his prize to the buccaneers at Puna, and remained with his own ship in the offing on the look-out.

The four days allowed for the payment of the ransom expired and no ransom was sent; neither did the buccaneers execute their sanguinary threat. It is worthy of remark that intreaty or intercession made to this set of buccaneers, so far from obtaining remission or favour, at all times produced the opposite effect, as if reminding them of their power instigated them to an imperious display of it. The lieutenant-governor of Guayaquil was in no haste to fulfil the terms of the treaty made by the governor, nor did he importune them with solicitations, and the whole business for a time lay at rest. The forbearance of the buccaneers may not unjustly be attributed to Davis having joined them.

On the 23rd the Spaniards paid to the buccaneers as much gold as amounted in value to 20,000 pieces of eight, and eighty packages of flour, as part of the ransom. The day following the lieutenant-governor sent word that they might receive 22,000 pieces of eight more for the release of the prisoners, and if that sum would not satisfy them they might do their worst, for that no greater would be paid them. Upon this message the buccaneers held a consultation whether they should cut off the heads of all the prisoners or take the 22,000 pieces of eight, and it was determined, not unanimously, but by a majority of voices, that it was better to take a little money than to cut off many heads.

Lussan, his own biographer and a young man, boasts of the pleasant manner in which he passed his time at Puna. " We made good cheer, being daily supplied with refreshments from Guayaquil. We had concerts of music : we had the best performers of the city among our prisoners. Some among us engaged in friendships with our women prisoners, who were not hard-hearted." This is said by way of prelude to a history which he gives of his own good fortune ; all which, whether true or otherwise, serves to show that among this abandoned crew the prisoners of both sexes were equally unprotected.

On the 26th the 22,000 pieces of eight were paid to the buccaneers, who selected a hundred prisoners of the most consideration to retain, and released the rest. The same day they quitted their anchorage at Puna, intending to anchor again at point Santa Elena and there to enter afresh into negotiation for ransom of prisoners, but in the evening two Spanish ships of war came in sight.

The engagement which ensued, and other proceedings of the buccaneers until Edward Davis parted company to return homeward by the south of America, has been related. It remains to give an account of the French buccaneers after the separation, to their finally quitting the South Sea.

CHAPTER XXIV.

Retreat of the French buccaneers across New Spain to the West Indies. All the buccaneers quit the South Sea.

THE party left by Davis consisted of 250 buccaneers, the greater number of whom were French, the rest were English, and their leaders Le Picard and George Hout. They had determined to quit the South Sea, and with that view to sail to the coast of New Spain, whence they proposed to march overland to the shore of the Caribbean Sea.

About the end of July they anchored in the Bay of Amapalla, and were joined there by thirty French buccaneers. These thirty were part of a crew which had formerly quitted Grogniet to cruise towards California. Others of that party were still on the coast to the north-west, and the buccaneers in Amapalla Bay put to sea in search of them, that all of their fraternity in the South Sea might be collected and depart together.

In the search after their former companions, they landed at different places on the coast of New Spain. Among their adventures here they took and remained four days in possession of the town of Tecoantepeque, but without any profit to themselves. At Guatulco they plundered some plantations, and obtained provisions in ransom for prisoners. Whilst they lay there at anchor they saw a vessel in the offing, which, from her appearance and manner of working her sails, they believed to contain the people they were seeking ; but the wind and sea set so strong on the shore at the time that neither their vessels nor boats could go out to ascertain what she was, and after that day they did not see her again.

In the middle of December they returned to the Bay of Amapalla, which they had fixed upon for the place of their departure from the shores of the South Sea. Their plan was to march by the town of Nueva Segovia, which had before been visited by buccaneers, and they now expected would furnish them with provisions. According to Lussan's information, the distance they would have to travel by land from Amapalla Bay was about sixty leagues, when they would come to the source of a river by which they could descend to the Caribbean Sea near to Cape Gracias a Dios.

Whilst they made preparation for their march they were anxious to obtain intelligence what force the Spaniards had in their proposed route, but the natives kept at a distance. On the 18th seventy buccaneers landed and marched into the country, of which adventure Lussan gives the account following. They travelled the whole day without meeting an inhabitant. They rested for the night, and next morning proceeded on their journey, but all seemed a desert, and about noon the majority of them were dissatisfied and turned back. Twenty went on, and soon after came to a beaten road on which they perceived three horsemen riding towards them, whom they way-laid so effectually as to take them all. By these men they learnt the way to a small town named Chiloteca, to which they went and there made fifty of the inhabitants prisoners. They took up their quarters in the church, where they also lodged their prisoners and intended to have rested during the night ; but after dark they heard much bustle in the town, which made them apprehensive the Spaniards were preparing to attack them, and the noise caused in the prisoners the appearance of a disposition to rise, upon which the buccaneers slew them all except four, whom they carried away with them, and reached the vessels without being molested in their retreat.

The prisoners were interrogated, and the accounts they gave confirmed the buccaneers in the opinion that they had no better chance of transporting themselves and their plunder to the North Sea than by immediately setting about the execution of the plan they had formed. To settle the order of the march they landed their riches and the stores necessary for their journey on one of the islands in the bay ; and that their number might not suffer diminution by the defection of any it was agreed to destroy the vessels, which was executed forthwith, with the reserve of one galley and the canoes, which were necessary for the transport of themselves and their effects to the mainland. They made a muster of their force, which they divided into four companies, each consisting of seventy men and every man having his arms and accoutrements. Whilst these matters were arranging a detachment of one hundred men was sent to the mainland to endeavour to get horses.

They had destroyed their vessels, and had not removed from the island, when a large Spanish armed ship anchored in Amapalla Bay, but she was not able to give them annoyance nor in the least to impede their operations. On the 1st of January, 1688, they passed over with their effects to the mainland, and the same day the party which had gone in search of horses returned bringing with them sixty-eight, which were divided equally among the four companies, to be employed in carrying stores and provisions, as were eighty prisoners who, besides carriers of stores, were made to carry the sick and wounded. Every buccaneer had his particular sack or package, which it was required should contain his ammunition; what else was at his own discretion.

Many of these buccaneers had more silver than they themselves were able to carry. There were also many who had neither silver nor gold, and were little encumbered with effects of their own. These light-freighted gentry were glad to be hired as porters to the rich, and the contract for carrying silver on this occasion was one half, that is to say, that on arriving at the North Sea there should be an equal division between the employer and the carrier. Carriage of gold or other valuables was according to particular agreement. Lussan, who no doubt was as sharp a rogue as any of his companions, relates of himself that he had been fortunate at play, and that his winnings added to his share of plunder amounted to 30,000 pieces of eight, the whole of which he had converted into gold and jewels; and that, whilst they were making ready for their march, he received warning from a friend that a gang had been formed by about twenty of the poorer buccaneers with the intention to waylay and strip those of their brethren who had been most fortunate. On considering the danger and great difficulty of having to guard against the machinations of hungry conspirators who were to be his fellow-travellers in a long journey, and might have opportunities to perpetrate their mischievous intentions during any fight with the Spaniards, Lussan came to the resolution of making a sacrifice of part of his riches to insure the remaining part, and to lessen the temptation to any individual to seek his death. To this end he divided his treasure into a number of small parcels, which he confided to the care of so many of his companions, making agreement with each for the carriage.

January the 2nd, in the morning, they began their march, an advanced guard being established, to consist of ten men from each company, who were to be relieved every morning by ten others. At night they rested at four leagues' distance, according to their estimation, from the border of the sea.

The first part of Lussan's account of this journey has little of adventure or description. The difficulties experienced were what had been foreseen, such as the inhabitants driving away cattle and removing provisions, setting fire to the dry grass when it could annoy them in their march, and sometimes the buccaneers were fired at by unseen shooters. They rested at villages and farms when they found any in their route, where, and also by making prisoners, they obtained provisions. When no habitations or buildings were at hand they generally encamped at night on a hill or in open ground. Very early in their march they were attended by a body of Spanish troops at a small distance, the music of whose trumpets afforded them entertainment every morning and evening. " But," says Lussan, " it was like the music of the enchanted palace of Psyche, which was heard without the musicians being visible."

On the forenoon of the 9th, notwithstanding their vigilance, the buccaneers were saluted with an unexpected volley of musketry, which killed two men ; and this was the only mischance that befel them in their march from the western sea to Segovia, which town they entered on the 11th of January without hindrance, and found it without inhabitants and cleared of every kind of provisions.

" The town of Segovia is situated in a vale, and is so surrounded with mountains that it seems to be a prisoner there. The churches are ill built. The place of arms, or parade, is large and handsome, as are many of the houses. It is distant from the shore of the South Sea forty leagues : the road is difficult, the country being extremely mountainous."

On the 12th they left Segovia, and without injuring the houses, a forbearance to which they had little accustomed themselves ; but present circumstances brought to their consideration that, if it should be their evil fortune to be called to account, it might be quite as well for them not to add the burning of Segovia to the reckoning.

The 13th, an hour before sunset, they ascended a hill which appeared a good station to occupy for the night. When they arrived at the summit they per-

ceived on the slope of the next mountain before them
a great number of horses grazing (Lussan says between
twelve and fifteen hundred), which at the first sight
they mistook for horned cattle, and congratulated
each other on the near prospect of a good meal; but
it was soon discovered they were horses, and that a
number of them were saddled : intrenchments also
were discerned near the same place, and finally troops.
This part of the country was a thick forest with deep
gullies, and not intersected with any path excepting
the road they were travelling, which led across the
mountain where the Spaniards were intrenched.   On
reconnoitring the position of the Spaniards, the road
beyond them was seen to the right of the intrenchments.   The buccaneers, on short consultation, determined that they would endeavour under cover of
the night to penetrate the wood to the right, so as
to arrive at the road beyond the Spanish camp and
come on it by surprise.

This plan was similar to that which they had projected at Guayaquil, and was a business exactly suited
to the habits and inclinations of these adventurers,
who more than any other of their calling, or perhaps
than the native tribes of North America, were practised
and expert in veiling their purpose so as not to awaken
suspicion : in concealing themselves by day and making
silent advances by night, and in all the arts by which
even the most wary may be ensnared.   Here,
immediately after fixing their plan, they began to
intrench and fortify the ground they occupied, and
made all the dispositions which troops usually do
who halt for the night.   This encampment, besides

impressing the Spaniards with the belief that they intended to pass the night in repose, was necessary to the securing their baggage and prisoners.

Rest seemed necessary and due to the buccaneers after a toilsome day's march, and so it was thought by the Spanish commander, who, seeing them fortify their quarters, doubted not that they meant to do themselves justice; but an hour after the close of day two hundred buccaneers departed from their camp. The moon shone out bright, which gave them light to penetrate the woods, whilst the woods gave them concealment from the Spaniards, and the Spaniards kept small look-out. Before midnight they were near enough to hear the Spaniards chanting litanies, and long before daylight were in the road beyond the Spanish encampment. They waited till the day broke, and then pushed for the camp, which, as had been conjectured, was entirely open on this side. Two Spanish sentinels discovered the approach of the enemy and gave alarm, but the buccaneers were immediately after in the camp, and the Spanish troops, disturbed from their sleep, had neither time nor recollection for any other measure than to save themselves by flight. They abandoned all the intrenchments, and the buccaneers, being masters of the pass, were soon joined by the party who had charge of the baggage and prisoners. In this affair the loss of the buccaneers was only two men killed and four wounded.

In the remaining part of their journey they met no serious obstruction, and were not at any time distressed by a scarcity of provisions. Lussan says they led from the Spanish encampment 900 horses, which served them for carriage, for present food, and to salt for future provision when they should arrive at the sea-shore.

On the 17th of January, which was the 16th of their journey, they came to the banks of a river, by which they were to descend to the Caribbean Sea. This river has its source among the mountains of Nueva Segovia, and falls into the sea to the south of Cape Gracias a Dios about fourteen leagues, according to D'Anville's map, in which it is called Rio de Yare Dampier makes it fall into the sea something more to the southward, and names it the Cape river.

The country here was not occupied nor frequented by the Spaniards, and was inhabited only in a few places by small tribes of native Americans. The buc-caneers cut down trees, and made rafts or catamarans for the conveyance of themselves and their effects down the stream. On account of the falls, the rafts were constructed each to carry no more than two persons with their luggage, and every man went provided with a pole to guide the raft clear of rocks and shallows.

In the commencement of this fresh-water naviga-tion their maritime experience, with all the pains they could take, did not prevent their getting into whirl-pools, were the rafts where overturned, with danger to the men and frequently with the loss of part of the lading. When they came to a fall which appeared more than usually dangerous they put ashore, took their raft to pieces, and carried all below the fall, where they re-accommodated matters and embarked again. The rapidity of the stream, meeting many obstructions, raised a foam and spray that kept everything on the rafts constantly wet; the salted horse-flesh was in a short time entirely spoilt, and their ammunition in a state not to be of service in supplying them with game. Fortunately for them the banks of the river abounded in banana-trees, both wild and in plantations.

When they first embarked on the river the rafts went in close company, but the irregularity and violence of the stream continually entangled and drove them against each other, on which account the method was changed and distances preserved. This gave opportunity to the desperadoes who had conspired against their companions to commence their operations, which they directed against five Englishmen, whom they killed and despoiled. The murderers absconded to the woods with their prey, and were not afterwards seen by the company.

The 20th of February they had passed all the falls, and were at a broad, deep and smooth part of the river where they found no other obstruction than trees and drift-wood floating. As they were near the sea many stopped and began to build canoes. Some English buccaneers, who went lower down the river, found at anchor an English vessel belonging to Jamaica, from which they learned that the French Government had just proclaimed an amnesty in favour of those who, since the peace made with Spain, had committed acts of piracy upon condition of their claiming the benefit of the proclamation within a specified time. A similar proclamation had been issued in the year 1687 by the English Government, but as it was not clear from the report made by the crew of the Jamaica vessel whether

it yet operated the English buccaneers would not
embark for Jamaica. They sent by two Mosquito
Indians an account of the news they had heard to the
French buccaneers, with notice that there was a vessel
at the mouth of the river capable of accommodating not
more than forty persons. Immediately on receiving
the intelligence above a hundred of the French set off
in all haste for the vessel, every one of whom pretended
to be of the forty. Those who first arrived on board
took up the anchor as speedily as they could and set
sail, whilst those who were behind called loudly for a
decision by lot or dice, but the first comers were content to rest their title on possession.

The English buccaneers remained for the present
with the Mosquito Indians near Cape Gracias a Dios,
"who," says Lussan, "have an affection for the English
on account of the many little commodities which they
bring them from the island of Jamaica". The greater
part of the French buccaneers went to the French
settlements, but seventy-five of them who went to
Jamaica were apprehended and detained prisoners by
the Duke of Albemarle, who was then governor, and
their effects sequestrated. They remained in prison
until the death of the duke, which happened in the
following year, when they were released, but neither
their arms nor plunder were returned to them.

The South Sea was now cleared of the main body
of the buccaneers. A few stragglers remained, concerning whom some scattered notices are found, of
which the following are the heads.

Seixas mentions an English frigate named "La
Pava" being wrecked in the Strait of Magalhanes in

the year 1687, and that her loss was occasioned by currents.* By the name being Spanish (signifying the hen) this vessel must have been a prize to the buccaneers.

In the narrative of the loss of the " Wager," by Bulkeley and Cummins, it is mentioned that they found at Port Desire cut on a brick in very legible characters "Captain Straiton, 16 cannon, 1687". Most probably this was meant of a buccaneer vessel.

At the time that the English and French buccaneers were crossing the isthmus in great numbers from the West Indies to the South Sea, two hundred French buccaneers departed from Hispaniola in a ship commanded by a Captain Le Sage, intending to go to the South Sea by the Strait of Magalhanes, but having chosen a wrong season of the year for that passage, and finding the winds unfavourable, they stood over to the coast of Africa, where they continued cruising two years, and returned to the West Indies with great booty obtained at the expense of the Hollanders.

The small crew of French buccaneers in the South Sea who were a part of those who had separated from Grogniet to cruise near California, and for whom Le Picard had sought in vain on the coast of New Spain, were necessitated by the smallness of their force and the bad state of their vessel to shelter themselves at the Tres Marias Islands in the entrance of the Gulf of California. It is said that they remained four years among those islands, at the end of which time they determined, rather than to pass the rest of their lives in so desolate a place, to sail southward,

* *Theatro Naval.* fol. 61, 1.

though with little other prospect or hope than that they should meet some of their former comrades, instead of which, on looking in at Arica on the coast of Peru, they found at anchor in the road a Spanish ship, which they took, and in her a large quantity of treasure. The buccaneers embarked in their prize and proceeded southward for the Atlantic, but were cast ashore in the Strait of Magalhanes. Part of the treasure and as much of the wreck of the vessel as served to construct two sloops were saved, with which, after so many perils, they arrived safely in the West Indies.

Le Sieur Froger, in his account of the voyage of M. de Gennes, has introduced a narrative of a party of French buccaneers or flibustiers going from St. Domingo to the South Sea in the year 1686, which is evidently a romance fabricated from the descriptions which had been given of their general courses and habits. These protégés of Le Sieur Froger, like the buccaneer crew from the Tres Marias Islands just mentioned, were reduced to great distress, took a rich prize afterwards on the coast of Peru, were returning to the Atlantic and lost their ship in the Strait of Magalhanes. They were ten months in the strait building a barque, which they loaded with the best of what they had saved of the cargo of their ship, and in the end arrived safe at Cayenne.* Funnel also mentions a report which he heard of a small crew of French buccaneers, not more than twenty, whose adventures were of the same cast, and who probably were the Tres Marias buccaneers.

* *Relation du Voyage de M. de Gennes*, p. 106. Paris, 1698.

It has been related that five buccaneers who had gamed away their money, unwilling to return poor out of the South Sea, landed at the island Juan Fernandez from Edward Davis's ship about the end of the year 1687 and were left there. In 1690 the English ship "Welfare," commanded by Captain John Strong, anchored at Juan Fernandez; of which voyage two journals have been preserved among the MSS. in the Sloane Collection in the British Museum, from which the following account is taken.

The "Welfare" arrived off the island on the evening of the 11th October, 1690. In the night those on board were surprised at seeing a fire on an elevated part of the land. Early next morning a boat was sent on shore, which soon returned, bringing off from the island two Englishmen. These were part of the five who had landed from Davis's ship. They piloted the "Welfare" to a good anchoring place.

In the three years that they had lived on Juan Fernandez they had not, until the arrival of the "Welfare," seen any other ships than Spaniards, which was a great disappointment to them. The Spaniards had landed and had endeavoured to take them, but they had found concealment in the woods, one excepted, who deserted from his companions and delivered himself up to the Spaniards. The four remaining, when they learned that the buccaneers had entirely quitted the South Sea, willingly embarked with Captain Strong, and with them four servants or slaves. Nothing is said of the manner in which they employed themselves whilst on the island except of their contriving subterraneous places of concealment that the Spaniards should not find them, and of their taming a great number of goats, so that at one time they had a tame stock of three hundred.

CHAPTER XXV.

Steps taken towards reducing the buccaneers and flibustiers under subordination to the regular governments. War of the Grand Alliance against France. The neutrality of the island St. Christopher broken.

WHILST these matters were passing in the Pacific Ocean small progress was made in the reform which had begun in the West Indies. The English governors, by a few examples of severity, restrained the English buccaneers from undertaking any enterprise of magnitude. With the French the case was different. The number of the flibustiers who absented themselves from Hispaniola to go to the South Sea alarmed the French Government for the safety of their colonies, and especially of their settlements in Hispaniola, the security and defence of which against the Spaniards they had almost wholly rested on its being the place of residence and the home of those adventurers. To persist in a rigorous policy against their cruising it was apprehended would make the rest of them quit Hispaniola, for which reason it was judged prudent to relax in the enforcement of the prohibitions; the flibustiers accordingly continued their courses as usual.

In 1686 Granmont and De Graaf prepared an armament against Campeachy. M. de Cussy, who was governor of Tortuga and the French part of Hispaniola, applied personally to them to relinquish their design; but as the force was collected, and all preparation made, neither the flibustiers nor their commanders would be dissuaded from the undertaking, and De Cussy submitted. Campeachy was plundered and burnt.

A measure was adopted by the French Government which certainly trenched on the honour of the regular military establishments of France, but was attended with success in bringing the flibustiers more under control and rendering them more manageable. This was the taking into the king's service some of the principal leaders of the flibustiers, and giving them commissions of advanced rank, either in the land service or in the French marine. A commission was made out for Granmont, appointing him commander on the south coast of St. Domingo, with the rank of Lieutenant du Roy. But of Granmont, as a buccaneer, it might be said, in the language of sportsmen, that he was game to the last. Before the commission arrived he received information of the honour intended him, and whilst yet in his state of liberty was seized with the wish to make one more cruise. He armed a ship and, with a crew of 180 flibustiers in her, put to sea. This was near the end of the year 1686, and what afterwards became of him and his followers is not known, for they were not again seen or heard of.

In the beginning of 1687 a commission arrived from France appointing De Graaf major in the king's

army in the West Indies.   He was then with a crew
of flibustiers near Carthagena.   In this cruise twenty-
five of his men, who landed in the Gulf of Darien,
were cut off by the Darien Indians.   De Graaf on his
return into port accepted his commission, and when
transformed to an officer in the king's army became,
like Morgan, a great scourge to the flibustiers and
Forbans.

In consequence of complaints made by the Spaniards,
a proclamation was issued at this time by the king of
Great Britain, James II., specified in the title to
be "for the more effectual reducing and suppressing
of pirates and privateers in America, as well on the
sea as on the land, who in great numbers have
committed frequent robberies, which hath occasioned
great prejudice and obstruction to trade and commerce".

A twenty years' truce had, in the year 1686, been
agreed upon between France and Spain, but scarcely
a twentieth part of that time was suffered to elapse before it was broken in the West Indies.   The flibustiers
of Hispaniola did not content themselves with their
customary practice: in 1688 they plundered the
Danish factory at the island St. Thomas, which is one
of the small islands called the Virgins near the east
end of Porto Rico.   This was an aggression beyond
the limits which they had professed to prescribe to
their depredatory system, and it is not shown that they
had received injury at the hands of the Danes.   Nevertheless, the French West-India histories say : "Our
flibustiers (*nos flibustiers*), in 1688, surprised the Danish
factory at St. Thomas.   The pillage was considerable,
and would have been more if they had known that the

chief part of the cash was kept in a vault under the hall, which was known to very few of the house.   They forgot on this occasion their ordinary practice, which is to put their prisoners to the torture to make them declare where the money is.   It is certain that if they had so done the hiding-place would have been revealed to them, in which, it was believed, there were more than 500,000 livres."   Such remarks show the strong prepossession which existed in favour of the buccaneers, and an eagerness undistinguishing and determined after the extraordinary.   Qualities the most common to the whole of mankind were received as wonderful when related of the buccaneers.   One of our encyclopedias, under the article "Buccaneer," says : "They were transported with an astonishing degree of enthusiasm whenever they saw a sail".

In this same year, 1688, war broke out in Europe between the French and Spaniards, and in a short time the English joined against the French.

England and France had at no period since the Norman conquest been longer without serious quarrel. On the accession of William III. to the crown of Great Britain it was generally believed that a war with France would ensue.   The French in the West Indies did not wait for its being declared, but attacked the English part of St. Christopher, the island on which, by joint agreement, had been made the original and confederated first settlements of the two nations in the West Indies.   The English inhabitants were driven from their possessions and obliged to retire to the island Nevis, which terminated the longest preserved union which history can show between the

English and French as subjects of different nations. In the commencement it was strongly cemented by the mutual want of support against a powerful enemy ; that motive for their adherence to each other had ceased to exist: yet in the reigns of Charles II. and James II. of England, an agreement had been made between England and France, that, if war should at any time break out between them, a neutrality should be observed by their subjects in the West Indies.

This war continued nearly to the end of King William's reign, and during that time the English and French buccaneers were engaged on opposite sides as auxiliaries to the regular forces of their respective nations, which completely separated them ; and it never afterwards happened that they again confederated in any buccaneer cause. They became more generally distinguished by different appellations, not consonant to their present situations and habits ; for the French adventurers, who were frequently occupied in hunting and at the boucan, were called the flibustiers of St. Domingo, and the English adventurers, who had nothing to do with the boucan, were called the buccaneers of Jamaica.

The French had not kept possession of St. Christopher quite a year when it was taken from them by the English. This was an unfortunate year for the French, who in it suffered a great defeat from the Spaniards in Hispaniola. Their governor, De Cussy, and 500 Frenchmen fell in battle, and the town of Cape François was demolished.

The French flibustiers at this time greatly annoyed Jamaica, making descents, in which they carried off such a number of negroes that in derision they nick-named Jamaica " Little Guinea ". The principal transactions in the West Indies were the attempts made by each party on the possessions of the other. In the course of these services De Graaf was accused of misconduct, tried, and deprived of his commission in the army ; but, though judged unfit for command in land service, out of respect to his maritime experience he was appointed captain of a frigate.

No one among the flibustiers was more dis-tinguished for courage and enterprise in this war than Jean Montauban, who commanded a ship of between thirty and forty guns. He sailed from the West Indies to Bordeaux in 1694. In February of the year following he departed from Bordeaux for the coast of Guinea, where in battle with an English ship of force both the ships were blown up. Mon-tauban and a few others escaped with their lives. This affair is not to be ranked among buccaneer exploits, Great Britain and France being at open war, and Montauban having a regular commission.

CHAPTER XXVI.

Siege and plunder of the city of Carthagena on the terra firma, by an armament from France, in conjunction with the flibustiers of St. Domingo.

IN 1697, at the suggestion of M. le Baron de Pointis, an officer of high rank in the French marine, a large armament was fitted out in France, jointly at the expense of the crown and of private contributors, for an expedition against the Spaniards in the West Indies. The chief command was given to M. de Pointis, and orders were sent out to the governor of the French settlements in Hispaniola (M. du Casse) to raise twelve hundred men in Tortuga and Hispaniola to assist in the expedition. The king's regular force in M. du Casse's government was small, and the men demanded were to be supplied principally from the flibustiers. The despatches containing the above orders arrived in January. It was thought necessary to specify to the flibustiers a limitation of time, and they were desired to keep from dispersing till the 15th of February, it being calculated that M. de Pointis would then, or before, certainly be at Hispaniola. De Pointis, however, did not arrive till the beginning of March, when he made Cape François, but did not anchor there, preferring

(355)

the western part of Hispaniola, "fresh water being better and more easy to be got at Cape Tiburon than at any other part". M. du Casse had with some difficulty kept the flibustiers together beyond the time specified, and they were soon dissatisfied with the deportment of the Baron de Pointis, which was more imperious than they had been accustomed to from any commander.

M. de Pointis published a history of his expedition, in which he relates that at the first meeting between him and M. du Casse he expressed himself dissatisfied at the small number of men provided ; "but," says he, " M. du Casse assured me that the buccaneers were at this time collected and would every man of them perform wonders. It is the good fortune of all the pirates in these parts to be called buccaneers. These freebooters are for the most part composed of those that desert from ships that come upon the coast. The advantage they bring to the governors, protects them against the prosecution of the law. All who are apprehended as vagabonds in France, and can give no account of themselves, are sent to these islands, where they are obliged to serve for three years. The first that gets them, obliges them to work in the plantations ; at the end of the term of servitude somebody lends them a gun, and to sea they go a-buccaneering." It is proper to hint here that when M. de Pointis published his narrative he was at enmity with the buccaneers, and had a personal interest in bringing the buccaneer character into dis-repute. Many of his remarks upon them, never-theless, are not less just than characteristic. He

continues his description : "They were formerly
altogether independent.   Of late years they have
been reduced under the government of the coast
of St. Domingo.   They have commissions given
them, for which they pay the tenth of all prizes, and
are now called the king's subjects.   The governors of
our settlements in St. Domingo, being enriched by
them, do mightily extol them for the damages they do
to the Spaniards.   This infamous profession, which an
impunity for all sorts of crimes renders so much beloved,
has within a few years lost us above six thousand men,
who might have improved and peopled the colony.
At present they are pleased to be called the king's
subjects, yet it is with so much arrogance as obliges
all who are desirous to make use of them, to court in
the most flattering terms.   This was not agreeable to
my disposition, and, considering them as his Majesty's
subjects which the governor was ordered to deliver to
me, I plainly told them that they should find me a
commander to lead them on, but not as a companion
to them."

The expedition, though it was not yet made known,
or even yet pretended to be determined against what
place it should be directed, was expected to yield both
honour and profit.   The buccaneers would not quarrel
with a promising enterprise under a spirited and experienced commander, for a little haughtiness in his
demeanour towards them ; but they demanded to
have clearly specified the share of the prize money and
plunder to which they should be entitled, and it was
stipulated by mutual agreement " that the flibustiers
and colonists should, man for man, have the same

shares of booty that were allowed to the men on board the king's ships ". As so many men were to embark from M. du Casse's government, he proposed to go at their head, and desired to know of M. de Pointis what rank would be allowed him. M. du Casse was a mariner by profession, and had the rank of captain in the French navy. De Pointis told him that the highest character he knew him in, was that which he derived from his commission as *Capitaine de Vaisseau*, and that if he embarked in the expedition he must be content to serve in that quality, according to his seniority.

M. du Casse nevertheless chose to go, though it was generally thought he was not allowed the honours and considerations which were his due as governor of the French colonies at St. Domingo, and commander of so large a portion of the men engaged in the expedition. It was settled that the flibustiers should embark partly in their own cruising vessels, and partly on board the ships of M. de Pointis' squadron, and should be furnished with six weeks' provisions. A review was made to prevent any but able men of the colony being taken ; negroes who served, if free, were to be allowed shares like other men ; if slaves and they were killed, their masters were to be paid for them.

Two copies of the agreement respecting the sharing of the booty were posted up in public places at Petit Goave, and a copy was delivered to M. du Casse, the governor. M. de Pointis consulted with M. du Casse what enterprise they should undertake, but the determination wholly rested with M. de Pointis. "There was added," M. de Pointis says,

"without my knowledge, to the directions sent to
Governor du Casse, that he was to give assistance to
our undertaking, without damage to, or endangering
his colony. This restriction did in some measure
deprive me of the power of commanding his forces,
seeing he had an opportunity of pretending to keep
them for the preservation of the colony." M. du
Casse made no pretences to withhold, but gave all the
assistance in his power. He was an advocate for attacking the city of St. Domingo. This was the wish
of most of the colonists, and perhaps was what would
have been of more advantage to France than any
other expedition they could have undertaken. But
the armament having been prepared principally at
private expense, it was reasonable for the contributors
to look to their own reimbursement. To attack the
city of St. Domingo was not approved; other plans
were proposed; but Carthagena seems to have been
the original object of the projectors of the expedition,
and the attack of that city was determined upon.
Before the flibustiers and other colonists embarked, a
disagreement happened which nearly made them refuse
altogether to join in the expedition. The officers of
De Pointis' fleet had imbibed the sentiments of their
commander respecting the flibustiers, or buccaneers,
and followed the example of his manner towards them.
The fleet was lying at Petit Goave, and M. de Pointis,
giving to himself the title of general of the armies of
France, by sea and by land in America, had placed a
guard in a fort there. M. du Casse, as he had received no orders from Europe to acknowledge any
superior within his government, might have considered

such an exercise of power to be an encroachment on his authority which it became him to resist; but he acted in this and in other instances like a man over-awed. The officer of M. de Pointis who commanded the guard on shore arrested a flibustier for disorderly behaviour, and held him prisoner in the fort. The flibustiers surrounded the fort in a tumultuous manner to demand his release, and the officer commanded his men to fire upon them, by which three of the flibustiers were killed. It required some address and civility on the part of M. de Pointis himself, as well as the assistance of M. du Casse, to appease the flibustiers; and the officer who had committed the offence was sent on board under arrest.

The force furnished from M. du Casse's government consisted of nearly 700 flibustiers, 170 soldiers from the garrisons, and as many volunteer inhabitants and negroes as made up about 1200 men. The whole armament consisted of seven large ships and eleven frigates, besides store ships and smaller vessels; and, reckoning persons of all classes, 6000 men.

The fleet arrived off Carthagena on 13th April, and the landing was effected on the 15th. It is not necessary to relate all the particulars of this siege, in which the buccaneers bore only a part. That part, however, was of essential importance.

M. de Pointis, in the commencement, appointed the whole of the flibustiers, without any mixture of the king's troops, to a service of great danger, which raised a suspicion of partiality, and of an intention to save the men he brought with him from Europe, as regarding them to be more peculiarly his own men.

An eminence about a mile to the eastward of the city of Carthagena, on which was a church named "Nuestra Senora de la Poupa," commands all the avenues and approaches on the land side to the city. "I had been assured," says M. de Pointis, "that if we did not seize the hill De la Poupa immediately on our arrival, all the treasure would be carried off. To get possession of this post I resolved to land the buccaneers in the night of the same day on which we came to anchor, they being proper for such an attempt, as being accustomed to marching and subsisting in the woods." M. de Pointis takes this occasion to accuse the buccaneers of behaving less heroically than M. du Casse had boasted they would, and that it was not without murmuring that they embarked in the boats in order to their landing. It is, however, due to them on the score of courage and exertion to remark, though in some degree it is in anticipation, that no part of the force under M. de Pointis showed more readiness or performed better service in the siege than the buccaneers.

There was uncertainty about the most proper place for landing, and M. de Pointis went himself in a boat to examine near the shore to the north of the city. The surf rolled in heavily, by which his boat was filled, and was with difficulty saved from being stranded on a rock. The proposed landing was given up as impracticable, and M. de Pointis became of opinion that Carthagena was approachable only by the lake which makes the harbour, the entrance to which, on account of its narrowness, was called the Bocca-chica, and was defended by a strong fort.

The fleet sailed for the Bocca-chica, and on the 15th some of the ships began to cannonade the fort. The first landing was effected at the same time by a corps of eighty negroes, without any mixture of the king's troops.   This was a second marked instance of the commander's partial attention to the preservation of the men he brought from France.   M. de Pointis despised the flibustiers, and probably regarded negroes as next to nothing.   He was glad, however, to receive them as his companions-in-arms, and it was in honour due from him to all under his command, as far as circumstances would admit, without injury to service, to share the dangers equally, or at least without partiality.

The 16th, which was the day next after the landing, the castle of Bocca-chica surrendered.   This was a piece of good fortune much beyond expectation, and was obtained principally by the dexterous management of a small party of the buccaneers, which drew commendation even from M. de Pointis.   "Among the chiefs of these buccaneers," he says, "there may be about twenty men who deserve to be distinguished for their courage, it not being my intention to comprehend them in the descriptions which I make of the others."

De Pointis conducted the siege with diligence and spirit.   The Church "Nuestra Senora de la Poupa" was taken possession of on the 17th, and on the 3rd of May the city capitulated.   The terms of the capitulation were :—

That all public effects and office accounts should be delivered to the captors.

That merchants should produce their books of

accounts, and deliver up all money and effects held by them for their correspondents.

That every inhabitant should be free to leave the city or to remain in his dwelling. That those who retired from the city should first deliver up all their property there to the captors. That those who chose to remain should declare faithfully, under penalty of entire confiscation, the gold, silver, and jewels in their possession : on which condition, and delivering up one-half, they should be permitted to retain the other half, and afterwards to be regarded as subjects of France.

That the churches and religious houses should be spared and protected.

The French general, on entering the town with his troops, went first to the cathedral to attend the *Te Deum*. He next sent for the superiors of the convents and religious houses, to whom he explained the meaning of the article of the capitulation, promising them protection, which was, that their houses should not be destroyed, but that it had no relation to money in their possession, which they were required to deliver up. Otherwise, he observed, it would be in their power to collect in their houses all the riches of the city. He caused it to be publicly rumoured that he was directed by the court to keep possession of Carthagena, and that it would be made a French colony. To give colour to this report, he appointed M. du Casse to be governor of the city. He strictly prohibited the troops from entering any house until it had undergone the visitation of officers appointed by himself, some of which officers it was supposed embezzled not less than 100,000 crowns each. A reward was proclaimed for

informers of concealed treasure, of one-tenth of all
treasure discovered by them. "The hope of securing
a part, with the fear of bad neighbours and false
friends, induced the inhabitants to be forward in dis-
closing their riches, and Tilleul, who was charged with
receiving the treasure, was not able to weigh the specie
fast enough."

M. du Casse, in the exercise of what he conceived
to be the duties of his new office of governor of
Carthagena, had begun to take cognisance of the
money which the inhabitants brought in according to
the capitulation; but M. de Pointis was desirous that
he should not be at any trouble on that head. High
words passed between them, in consequence of which
Du Casse declined further interference in what was
transacting, and retired to a house in the suburbs. This
was quitting the field to an antagonist who would not
fail to take advantage of it; whose refusal to admit
other witnesses to the receipt of money than those
of his own appointment, was a strong indication,
whatever contempt he might profess or really feel for
the flibustiers, that he was himself of as staunch flibustier
principles as any one of the gentry of the coast. Some
time afterwards, however, M. du Casse thought proper
to send a formal representation to the general, that it
was nothing more than just, that some person of the
colony should be present at the receipt of the money.
The general returned answer that what M. du Casse
proposed, was in itself a matter perfectly indifferent,
but that it would be an insult to his own dignity, and
therefore he could not permit it.

The public collection of plunder by authority did

not save the city from private pillage. In a short
time all the plate disappeared from the churches.
Houses were forcibly entered by the troops, and as
much violence committed as if no capitulation had been
granted. M. de Pointis, when complained to by the
aggrieved inhabitants, gave orders for the prevention
of outrage, but was at no pains to make them observed.
It appears that the flibustiers were most implicated in
these disorders. Many of the inhabitants who had
complied with the terms of the capitulation, seeing the
violences everywhere committed, hired flibustiers to be
guards in their houses, hoping, that by being well paid,
they would be satisfied, and protect them against others.
Some observed this compact and were faithful guardians,
but the greater number robbed those they undertook
to defend. For this, among other reasons, De Pointis
resolved to rid the city of them. On a report, which it
is said he himself caused to be spread, that an army of
10,000 Indians were approaching Carthagena, he ordered
the flibustiers out to meet them. Without suspecting
any deception they went forth, and were some days
absent seeking the reported enemy. As they were on
their return, a message met them from the general, purporting that he apprehended their presence in the city
would occasion some disturbance, and he therefore desired them to stop without the gates. On receiving
this message they broke out into imprecations, and
resolved not to delay their return to the city nor to be
kept longer in ignorance of what was passing there.
When they arrived at the gates they found them shut
and guarded by the king's troops. Whilst they delibe-
rated on what they should next do, another message,

more conciliating in language than the former, came to them from M. de Pointis, in which he said that it was by no means his intention to interdict them from entering Carthagena ; that he only wished they would not enter so soon, nor all at one time, for fear of frightening the inhabitants, who greatly dreaded their presence. The flibustiers knew not how to help themselves, and were necessitated to take up their quarters without the city walls, where they were kept fifteen days, by which time the collection of treasure from the inhabitants was completed, the money weighed, secured in chests, and great part embarked. De Pointis says : " As fast as the money was brought in, it was immediately carried on board the king's ships ". The uneasiness and impatience of the flibustiers for distribution of the booty may easily be imagined. On their re-admission to the city the merchandise was put up to sale by auction, and the produce joined to the former collection ; but no distribution took place, and the flibustiers were loud in their importunities. M. de Pointis assigned as a reason for the delay, that the clerks employed in the business had not made up the accounts. He says in his narrative : " I was not so ill served by my spies as not to be informed of the seditious discourses held by some wholly abandoned to their own interests upon the money being carried on board the king's ships ". To allay the ferment, he ordered considerable gratifications to be paid to the buccaneer captains, also compensation to the buccaneers who had been maimed or wounded, and rewards to be given to some who had most distinguished themselves during the siege ; and he spoke with so much appearance of frankness of his intention, as soon as ever he should receive the account of the whole, to make a division which should be satisfactory to all parties, that the buccaneers were persuaded to remain quiet.

The value of the plunder is variously reported. Much of the riches of the city had been carried away on the first alarm of the approach of an enemy. De Pointis says 110 mules laden with gold went out in the course of four days. "Nevertheless, the honour acquired to his Majesty's arms, besides near eight or nine millions that could not escape us, consoled us for the rest." Whether these eight or nine millions were crowns or livres M. de Pointis' account does not specify. It is not improbable he meant it should be understood as livres. Many were of opinion that the value of the booty was not less than forty millions of livres ; M. du Casse estimated it at above twenty millions, besides merchandise.

M. de Pointis now made known that on account of the unhealthiness of the situation he had changed his intention of leaving a garrison and keeping Carthagena, for that already more Frenchmen had died there by sickness than he had lost in the siege. He ordered the cannon of the Bocca-chica castle to be taken on board the ships, and the castle to be demolished. On the 25th of May orders were issued for the troops to embark ; and at the same time he embarked himself without having given any previous notice of his intention so to do to M. du Casse, from whom he had parted but a few minutes before. The ships of the king's fleet began to take up their anchors to move towards the entrance of the harbour, and M. de Pointis sent an order to M. du Casse for the buccaneers and the people of the colony to embark on board their own vessels.

M. du Casse sent two of his principal officers to the general to demand that justice should be done to the colonists. Still the accounts were said not to be ready; but on the 29th, the king's fleet being ready for sea, M. de Pointis sent to M. du Casse the commissary's account, which stated the share of the booty due to the colonists, including the governor and the buccaneers, to be 40,000 crowns.

What the customary manner of dividing prize money in the French navy was at that time is not to be understood from the statement given by De Pointis, which says "that the king had been pleased to allow to the several ships' companies a tenth of the first million, and a thirtieth part of all the rest". Here it is not specified whether the million of which the ships' companies were to be allowed one-tenth is to be understood a million of louis, a million crowns, or a million livres. The difference of construction in a large capture would be nearly as three to one. It requires explanation likewise what persons are meant to be included in the term "ships' companies". Sometimes it is used to signify the common seamen, without including the officers, and for them the one-tenth is certainly not too large a share. That in any military service, public or private, one-tenth of captures or of plunder should be deemed adequate gratification for the services of all the captors, officers included, seems scarcely credible. In the Carthagena expedition it is also to be observed that the dues of the crown were in some measure compromised by the admission of private contributions towards defraying the expense. The flibustiers had contributed by furnishing their own vessels to the service.

Du Casse, when he saw the account, did not immediately communicate it to his colonists, deterred at first probably by something like shame and an apprehension that they would reproach him with weakness for having yielded so much as he had all along done to the insulting and imperious pretensions of De Pointis. Afterwards, through discretion, he delayed making the matter public until the colonists had all embarked and their vessels had sailed from the city. He then sent for the captains and acquainted them with the distribution intended by M. de Pointis, and they informed their crews.

CHAPTER XXVII.

Second plunder of Carthagena. Peace of Ryswick, in 1697. Entire suppression of the buccaneers and flibustiers.

THE share which M. de Pointis had allotted of the plunder of Carthagena to the buccaneers fell so short of their calculations, and was felt as so great an aggravation of the contemptuous treatment they had before received, that their rage was excessive, and in their first transports they proposed to board the "Sceptre," a ship of 84 guns, on board which M. de Pointis carried his flag. This was too desperate a scheme to be persevered in. After much deliberation, one among them exclaimed : " It is useless to trouble ourselves any farther about such a villain as De Pointis ; let him go with what he has got ; he has left us our share at Carthagena, and thither we must return to seek it ". The proposition was received with general applause by these remorseless robbers, whose desire for vengeance on De Pointis was all at once obliterated by the mention of an object that awakened their greediness for plunder. They got their vessels under sail, and stood back to the devoted city, doomed by them to pay the forfeit for the dishonesty of their countryman.

The matter was consulted and determined upon without M. du Casse being present, and the ship in which he had embarked was left by the rest without company. When he perceived what they were bent upon, he sent orders to them to desist, which he accompanied with a promise to demand redress for them in France; but neither the doubtful prospect of distant redress held out, nor respect for his orders, had any effect in restraining them. M. du Casse sent an officer to M. de Pointis, who had not yet sailed from the entrance of Carthagena harbour, to inform him that the buccaneers, in defiance of all order and in breach of the capitulation which had been granted to the city, were returning thither to plunder it again; but M. de Pointis in sending the commissary's account had closed his intercourse with the buccaneers and with the colonists, at least for the remainder of his expedition. M. du Casse's officer was told that the general was so ill that he could not be spoken with. The officer went to the next senior captain in command of the fleet, who, on being informed of the matter, said "the buccaneers were great rogues, and ought to be hanged"; but as no step could be taken to prevent the mischief without delaying the sailing of the fleet, the chief commanders of which were impatient to see their booty in a place of greater security, none was taken, and on the 1st of June the king's fleet sailed for France, leaving Carthagena to the discretion of the buccaneers. M. de Pointis claims being ignorant of what was transacting. "On the 30th of May," he says, "I was taken so ill that all I could do, before I fell into a condition that deprived me of my intellect, was to acquaint Captain Levi that I committed the care of the squadron to him."

If M. de Pointis acted fairly by the people who came from France and returned with him, it must be supposed that in his sense of right and wrong he held the belief that "to rob a rogue is no breach of honesty". But it was said of him, "Il etoit capable de former un grand dessein, et de rien epargner pour le faire réussir "; the English phrase for which is, "he would stick at nothing".

On the 1st of June M. du Casse also sailed from Carthagena to return to St. Domingo. Thus were the flibustiers abandoned to their own will by all the authorities whose duty it was to have restrained them.

The inhabitants of Carthagena, seeing the buccaneer ships returning to the city, waited in the most anxious suspense to learn the cause. The flibustiers on landing seized on all the male inhabitants they could lay hold of, and shut them up in the great church. They posted up a kind of manifesto in different parts of the city, setting forth the justice of their second invasion of Carthagena, which they grounded on the perfidy of the French general, De Pointis ("que nous vous permettons de charger de toutes les maledictions imaginables "), and on their own necessities. Finally, they demanded five millions of livres as the price of their departing again without committing disorder. It seems strange that the buccaneers could expect to raise so much money in a place so recently plundered. Nevertheless, by terrifying their prisoners, putting some to the torture, ransacking the tombs, and other means equally abhorrent, in four days' time they had nearly made up the proposed sum. It happened that two flibustiers killed two women of Carthagena in some manner, or under some circumstances, that gave general offence, and raised indignation in the rest of the flibustiers, who held a kind of trial and condemned them to be shot, which was done in presence of many of the inhabitants. The buccaneer histories praise this as an act of extraordinary justice, and a set-off against their cruelties and robberies, such as gained them the esteem even of the Spaniards. The punishment, however merited, was a matter of caprice. It is no-where pretended that they ever made a law to themselves to forbid their murdering their prisoners; in very many instances they had not refrained, and in no former instance had it been attended with punishment. The putting these two murderers to death, therefore, as it related to themselves, was an arbitrary and lawless act. If the women had been murdered for the purpose of coming at their money, it could not have incurred blame from the rest. These remarks are not intended in disapprobation of the act, which was very well, but too highly extolled.

Having almost completed their collection, they began to dispute about the division, the flibustiers pretending that the more regular settlers of the colony (being but landsmen) were not entitled to an equal share with themselves, when a barque arrived from Martinico which was sent expressly to give them notice that a fleet of English and Dutch ships of war had just arrived in the West Indies. This news made them hasten their departure, and shortened or put an end to their disputes; for, previous to sailing, they made a division of the gold and silver, in which each man shared nearly a thousand crowns, the merchandise and negroes being reserved for future division, and which it was expected would produce much more.

The commanders of the English and Dutch squadrons, on arriving at Barbadoes, learnt that the French had taken Carthagena. They sailed on for that place, and had almost reached it when they came in sight of De Pointis' squadron, to which they gave chase, but which escaped from them by superior sailing.

On the 3rd or 4th of June the flibustiers sailed from Carthagena in nine vessels, and had proceeded thirty leagues of their route towards Hispaniola when they came in sight of the English and Dutch fleet. They dispersed, everyone using his best endeavours to save himself by flight. The two richest ships were taken; two were driven on shore and wrecked, one of them near Carthagena, and her crew fell into the hands of the Spaniards, who would have been justified in treating them as pirates, but they were only made to work on the fortifications. The five others had the good fortune to reach Isle Avache. To conclude the history of the Carthagena expedition, a suit was instituted in France against M. de Pointis and the *armateurs* in behalf of the colonists and flibustiers, and a decree was obtained in their favour for 1,400,000 livres; but the greater part of the sum was swallowed up by the expenses of the suit and the embezzlements of agents.

The Carthagena expedition was the last transaction in which the flibustiers or buccaneers made a conspicuous figure. It turned out to their disadvantage in many respects, but chiefly in stripping them of public favour. In September, 1697, an end was put to the war by a treaty signed at Ryswick. By this treaty the part of the island St. Christopher which had belonged to the French was restored to them.

In earlier times, peace, by releasing the buccaneers from public demands on their services, left them free to pursue their own projects with an understood licence or privilege to cruise or form any other enterprise against the Spaniards without danger of being subjected to enquiry; but the aspect of affairs in this respect was now greatly altered. The treaty of 1670 between Great Britain and Spain, with the late alliance of those powers against France, had put an end to buccaneering in Jamaica; the scandal of the second plunder of Carthagena lay heavy on the flibustiers of St. Domingo; and a circumstance, in which both Great Britain and France were deeply interested, went yet more strongly to the entire suppression of the cruisings of the buccaneers and to the dissolution of their piratical union; this was, that the king of Spain, Charles II., was in a weak state of health, without issue, and the succession to the crown of Spain was believed to depend upon his will. On this last account the kings of Great Britain and France were earnest in their endeavours to give satisfaction to Spain. Louis XIV. sent back from France to Carthagena the silver ornaments of which the churches had been stripped, and distinction was no longer admitted in the French settlements between flibustier and pirate. The flibustiers themselves had grown tired of preserving the distinction; for, after the peace of Ryswick

had been fully notified in the West Indies, they continued to seize and plunder the ships of the English
and Dutch, till complaint was made to the French
governor of St. Domingo, M. du Casse, who thought
proper to make indemnification to the sufferers.
Fresh prohibitions and proclamations were issued, and
encouragement was given to the adventurers to become planters. The French were desirous to obtain
permission to trade in the Spanish ports of the *terra
firma*. Charlevoix says: "The Spaniards were charmed
by the sending back the ornaments taken from the
churches at Carthagena, and it was hoped to gain
them entirely by putting a stop to the cruisings o
the flibustiers. The commands of the king were strict
and precise on this head; that the governor should
persuade the flibustiers to make themselves inhabitants, and in default of prevailing by persuasion, to use
force."

Many flibustiers and buccaneers did turn planters,
or followed their profession of mariner in the ships of
merchants. Attachment to old habits, difficulties in
finding employment, and being provided with vessels
fit for cruising, made many persist in their former
courses. The evil most grievously felt by them was
their proscribed state, which left them no place in the
West Indies where they might riot with safety and to
their liking, in the expenditure of their booty. Not
having the same inducement as formerly to limit themselves to the plundering one people, they extended
their scope of action, and robbed vessels of all nations.
Most of those who were in good vessels, quitted the
West Indian seas, and went roving to different parts

of the world. Mention is made of pirates or buccaneers being in the South Sea in the year 1697, but their particular deeds are not related; and Robert Drury, who was shipwrecked at Madagascar in the year 1702, relates: "King Samuel's messenger then desired to know what they demanded for me. To which Deaan Crindo sent word that they required two buccaneer guns."

At the time of the Peace of Ryswick the Darien Indians, having quarrelled with the Spaniards, had become reconciled to the flibustiers, and several of the old flibustiers afterwards settled on the isthmus and married Darien women.

One of the Lucayas, or Bahama Islands, had been settled by the English, under the name of Providence Island. It afforded good anchorage, and the strength of the settlement was small, which were conveniencies to pirates that induced them to frequent it; and, according to the proverbial effect of evil communication, the inhabitants were tempted to partake of their plunder and assist in their robberies by purchasing their prize goods, and supplying them with all kinds of stores and necessaries. This was for several years so gainful a business to the settlement, as to cause it to be proverbial in the West Indies that "shipwrecks and pirates were the only hopes of the island Providence".

In three years after the peace of Ryswick Charles II. of Spain died, and a prince of the house of Bourbon mounted the Spanish throne, which produced a close union of interests between France and Spain. The ports of Spanish America, both in the West Indies and in the South Sea, were laid open to the merchants of France. The *Noticia de las Expediciones al Magal-hanes* notices the great resort of the French to the Pacific Ocean, " who in an extraordinary manner en-riched themselves during the war of the Spanish succession ". In the French settlements in the West Indies the name of flibustier, because it implied enmity to the Spaniards, was no longer tolerated.

On the breaking out of the war between Great Britain and France which followed the Spanish succes-sion, the English drove the French out of St. Christo-pher, and it has since remained wholly to Great Britain. M. le Comte de Gennes, a commander in the French navy, who a few years before had made an unsuccessful voyage to the Strait of Magalhanes, was the governor of the French part of the island at the time of the surrender.*

During this war the governors of Providence exer-cised their authority in granting commissions or letters of reprisal, and created Admiralty courts for the con-demnation of captured vessels : for under some of the governors no vessels brought to the adjudication of the court escaped that sentence. These were indirect acts of piracy.

The last achievement related of the flibustiers happened in 1702, when a party of Englishmen, having

---

* Père Labat relates a story of a ridiculous effort in mechanical ingenuity, in which M. de Gennes succeeded whilst he was governor at St. Christopher. He made an automaton in the likeness of a soldier, which marched and performed sundry actions. It was jocosely said that M. de Gennes might have defended his government with troops of his own making. His automaton soldier ate victuals placed before it, which it digested by means of a dissolvent. (P. Labat, vol. v. p. 349).

commissions from the governor of Jamaica, landed on the isthmus near the Samballas Islands, where they were joined by some of the old flibustiers who lived among the Darien Indians, and also by 300 of the Indians. They marched to some mines, from which they drove the Spaniards and took 70 negroes. They kept the negroes at work in the mines twenty-one days; but in all this exploit they obtained no more than about eighty pounds' weight of gold.

Here, then, terminates the history of the buccaneers of America. Their distinctive mark, which they undeviatingly preserved for nearly two centuries, was their waging constant war against the Spaniards, and against them only. Many peculiarities have been attributed to the buccaneers in other respects, some of which can apply only to their situation as hunters of cattle, and some existed rather in the writer's fancy than in reality. Mariners are generally credited with being more eccentric in their caprices than other men, which, if true, is to be accounted for by the circumstances of their profession; and it happens that they are most subjected to observation at the times when they are fresh in the possession of liberty and money, earned by long confinement and labour.

It may be said of the buccaneers that they were in general courageous, according to the character of their leader, often rash, alternately negligent and vigilant, and always addicted to pleasure and idleness. It will help to illustrate the manners and qualifications of the buccaneers in the South Sea, to give an extract from the concluding part of Dampier's manuscript journal of his voyage round the world with the buccaneers, and will also establish a fact which has been mentioned before only as a matter surmised. Dampier says :—

"The 20th September, 1691, arrived in the Downs, to my great joy and satisfaction, having in my voyage ran clear round the globe. I might have been master of the ship we first sailed in if I would have accepted it, for it was known to most men on board that I kept a journal, and all that knew me did ever judge my accounts were kept as correct as any man's. Besides, that most, if not all, others who kept journals in the voyage lost them before they got to Europe, whereas I preserved my writing. Yet I see that some men are not so well pleased with my account as if it came from any of the commanders that were in the South Sea, though most of them, I think all but Captain Swan, were incapable of keeping a sea journal and took no account of any action, neither did they make any observations. But I am only to answer for myself, and, if I have not given satisfaction to my friends in what I have written, the fault is in the meanness of my information, and not in me, who have been faithful as to what came to my knowledge."

Countenanced as the buccaneers were, it is not in the least surprising that they became so numerous. With the same degree of encouragement at the present time, the seas would be filled with such adventurers. It was fortunate for the Spaniards, and perhaps for the other maritime nations of Europe, that the buccaneers did not make conquest and settlement so much their object as they did plunder, and that they took no step towards making themselves independent whilst it was

in their power. Among their chiefs were some of good
capacity ; but only two of them, Mansvelt and Morgan,
appear to have contemplated any scheme of regular
settlement independent of the European governments,
and the time was then gone by. Before Tortuga was
taken possession of for the crown of France such a
project might have been undertaken with great advantage. The English and French buccaneers were then
united ; England was deeply engaged and fully occupied
by a civil war ; and the jealousy which the Spaniards
entertained of the encroachments of the French in the
West Indies, kept at a distance all probability of their
coalescing to suppress the buccaneers. If they had
chosen at that time to have formed for themselves any
regular mode of government, it appears not very
improbable that they might have become a powerful
independent State.

In the history of so much robbery and outrage
the rapacity shown in some instances by the European
governments in their West-India transactions, and by
governors of their appointment, appears in a worse
light than that of the buccaneers, from whom, they
being professed ruffians, nothing better was expected.
The superior attainments of Europeans, though they
have done much towards their own civilisation, chiefly
in humanising their institutions, have, in their dealings
with the inhabitants of the rest of the globe, with few
exceptions, been made the instruments of usurpation
and extortion.

After the suppression of the buccaneers, and partly
from their relics, arose a race of pirates of a more
desperate cast, so rendered by the increased danger of

their occupation, who for a number of years preyed upon the commerce of all nations, till they were hunted down and, it may be said, exterminated.   Of one crew of pirates who were brought before a court of justice, fifty-two men were condemned and executed at one time in the year 1722.

FINIS.

A CATALOG OF SELECTED DOVER
BOOKS IN ALL FIELDS OF INTEREST

CONCERNING THE SPIRITUAL IN ART, Wassily Kandinsky. Pioneering work by father of abstract art. Thoughts on color theory, nature of art. Analysis of earlier masters. 12 illustrations. 80pp. of text. 5⅜ x 8½. 23411-8

ANIMALS: 1,419 Copyright-Free Illustrations of Mammals, Birds, Fish, Insects, etc., Jim Harter (ed.). Clear wood engravings present, in extremely lifelike poses, over 1,000 species of animals. One of the most extensive pictorial sourcebooks of its kind. Captions. Index. 284pp. 9 x 12. 23766-4

CELTIC ART: The Methods of Construction, George Bain. Simple geometric techniques for making Celtic interlacements, spirals, Kells-type initials, animals, humans, etc. Over 500 illustrations. 160pp. 9 x 12. (Available in U.S. only.) 22923-8

AN ATLAS OF ANATOMY FOR ARTISTS, Fritz Schider. Most thorough reference work on art anatomy in the world. Hundreds of illustrations, including selections from works by Vesalius, Leonardo, Goya, Ingres, Michelangelo, others. 593 illustrations. 192pp. 7⅛ x 10¼. 20241-0

CELTIC HAND STROKE-BY-STROKE (Irish Half-Uncial from "The Book of Kells"): An Arthur Baker Calligraphy Manual, Arthur Baker. Complete guide to creating each letter of the alphabet in distinctive Celtic manner. Covers hand position, strokes, pens, inks, paper, more. Illustrated. 48pp. 8¼ x 11. 24336-2

EASY ORIGAMI, John Montroll. Charming collection of 32 projects (hat, cup, pelican, piano, swan, many more) specially designed for the novice origami hobbyist. Clearly illustrated easy-to-follow instructions insure that even beginning papercrafters will achieve successful results. 48pp. 8¼ x 11. 27298-2

THE COMPLETE BOOK OF BIRDHOUSE CONSTRUCTION FOR WOODWORKERS, Scott D. Campbell. Detailed instructions, illustrations, tables. Also data on bird habitat and instinct patterns. Bibliography. 3 tables. 63 illustrations in 15 figures. 48pp. 5¼ x 8½. 24407-5

BLOOMINGDALE'S ILLUSTRATED 1886 CATALOG: Fashions, Dry Goods and Housewares, Bloomingdale Brothers. Famed merchants' extremely rare catalog depicting about 1,700 products: clothing, housewares, firearms, dry goods, jewelry, more. Invaluable for dating, identifying vintage items. Also, copyright-free graphics for artists, designers. Co-published with Henry Ford Museum & Greenfield Village. 160pp. 8¼ x 11. 25780-0

HISTORIC COSTUME IN PICTURES, Braun & Schneider. Over 1,450 costumed figures in clearly detailed engravings–from dawn of civilization to end of 19th century. Captions. Many folk costumes. 256pp. 8⅜ x 11¾. 23150-X

STICKLEY CRAFTSMAN FURNITURE CATALOGS, Gustav Stickley and L. & J. G. Stickley. Beautiful, functional furniture in two authentic catalogs from 1910. 594 illustrations, including 277 photos, show settles, rockers, armchairs, reclining chairs, bookcases, desks, tables. 183pp. 6½ x 9¼. 23838-5

AMERICAN LOCOMOTIVES IN HISTORIC PHOTOGRAPHS: 1858 to 1949, Ron Ziel (ed.). A rare collection of 126 meticulously detailed official photographs, called "builder portraits," of American locomotives that majestically chronicle the rise of steam locomotive power in America. Introduction. Detailed captions. xi+ 129pp. 9 x 12. 27393-8

AMERICA'S LIGHTHOUSES: An Illustrated History, Francis Ross Holland, Jr. Delightfully written, profusely illustrated fact-filled survey of over 200 American lighthouses since 1716. History, anecdotes, technological advances, more. 240pp. 8 x 10¾. 25576-X

TOWARDS A NEW ARCHITECTURE, Le Corbusier. Pioneering manifesto by founder of "International School." Technical and aesthetic theories, views of industry, economics, relation of form to function, "mass-production split" and much more. Profusely illustrated. 320pp. 6⅛ x 9¼. (Available in U.S. only.) 25023-7

HOW THE OTHER HALF LIVES, Jacob Riis. Famous journalistic record, exposing poverty and degradation of New York slums around 1900, by major social reformer. 100 striking and influential photographs. 233pp. 10 x 7⅞ 22012-5

FRUIT KEY AND TWIG KEY TO TREES AND SHRUBS, William M. Harlow. One of the handiest and most widely used identification aids. Fruit key covers 120 deciduous and evergreen species; twig key 160 deciduous species. Easily used. Over 300 photographs. 126pp. 5⅜ x 8½. 20511-8

COMMON BIRD SONGS, Dr. Donald J. Borror. Songs of 60 most common U.S. birds: robins, sparrows, cardinals, bluejays, finches, more—arranged in order of increasing complexity. Up to 9 variations of songs of each species. Cassette and manual 99911-4

ORCHIDS AS HOUSE PLANTS, Rebecca Tyson Northen. Grow cattleyas and many other kinds of orchids—in a window, in a case, or under artificial light. 63 illustrations. 148pp. 5⅜ x 8½. 23261-1

MONSTER MAZES, Dave Phillips. Masterful mazes at four levels of difficulty. Avoid deadly perils and evil creatures to find magical treasures. Solutions for all 32 exciting illustrated puzzles. 48pp. 8¼ x 11. 26005-4

MOZART'S DON GIOVANNI (DOVER OPERA LIBRETTO SERIES), Wolfgang Amadeus Mozart. Introduced and translated by Ellen H. Bleiler. Standard Italian libretto, with complete English translation. Convenient and thoroughly portable—an ideal companion for reading along with a recording or the performance itself. Introduction. List of characters. Plot summary. 121pp. 5¼ x 8½. 24944-1

TECHNICAL MANUAL AND DICTIONARY OF CLASSICAL BALLET, Gail Grant. Defines, explains, comments on steps, movements, poses and concepts. 15-page pictorial section. Basic book for student, viewer. 127pp. 5⅜ x 8½. 21843-0

THE CLARINET AND CLARINET PLAYING, David Pino. Lively, comprehensive work features suggestions about technique, musicianship, and musical interpretation, as well as guidelines for teaching, making your own reeds, and preparing for public performance. Includes an intriguing look at clarinet history. "A godsend," *The Clarinet*, Journal of the International Clarinet Society. Appendixes. 7 illus. 320pp. 5⅜ x 8½. 40270-3

HOLLYWOOD GLAMOR PORTRAITS, John Kobal (ed.). 145 photos from 1926-49. Harlow, Gable, Bogart, Bacall; 94 stars in all. Full background on photographers, technical aspects. 160pp. 8⅜ x 11¼. 23352-9

THE ANNOTATED CASEY AT THE BAT: A Collection of Ballads about the Mighty Casey/Third, Revised Edition, Martin Gardner (ed.). Amusing sequels and parodies of one of America's best-loved poems: Casey's Revenge, Why Casey Whiffed, Casey's Sister at the Bat, others. 256pp. 5⅜ x 8½. 28598-7

THE RAVEN AND OTHER FAVORITE POEMS, Edgar Allan Poe. Over 40 of the author's most memorable poems: "The Bells," "Ulalume," "Israfel," "To Helen," "The Conqueror Worm," "Eldorado," "Annabel Lee," many more. Alphabetic lists of titles and first lines. 64pp. 5³⁄₁₆ x 8¼. 26685-0

PERSONAL MEMOIRS OF U. S. GRANT, Ulysses Simpson Grant. Intelligent, deeply moving firsthand account of Civil War campaigns, considered by many the finest military memoirs ever written. Includes letters, historic photographs, maps and more. 528pp. 6⅛ x 9¼. 28587-1

ANCIENT EGYPTIAN MATERIALS AND INDUSTRIES, A. Lucas and J. Harris. Fascinating, comprehensive, thoroughly documented text describes this ancient civilization's vast resources and the processes that incorporated them in daily life, including the use of animal products, building materials, cosmetics, perfumes and incense, fibers, glazed ware, glass and its manufacture, materials used in the mummification process, and much more. 544pp. 6⅛ x 9¼. (Available in U.S. only.) 40446-3

RUSSIAN STORIES/RUSSKIE RASSKAZY: A Dual-Language Book, edited by Gleb Struve. Twelve tales by such masters as Chekhov, Tolstoy, Dostoevsky, Pushkin, others. Excellent word-for-word English translations on facing pages, plus teaching and study aids, Russian/English vocabulary, biographical/critical introductions, more. 416pp. 5⅜ x 8½. 26244-8

PHILADELPHIA THEN AND NOW: 60 Sites Photographed in the Past and Present, Kenneth Finkel and Susan Oyama. Rare photographs of City Hall, Logan Square, Independence Hall, Betsy Ross House, other landmarks juxtaposed with contemporary views. Captures changing face of historic city. Introduction. Captions. 128pp. 8¼ x 11. 25790-8

AIA ARCHITECTURAL GUIDE TO NASSAU AND SUFFOLK COUNTIES, LONG ISLAND, The American Institute of Architects, Long Island Chapter, and the Society for the Preservation of Long Island Antiquities. Comprehensive, well-researched and generously illustrated volume brings to life over three centuries of Long Island's great architectural heritage. More than 240 photographs with authoritative, extensively detailed captions. 176pp. 8¼ x 11. 26946-9

NORTH AMERICAN INDIAN LIFE: Customs and Traditions of 23 Tribes, Elsie Clews Parsons (ed.). 27 fictionalized essays by noted anthropologists examine religion, customs, government, additional facets of life among the Winnebago, Crow, Zuni, Eskimo, other tribes. 480pp. 6⅛ x 9¼. 27377-6

FRANK LLOYD WRIGHT'S DANA HOUSE, Donald Hoffmann. Pictorial essay of residential masterpiece with over 160 interior and exterior photos, plans, elevations, sketches and studies. 128pp. 9¼ x 10¾. 29120-0

THE MALE AND FEMALE FIGURE IN MOTION: 60 Classic Photographic Sequences, Eadweard Muybridge. 60 true-action photographs of men and women walking, running, climbing, bending, turning, etc., reproduced from rare 19th-century masterpiece. vi + 121pp. 9 x 12. 24745-7

1001 QUESTIONS ANSWERED ABOUT THE SEASHORE, N. J. Berrill and Jacquelyn Berrill. Queries answered about dolphins, sea snails, sponges, starfish, fishes, shore birds, many others. Covers appearance, breeding, growth, feeding, much more. 305pp. 5¼ x 8¼. 23366-9

ATTRACTING BIRDS TO YOUR YARD, William J. Weber. Easy-to-follow guide offers advice on how to attract the greatest diversity of birds: birdhouses, feeders, water and waterers, much more. 96pp. 5³⁄₁₆ x 8¼. 28927-3

MEDICINAL AND OTHER USES OF NORTH AMERICAN PLANTS: A Historical Survey with Special Reference to the Eastern Indian Tribes, Charlotte Erichsen-Brown. Chronological historical citations document 500 years of usage of plants, trees, shrubs native to eastern Canada, northeastern U.S. Also complete identifying information. 343 illustrations. 544pp. 6½ x 9¼. 25951-X

STORYBOOK MAZES, Dave Phillips. 23 stories and mazes on two-page spreads: Wizard of Oz, Treasure Island, Robin Hood, etc. Solutions. 64pp. 8¼ x 11. 23628-5

AMERICAN NEGRO SONGS: 230 Folk Songs and Spirituals, Religious and Secular, John W. Work. This authoritative study traces the African influences of songs sung and played by black Americans at work, in church, and as entertainment. The author discusses the lyric significance of such songs as "Swing Low, Sweet Chariot," "John Henry," and others and offers the words and music for 230 songs. Bibliography. Index of Song Titles. 272pp. 6½ x 9¼. 40271-1

MOVIE-STAR PORTRAITS OF THE FORTIES, John Kobal (ed.). 163 glamor, studio photos of 106 stars of the 1940s: Rita Hayworth, Ava Gardner, Marlon Brando, Clark Gable, many more. 176pp. 8⅜ x 11¼. 23546-7

BENCHLEY LOST AND FOUND, Robert Benchley. Finest humor from early 30s, about pet peeves, child psychologists, post office and others. Mostly unavailable elsewhere. 73 illustrations by Peter Arno and others. 183pp. 5⅜ x 8½. 22410-4

YEKL and THE IMPORTED BRIDEGROOM AND OTHER STORIES OF YIDDISH NEW YORK, Abraham Cahan. Film Hester Street based on *Yekl* (1896). Novel, other stories among first about Jewish immigrants on N.Y.'s East Side. 240pp. 5⅜ x 8½. 22427-9

SELECTED POEMS, Walt Whitman. Generous sampling from *Leaves of Grass*. Twenty-four poems include "I Hear America Singing," "Song of the Open Road," "I Sing the Body Electric," "When Lilacs Last in the Dooryard Bloom'd," "O Captain! My Captain!"—all reprinted from an authoritative edition. Lists of titles and first lines. 128pp. 5³⁄₁₆ x 8¼. 26878-0

THE BEST TALES OF HOFFMANN, E. T. A. Hoffmann. 10 of Hoffmann's most important stories: "Nutcracker and the King of Mice," "The Golden Flowerpot," etc. 458pp. 5⅜ x 8½. 21793-0

FROM FETISH TO GOD IN ANCIENT EGYPT, E. A. Wallis Budge. Rich detailed survey of Egyptian conception of "God" and gods, magic, cult of animals, Osiris, more. Also, superb English translations of hymns and legends. 240 illustrations. 545pp. 5⅜ x 8½. 25803-3

FRENCH STORIES/CONTES FRANÇAIS: A Dual-Language Book, Wallace Fowlie. Ten stories by French masters, Voltaire to Camus: "Micromegas" by Voltaire; "The Atheist's Mass" by Balzac; "Minuet" by de Maupassant; "The Guest" by Camus, six more. Excellent English translations on facing pages. Also French-English vocabulary list, exercises, more. 352pp. 5⅜ x 8½. 26443-2

CHICAGO AT THE TURN OF THE CENTURY IN PHOTOGRAPHS: 122 Historic Views from the Collections of the Chicago Historical Society, Larry A. Viskochil. Rare large-format prints offer detailed views of City Hall, State Street, the Loop, Hull House, Union Station, many other landmarks, circa 1904-1913. Introduction. Captions. Maps. 144pp. 9⅜ x 12¼. 24656-6

OLD BROOKLYN IN EARLY PHOTOGRAPHS, 1865-1929, William Lee Younger. Luna Park, Gravesend race track, construction of Grand Army Plaza, moving of Hotel Brighton, etc. 157 previously unpublished photographs. 165pp. 8⅞ x 11¾. 23587-4

THE MYTHS OF THE NORTH AMERICAN INDIANS, Lewis Spence. Rich anthology of the myths and legends of the Algonquins, Iroquois, Pawnees and Sioux, prefaced by an extensive historical and ethnological commentary. 36 illustrations. 480pp. 5⅜ x 8½. 25967-6

AN ENCYCLOPEDIA OF BATTLES: Accounts of Over 1,560 Battles from 1479 B.C. to the Present, David Eggenberger. Essential details of every major battle in recorded history from the first battle of Megiddo in 1479 B.C. to Grenada in 1984. List of Battle Maps. New Appendix covering the years 1967-1984. Index. 99 illustrations. 544pp. 6½ x 9¼. 24913-1

SAILING ALONE AROUND THE WORLD, Captain Joshua Slocum. First man to sail around the world, alone, in small boat. One of great feats of seamanship told in delightful manner. 67 illustrations. 294pp. 5⅜ x 8½. 20326-3

ANARCHISM AND OTHER ESSAYS, Emma Goldman. Powerful, penetrating, prophetic essays on direct action, role of minorities, prison reform, puritan hypocrisy, violence, etc. 271pp. 5⅜ x 8½. 22484-8

MYTHS OF THE HINDUS AND BUDDHISTS, Ananda K. Coomaraswamy and Sister Nivedita. Great stories of the epics; deeds of Krishna, Shiva, taken from puranas, Vedas, folk tales; etc. 32 illustrations. 400pp. 5⅜ x 8½. 21759-0

THE TRAUMA OF BIRTH, Otto Rank. Rank's controversial thesis that anxiety neurosis is caused by profound psychological trauma which occurs at birth. 256pp. 5⅜ x 8½. 27974-X

A THEOLOGICO-POLITICAL TREATISE, Benedict Spinoza. Also contains unfinished Political Treatise. Great classic on religious liberty, theory of government on common consent. R. Elwes translation. Total of 421pp. 5⅜ x 8½. 20249-6

MY BONDAGE AND MY FREEDOM, Frederick Douglass. Born a slave, Douglass became outspoken force in antislavery movement. The best of Douglass' autobiographies. Graphic description of slave life. 464pp. 5⅜ x 8½.   22457-0

FOLLOWING THE EQUATOR: A Journey Around the World, Mark Twain. Fascinating humorous account of 1897 voyage to Hawaii, Australia, India, New Zealand, etc. Ironic, bemused reports on peoples, customs, climate, flora and fauna, politics, much more. 197 illustrations. 720pp. 5⅜ x 8½.   26113-1

THE PEOPLE CALLED SHAKERS, Edward D. Andrews. Definitive study of Shakers: origins, beliefs, practices, dances, social organization, furniture and crafts, etc. 33 illustrations. 351pp. 5⅜ x 8½.   21081-2

THE MYTHS OF GREECE AND ROME, H. A. Guerber. A classic of mythology, generously illustrated, long prized for its simple, graphic, accurate retelling of the principal myths of Greece and Rome, and for its commentary on their origins and significance. With 64 illustrations by Michelangelo, Raphael, Titian, Rubens, Canova, Bernini and others. 480pp. 5⅜ x 8½.   27584-1

PSYCHOLOGY OF MUSIC, Carl E. Seashore. Classic work discusses music as a medium from psychological viewpoint. Clear treatment of physical acoustics, auditory apparatus, sound perception, development of musical skills, nature of musical feeling, host of other topics. 88 figures. 408pp. 5⅜ x 8½.   21851-1

THE PHILOSOPHY OF HISTORY, Georg W. Hegel. Great classic of Western thought develops concept that history is not chance but rational process, the evolution of freedom. 457pp. 5⅜ x 8½.   20112-0

THE BOOK OF TEA, Kakuzo Okakura. Minor classic of the Orient: entertaining, charming explanation, interpretation of traditional Japanese culture in terms of tea ceremony. 94pp. 5⅜ x 8½.   20070-1

LIFE IN ANCIENT EGYPT, Adolf Erman. Fullest, most thorough, detailed older account with much not in more recent books, domestic life, religion, magic, medicine, commerce, much more. Many illustrations reproduce tomb paintings, carvings, hieroglyphs, etc. 597pp. 5⅜ x 8½.   22632-8

SUNDIALS, Their Theory and Construction, Albert Waugh. Far and away the best, most thorough coverage of ideas, mathematics concerned, types, construction, adjusting anywhere. Simple, nontechnical treatment allows even children to build several of these dials. Over 100 illustrations. 230pp. 5⅜ x 8½.   22947-5

THEORETICAL HYDRODYNAMICS, L. M. Milne-Thomson. Classic exposition of the mathematical theory of fluid motion, applicable to both hydrodynamics and aerodynamics. Over 600 exercises. 768pp. 6⅛ x 9¼.   68970-0

SONGS OF EXPERIENCE: Facsimile Reproduction with 26 Plates in Full Color, William Blake. 26 full-color plates from a rare 1826 edition. Includes "The Tyger," "London," "Holy Thursday," and other poems. Printed text of poems. 48pp. 5¼ x 7.   24636-1

OLD-TIME VIGNETTES IN FULL COLOR, Carol Belanger Grafton (ed.). Over 390 charming, often sentimental illustrations, selected from archives of Victorian graphics—pretty women posing, children playing, food, flowers, kittens and puppies, smiling cherubs, birds and butterflies, much more. All copyright-free. 48pp. 9¼ x 12¼.   27269-9

PERSPECTIVE FOR ARTISTS, Rex Vicat Cole. Depth, perspective of sky and sea, shadows, much more, not usually covered. 391 diagrams, 81 reproductions of drawings and paintings. 279pp. 5⅜ x 8½.   22487-2

DRAWING THE LIVING FIGURE, Joseph Sheppard. Innovative approach to artistic anatomy focuses on specifics of surface anatomy, rather than muscles and bones. Over 170 drawings of live models in front, back and side views, and in widely varying poses. Accompanying diagrams. 177 illustrations. Introduction. Index. 144pp. 8⅜ x11¼.   26723-7

GOTHIC AND OLD ENGLISH ALPHABETS: 100 Complete Fonts, Dan X. Solo. Add power, elegance to posters, signs, other graphics with 100 stunning copyright-free alphabets: Blackstone, Dolbey, Germania, 97 more–including many lower-case, numerals, punctuation marks. 104pp. 8⅛ x 11.   24695-7

HOW TO DO BEADWORK, Mary White. Fundamental book on craft from simple projects to five-bead chains and woven works. 106 illustrations. 142pp. 5⅜ x 8.
                                                                            20697-1

THE BOOK OF WOOD CARVING, Charles Marshall Sayers. Finest book for beginners discusses fundamentals and offers 34 designs. "Absolutely first rate . . . well thought out and well executed."–E. J. Tangerman. 118pp. 7¾ x 10⅝.   23654-4

ILLUSTRATED CATALOG OF CIVIL WAR MILITARY GOODS: Union Army Weapons, Insignia, Uniform Accessories, and Other Equipment, Schuyler, Hartley, and Graham. Rare, profusely illustrated 1846 catalog includes Union Army uniform and dress regulations, arms and ammunition, coats, insignia, flags, swords, rifles, etc. 226 illustrations. 160pp. 9 x 12.   24939-5

WOMEN'S FASHIONS OF THE EARLY 1900s: An Unabridged Republication of "New York Fashions, 1909," National Cloak & Suit Co. Rare catalog of mail-order fashions documents women's and children's clothing styles shortly after the turn of the century. Captions offer full descriptions, prices. Invaluable resource for fashion, costume historians. Approximately 725 illustrations. 128pp. 8⅜ x 11¼.   27276-1

THE 1912 AND 1915 GUSTAV STICKLEY FURNITURE CATALOGS, Gustav Stickley. With over 200 detailed illustrations and descriptions, these two catalogs are essential reading and reference materials and identification guides for Stickley furniture. Captions cite materials, dimensions and prices. 112pp. 6½ x 9¼.   26676-1

EARLY AMERICAN LOCOMOTIVES, John H. White, Jr. Finest locomotive engravings from early 19th century: historical (1804–74), main-line (after 1870), special, foreign, etc. 147 plates. 142pp. 11⅜ x 8¼.   22772-3

THE TALL SHIPS OF TODAY IN PHOTOGRAPHS, Frank O. Braynard. Lavishly illustrated tribute to nearly 100 majestic contemporary sailing vessels: Amerigo Vespucci, Clearwater, Constitution, Eagle, Mayflower, Sea Cloud, Victory, many more. Authoritative captions provide statistics, background on each ship. 190 black-and-white photographs and illustrations. Introduction. 128pp. 8⅞ x 11¾.
                                                                            27163-3

LITTLE BOOK OF EARLY AMERICAN CRAFTS AND TRADES, Peter Stockham (ed.). 1807 children's book explains crafts and trades: baker, hatter, cooper, potter, and many others. 23 copperplate illustrations. 140pp. 4⅝ x 6.   23336-7

VICTORIAN FASHIONS AND COSTUMES FROM HARPER'S BAZAR, 1867–1898, Stella Blum (ed.). Day costumes, evening wear, sports clothes, shoes, hats, other accessories in over 1,000 detailed engravings. 320pp. 9⅜ x 12¼. 22990-4

GUSTAV STICKLEY, THE CRAFTSMAN, Mary Ann Smith. Superb study surveys broad scope of Stickley's achievement, especially in architecture. Design philosophy, rise and fall of the Craftsman empire, descriptions and floor plans for many Craftsman houses, more. 86 black-and-white halftones. 31 line illustrations. Introduction 208pp. 6½ x 9¼.   27210-9

THE LONG ISLAND RAIL ROAD IN EARLY PHOTOGRAPHS, Ron Ziel. Over 220 rare photos, informative text document origin (1844) and development of rail service on Long Island. Vintage views of early trains, locomotives, stations, passengers, crews, much more. Captions. 8⅞ x 11¾.   26301-0

VOYAGE OF THE LIBERDADE, Joshua Slocum. Great 19th-century mariner's thrilling, first-hand account of the wreck of his ship off South America, the 35-foot boat he built from the wreckage, and its remarkable voyage home. 128pp. 5⅜ x 8½.
40022-0

TEN BOOKS ON ARCHITECTURE, Vitruvius. The most important book ever written on architecture. Early Roman aesthetics, technology, classical orders, site selection, all other aspects. Morgan translation. 331pp. 5⅜ x 8½.   20645-9

THE HUMAN FIGURE IN MOTION, Eadweard Muybridge. More than 4,500 stopped-action photos, in action series, showing undraped men, women, children jumping, lying down, throwing, sitting, wrestling, carrying, etc. 390pp. 7⅞ x 10⅝.
20204-6 Clothbd.

TREES OF THE EASTERN AND CENTRAL UNITED STATES AND CANADA, William M. Harlow. Best one-volume guide to 140 trees. Full descriptions, woodlore, range, etc. Over 600 illustrations. Handy size. 288pp. 4½ x 6⅜.   20395-6

SONGS OF WESTERN BIRDS, Dr. Donald J. Borror. Complete song and call repertoire of 60 western species, including flycatchers, juncoes, cactus wrens, many more–includes fully illustrated booklet.   Cassette and manual 99913-0

GROWING AND USING HERBS AND SPICES, Milo Miloradovich. Versatile handbook provides all the information needed for cultivation and use of all the herbs and spices available in North America. 4 illustrations. Index. Glossary. 236pp. 5⅜ x 8½.
25058-X

BIG BOOK OF MAZES AND LABYRINTHS, Walter Shepherd. 50 mazes and labyrinths in all–classical, solid, ripple, and more–in one great volume. Perfect inexpensive puzzler for clever youngsters. Full solutions. 112pp. 8⅛ x 11.   22951-3

PIANO TUNING, J. Cree Fischer. Clearest, best book for beginner, amateur. Simple repairs, raising dropped notes, tuning by easy method of flattened fifths. No previous skills needed. 4 illustrations. 201pp. 5⅜ x 8½. 23267-0

HINTS TO SINGERS, Lillian Nordica. Selecting the right teacher, developing confidence, overcoming stage fright, and many other important skills receive thoughtful discussion in this indispensible guide, written by a world-famous diva of four decades' experience. 96pp. 5⅜ x 8½. 40094-8

THE COMPLETE NONSENSE OF EDWARD LEAR, Edward Lear. All nonsense limericks, zany alphabets, Owl and Pussycat, songs, nonsense botany, etc., illustrated by Lear. Total of 320pp. 5⅜ x 8½. (Available in U.S. only.) 20167-8

VICTORIAN PARLOUR POETRY: An Annotated Anthology, Michael R. Turner. 117 gems by Longfellow, Tennyson, Browning, many lesser-known poets. "The Village Blacksmith," "Curfew Must Not Ring Tonight," "Only a Baby Small," dozens more, often difficult to find elsewhere. Index of poets, titles, first lines. xxiii + 325pp. 5⅝ x 8¼. 27044-0

DUBLINERS, James Joyce. Fifteen stories offer vivid, tightly focused observations of the lives of Dublin's poorer classes. At least one, "The Dead," is considered a masterpiece. Reprinted complete and unabridged from standard edition. 160pp. 5³⁄₁₆ x 8¼. 26870-5

GREAT WEIRD TALES: 14 Stories by Lovecraft, Blackwood, Machen and Others, S. T. Joshi (ed.). 14 spellbinding tales, including "The Sin Eater," by Fiona McLeod, "The Eye Above the Mantel," by Frank Belknap Long, as well as renowned works by R. H. Barlow, Lord Dunsany, Arthur Machen, W. C. Morrow and eight other masters of the genre. 256pp. 5⅜ x 8½. (Available in U.S. only.) 40436-6

THE BOOK OF THE SACRED MAGIC OF ABRAMELIN THE MAGE, translated by S. MacGregor Mathers. Medieval manuscript of ceremonial magic. Basic document in Aleister Crowley, Golden Dawn groups. 268pp. 5⅜ x 8½. 23211-5

NEW RUSSIAN-ENGLISH AND ENGLISH-RUSSIAN DICTIONARY, M. A. O'Brien. This is a remarkably handy Russian dictionary, containing a surprising amount of information, including over 70,000 entries. 366pp. 4½ x 6⅛. 20208-9

HISTORIC HOMES OF THE AMERICAN PRESIDENTS, Second, Revised Edition, Irvin Haas. A traveler's guide to American Presidential homes, most open to the public, depicting and describing homes occupied by every American President from George Washington to George Bush. With visiting hours, admission charges, travel routes. 175 photographs. Index. 160pp. 8¼ x 11. 26751-2

NEW YORK IN THE FORTIES, Andreas Feininger. 162 brilliant photographs by the well-known photographer, formerly with *Life* magazine. Commuters, shoppers, Times Square at night, much else from city at its peak. Captions by John von Hartz. 181pp. 9¼ x 10¾. 23585-8

INDIAN SIGN LANGUAGE, William Tomkins. Over 525 signs developed by Sioux and other tribes. Written instructions and diagrams. Also 290 pictographs. 111pp. 6⅛ x 9¼. 22029-X

ANATOMY: A Complete Guide for Artists, Joseph Sheppard. A master of figure drawing shows artists how to render human anatomy convincingly. Over 460 illustrations. 224pp. 8⅜ x 11¼. 27279-6

MEDIEVAL CALLIGRAPHY: Its History and Technique, Marc Drogin. Spirited history, comprehensive instruction manual covers 13 styles (ca. 4th century through 15th). Excellent photographs; directions for duplicating medieval techniques with modern tools. 224pp. 8⅜ x 11¼. 26142-5

DRIED FLOWERS: How to Prepare Them, Sarah Whitlock and Martha Rankin. Complete instructions on how to use silica gel, meal and borax, perlite aggregate, sand and borax, glycerine and water to create attractive permanent flower arrangements. 12 illustrations. 32pp. 5⅜ x 8½. 21802-3

EASY-TO-MAKE BIRD FEEDERS FOR WOODWORKERS, Scott D. Campbell. Detailed, simple-to-use guide for designing, constructing, caring for and using feeders. Text, illustrations for 12 classic and contemporary designs. 96pp. 5⅜ x 8½. 25847-5

SCOTTISH WONDER TALES FROM MYTH AND LEGEND, Donald A. Mackenzie. 16 lively tales tell of giants rumbling down mountainsides, of a magic wand that turns stone pillars into warriors, of gods and goddesses, evil hags, powerful forces and more. 240pp. 5⅜ x 8½. 29677-6

THE HISTORY OF UNDERCLOTHES, C. Willett Cunnington and Phyllis Cunnington. Fascinating, well-documented survey covering six centuries of English undergarments, enhanced with over 100 illustrations: 12th-century laced-up bodice, footed long drawers (1795), 19th-century bustles, 19th century corsets for men, Victorian "bust improvers," much more. 272pp. 5⅝ x 8¼. 27124-2

ARTS AND CRAFTS FURNITURE: The Complete Brooks Catalog of 1912, Brooks Manufacturing Co. Photos and detailed descriptions of more than 150 now very collectible furniture designs from the Arts and Crafts movement depict davenports, settees, buffets, desks, tables, chairs, bedsteads, dressers and more, all built of solid, quarter-sawed oak. Invaluable for students and enthusiasts of antiques, Americana and the decorative arts. 80pp. 6½ x 9¼. 27471-3

WILBUR AND ORVILLE: A Biography of the Wright Brothers, Fred Howard. Definitive, crisply written study tells the full story of the brothers' lives and work. A vividly written biography, unparalleled in scope and color, that also captures the spirit of an extraordinary era. 560pp. 6⅛ x 9¼. 40297-5

THE ARTS OF THE SAILOR: Knotting, Splicing and Ropework, Hervey Garrett Smith. Indispensable shipboard reference covers tools, basic knots and useful hitches; handsewing and canvas work, more. Over 100 illustrations. Delightful reading for sea lovers. 256pp. 5⅜ x 8½. 26440-8

FRANK LLOYD WRIGHT'S FALLINGWATER: The House and Its History, Second, Revised Edition, Donald Hoffmann. A total revision–both in text and illustrations–of the standard document on Fallingwater, the boldest, most personal architectural statement of Wright's mature years, updated with valuable new material from the recently opened Frank Lloyd Wright Archives. "Fascinating"–*The New York Times.* 116 illustrations. 128pp. 9¼ x 10¾. 27430-6

PHOTOGRAPHIC SKETCHBOOK OF THE CIVIL WAR, Alexander Gardner. 100 photos taken on field during the Civil War. Famous shots of Manassas Harper's Ferry, Lincoln, Richmond, slave pens, etc. 244pp. 10⅝ x 8¼.   22731-6

FIVE ACRES AND INDEPENDENCE, Maurice G. Kains. Great back-to-the-land classic explains basics of self-sufficient farming. The one book to get. 95 illustrations. 397pp. 5⅜ x 8½.   20974-1

SONGS OF EASTERN BIRDS, Dr. Donald J. Borror. Songs and calls of 60 species most common to eastern U.S.: warblers, woodpeckers, flycatchers, thrushes, larks, many more in high-quality recording.   Cassette and manual 99912-2

A MODERN HERBAL, Margaret Grieve. Much the fullest, most exact, most useful compilation of herbal material. Gigantic alphabetical encyclopedia, from aconite to zedoary, gives botanical information, medical properties, folklore, economic uses, much else. Indispensable to serious reader. 161 illustrations. 888pp. 6½ x 9¼. 2-vol. set. (Available in U.S. only.)   Vol. I: 22798-7
Vol. II: 22799-5

HIDDEN TREASURE MAZE BOOK, Dave Phillips. Solve 34 challenging mazes accompanied by heroic tales of adventure. Evil dragons, people-eating plants, blood-thirsty giants, many more dangerous adversaries lurk at every twist and turn. 34 mazes, stories, solutions. 48pp. 8¼ x 11.   24566-7

LETTERS OF W. A. MOZART, Wolfgang A. Mozart. Remarkable letters show bawdy wit, humor, imagination, musical insights, contemporary musical world; includes some letters from Leopold Mozart. 276pp. 5⅜ x 8½.   22859-2

BASIC PRINCIPLES OF CLASSICAL BALLET, Agrippina Vaganova. Great Russian theoretician, teacher explains methods for teaching classical ballet. 118 illustrations. 175pp. 5⅜ x 8½.   22036-2

THE JUMPING FROG, Mark Twain. Revenge edition. The original story of The Celebrated Jumping Frog of Calaveras County, a hapless French translation, and Twain's hilarious "retranslation" from the French. 12 illustrations. 66pp. 5⅜ x 8½.   22686-7

BEST REMEMBERED POEMS, Martin Gardner (ed.). The 126 poems in this superb collection of 19th- and 20th-century British and American verse range from Shelley's "To a Skylark" to the impassioned "Renascence" of Edna St. Vincent Millay and to Edward Lear's whimsical "The Owl and the Pussycat." 224pp. 5⅜ x 8½.   27165-X

COMPLETE SONNETS, William Shakespeare. Over 150 exquisite poems deal with love, friendship, the tyranny of time, beauty's evanescence, death and other themes in language of remarkable power, precision and beauty. Glossary of archaic terms. 80pp. 5¹⁵⁄₁₆ x 8¼.   26686-9

THE BATTLES THAT CHANGED HISTORY, Fletcher Pratt. Eminent historian profiles 16 crucial conflicts, ancient to modern, that changed the course of civilization. 352pp. 5⅜ x 8½.   41129-X

THE WIT AND HUMOR OF OSCAR WILDE, Alvin Redman (ed.). More than 1,000 ripostes, paradoxes, wisecracks: Work is the curse of the drinking classes; I can resist everything except temptation; etc. 258pp. 5⅜ x 8½. 20602-5

SHAKESPEARE LEXICON AND QUOTATION DICTIONARY, Alexander Schmidt. Full definitions, locations, shades of meaning in every word in plays and poems. More than 50,000 exact quotations. 1,485pp. 6½ x 9¼. 2-vol. set.
Vol. 1: 22726-X
Vol. 2: 22727-8

SELECTED POEMS, Emily Dickinson. Over 100 best-known, best-loved poems by one of America's foremost poets, reprinted from authoritative early editions. No comparable edition at this price. Index of first lines. 64pp. 5³⁄₁₆ x 8¼. 26466-1

THE INSIDIOUS DR. FU-MANCHU, Sax Rohmer. The first of the popular mystery series introduces a pair of English detectives to their archnemesis, the diabolical Dr. Fu-Manchu. Flavorful atmosphere, fast-paced action, and colorful characters enliven this classic of the genre. 208pp. 5³⁄₁₆ x 8¼. 29898-1

THE MALLEUS MALEFICARUM OF KRAMER AND SPRENGER, translated by Montague Summers. Full text of most important witchhunter's "bible," used by both Catholics and Protestants. 278pp. 6⅝ x 10. 22802-9

SPANISH STORIES/CUENTOS ESPAÑOLES: A Dual-Language Book, Angel Flores (ed.). Unique format offers 13 great stories in Spanish by Cervantes, Borges, others. Faithful English translations on facing pages. 352pp. 5⅜ x 8½. 25399-6

GARDEN CITY, LONG ISLAND, IN EARLY PHOTOGRAPHS, 1869–1919, Mildred H. Smith. Handsome treasury of 118 vintage pictures, accompanied by carefully researched captions, document the Garden City Hotel fire (1899), the Vanderbilt Cup Race (1908), the first airmail flight departing from the Nassau Boulevard Aerodrome (1911), and much more. 96pp. 8⅞ x 11¾. 40669-5

OLD QUEENS, N.Y., IN EARLY PHOTOGRAPHS, Vincent F. Seyfried and William Asadorian. Over 160 rare photographs of Maspeth, Jamaica, Jackson Heights, and other areas. Vintage views of DeWitt Clinton mansion, 1939 World's Fair and more. Captions. 192pp. 8⅞ x 11. 26358-4

CAPTURED BY THE INDIANS: 15 Firsthand Accounts, 1750-1870, Frederick Drimmer. Astounding true historical accounts of grisly torture, bloody conflicts, relentless pursuits, miraculous escapes and more, by people who lived to tell the tale. 384pp. 5⅜ x 8½. 24901-8

THE WORLD'S GREAT SPEECHES (Fourth Enlarged Edition), Lewis Copeland, Lawrence W. Lamm, and Stephen J. McKenna. Nearly 300 speeches provide public speakers with a wealth of updated quotes and inspiration–from Pericles' funeral oration and William Jennings Bryan's "Cross of Gold Speech" to Malcolm X's powerful words on the Black Revolution and Earl of Spenser's tribute to his sister, Diana, Princess of Wales. 944pp. 5⅜ x 8⅜. 40903-1

THE BOOK OF THE SWORD, Sir Richard F. Burton. Great Victorian scholar/adventurer's eloquent, erudite history of the "queen of weapons"–from prehistory to early Roman Empire. Evolution and development of early swords, variations (sabre, broadsword, cutlass, scimitar, etc.), much more. 336pp. 6⅛ x 9¼. 25434-8

CATALOG OF DOVER BOOKS

AUTOBIOGRAPHY: The Story of My Experiments with Truth, Mohandas K. Gandhi. Boyhood, legal studies, purification, the growth of the Satyagraha (nonviolent protest) movement. Critical, inspiring work of the man responsible for the freedom of India. 480pp. 5⅜ x 8½. (Available in U.S. only.) 24593-4

CELTIC MYTHS AND LEGENDS, T. W. Rolleston. Masterful retelling of Irish and Welsh stories and tales. Cuchulain, King Arthur, Deirdre, the Grail, many more. First paperback edition. 58 full-page illustrations. 512pp. 5⅜ x 8½. 26507-2

THE PRINCIPLES OF PSYCHOLOGY, William James. Famous long course complete, unabridged. Stream of thought, time perception, memory, experimental methods; great work decades ahead of its time. 94 figures. 1,391pp. 5⅜ x 8½. 2-vol. set.
Vol. I: 20381-6 Vol. II: 20382-4

THE WORLD AS WILL AND REPRESENTATION, Arthur Schopenhauer. Definitive English translation of Schopenhauer's life work, correcting more than 1,000 errors, omissions in earlier translations. Translated by E. F. J. Payne. Total of 1,269pp. 5⅜ x 8½. 2-vol. set. Vol. 1: 21761-2 Vol. 2: 21762-0

MAGIC AND MYSTERY IN TIBET, Madame Alexandra David-Neel. Experiences among lamas, magicians, sages, sorcerers, Bonpa wizards. A true psychic discovery. 32 illustrations. 321pp. 5⅜ x 8½. (Available in U.S. only.) 22682-4

THE EGYPTIAN BOOK OF THE DEAD, E. A. Wallis Budge. Complete reproduction of Ani's papyrus, finest ever found. Full hieroglyphic text, interlinear transliteration, word-for-word translation, smooth translation. 533pp. 6½ x 9¼. 21866-X

MATHEMATICS FOR THE NONMATHEMATICIAN, Morris Kline. Detailed, college-level treatment of mathematics in cultural and historical context, with numerous exercises. Recommended Reading Lists. Tables. Numerous figures. 641pp. 5⅜ x 8½.
24823-2

PROBABILISTIC METHODS IN THE THEORY OF STRUCTURES, Isaac Elishakoff. Well-written introduction covers the elements of the theory of probability from two or more random variables, the reliability of such multivariable structures, the theory of random function, Monte Carlo methods of treating problems incapable of exact solution, and more. Examples. 502pp. 5⅜ x 8½. 40691-1

THE RIME OF THE ANCIENT MARINER, Gustave Doré, S. T. Coleridge. Doré's finest work; 34 plates capture moods, subtleties of poem. Flawless full-size reproductions printed on facing pages with authoritative text of poem. "Beautiful. Simply beautiful."–*Publisher's Weekly*. 77pp. 9¼ x 12. 22305-1

NORTH AMERICAN INDIAN DESIGNS FOR ARTISTS AND CRAFTSPEOPLE, Eva Wilson. Over 360 authentic copyright-free designs adapted from Navajo blankets, Hopi pottery, Sioux buffalo hides, more. Geometrics, symbolic figures, plant and animal motifs, etc. 128pp. 8⅜ x 11. (Not for sale in the United Kingdom.) 25341-4

SCULPTURE: Principles and Practice, Louis Slobodkin. Step-by-step approach to clay, plaster, metals, stone; classical and modern. 253 drawings, photos. 255pp. 8⅛ x 11.
22960-2

THE INFLUENCE OF SEA POWER UPON HISTORY, 1660–1783, A. T. Mahan. Influential classic of naval history and tactics still used as text in war colleges. First paperback edition. 4 maps. 24 battle plans. 640pp. 5⅜ x 8½. 25509-3

CATALOG OF DOVER BOOKS

THE STORY OF THE TITANIC AS TOLD BY ITS SURVIVORS, Jack Winocour (ed.). What it was really like. Panic, despair, shocking inefficiency, and a little heroism. More thrilling than any fictional account. 26 illustrations. 320pp. 5⅜ x 8½.
20610-6

FAIRY AND FOLK TALES OF THE IRISH PEASANTRY, William Butler Yeats (ed.). Treasury of 64 tales from the twilight world of Celtic myth and legend: "The Soul Cages," "The Kildare Pooka," "King O'Toole and his Goose," many more. Introduction and Notes by W. B. Yeats. 352pp. 5⅜ x 8½.
26941-8

BUDDHIST MAHAYANA TEXTS, E. B. Cowell and others (eds.). Superb, accurate translations of basic documents in Mahayana Buddhism, highly important in history of religions. The Buddha-karita of Asvaghosha, Larger Sukhavativyuha, more. 448pp. 5⅜ x 8½.
25552-2

ONE TWO THREE . . . INFINITY: Facts and Speculations of Science, George Gamow. Great physicist's fascinating, readable overview of contemporary science: number theory, relativity, fourth dimension, entropy, genes, atomic structure, much more. 128 illustrations. Index. 352pp. 5⅜ x 8½.
25664-2

EXPERIMENTATION AND MEASUREMENT, W. J. Youden. Introductory manual explains laws of measurement in simple terms and offers tips for achieving accuracy and minimizing errors. Mathematics of measurement, use of instruments, experimenting with machines. 1994 edition. Foreword. Preface. Introduction. Epilogue. Selected Readings. Glossary. Index. Tables and figures. 128pp. 5⅜ x 8½.
40451-X

DALÍ ON MODERN ART: The Cuckolds of Antiquated Modern Art, Salvador Dalí. Influential painter skewers modern art and its practitioners. Outrageous evaluations of Picasso, Cézanne, Turner, more. 15 renderings of paintings discussed. 44 calligraphic decorations by Dalí. 96pp. 5⅜ x 8½. (Available in U.S. only.)
29220-7

ANTIQUE PLAYING CARDS: A Pictorial History, Henry René D'Allemagne. Over 900 elaborate, decorative images from rare playing cards (14th–20th centuries): Bacchus, death, dancing dogs, hunting scenes, royal coats of arms, players cheating, much more. 96pp. 9¼ x 12¼.
29265-7

MAKING FURNITURE MASTERPIECES: 30 Projects with Measured Drawings, Franklin H. Gottshall. Step-by-step instructions, illustrations for constructing handsome, useful pieces, among them a Sheraton desk, Chippendale chair, Spanish desk, Queen Anne table and a William and Mary dressing mirror. 224pp. 8⅛ x 11¼.
29338-6

THE FOSSIL BOOK: A Record of Prehistoric Life, Patricia V. Rich et al. Profusely illustrated definitive guide covers everything from single-celled organisms and dinosaurs to birds and mammals and the interplay between climate and man. Over 1,500 illustrations. 760pp. 7½ x 10⅛.
29371-8